MEN IN MOTION

MEN IN MOTION

By HENRY J. TAYLOR

Author of TIME RUNS OUT

DOUBLEDAY, DORAN AND COMPANY, INC.

Garden City 1943 *New York*

PRINTED AT THE *Country Life Press*, GARDEN CITY, N. Y., U. S. A.

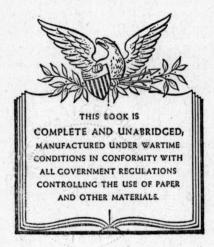

THIS BOOK IS
COMPLETE AND UNABRIDGED,
MANUFACTURED UNDER WARTIME
CONDITIONS IN CONFORMITY WITH
ALL GOVERNMENT REGULATIONS
CONTROLLING THE USE OF PAPER
AND OTHER MATERIALS.

To The Memory Of
My Father

Contents

CHAPTER   PAGE

1. In Sir Arthur Tedder's Cairo Garden 1
2. Napoleon Had an American Problem 11
3. Duluth's Dogs Bark in Accra 20
4. The Hudson Tube Age Begins 29
5. Woodrow Wilson Lived on S Street 39
6. Europe, an Impoverished Peninsula 49
7. The Idea Spreads to America 60
8. The Nazi Pigs Were in the Pasture 65
9. This Life Is New 80
10. Europeans Stop the Clock in Africa 89
11. Europeans Can Make This Contribution 97
12. The Farmer at the Zoo 111
13. General Valin Rides the Ammunition 123
14. Diver Ellsberg on the Nile 137
15. The Evacuation of Cairo 147
16. Our Fundamental Strategy 159
17. Rommel Won the Sand and Lost the Air 169
18. *A* for Africa, *E* for Eisenhower, *F* for France . . . 181

vii

Contents

CHAPTER | PAGE

19. With the R.A.F. in the Desert 192

20. "This Is It" 201

21. Palestine, Syria, and the Jews 211

22. Atatürk Is Turkey 229

23. Marshal Chakmak Calls the Russian Turn 238

24. The German Underground and Saracoglu 249

25. Von Papen Is Germany 258

26. The Great European Dilemma 273

27. Our Boundless Future 286

Index 299

MEN IN MOTION

CHAPTER 1

In Sir Arthur Tedder's Cairo Garden

CAIRO IS QUITE A PLACE. It was always as colorful as the pages of the *Arabian Nights*. Now war supercharges its air of romance and mystery with suspense and vitality.

The streets are a melee of dust-covered army material and all the trappings of desert fighting, mixed in with open-air streetcars, bicycle bells, backfires, bagpipes and flutes, Rolls-Royces, donkeys, newsboys, and bootblacks—especially bootblacks.

Assyrian vendors walk among the troops and tanks, selling stale coffee from immense brass carafes. Keen-eyed Arabs with inflexible faces move as quietly as shadows. Egyptians and soldiers crowd the sidewalk cafés, play cards or dominoes, or just sit and listen to music, laughter, and noise. Bearded Sikhs walk in shorts. Women of the Italian secret police, E. Phillips Oppenheim characters, flirt on the veranda of Shepheard's Hotel.

Cairo is a city of horse-drawn cabs, like those which stand in front of the Plaza on Fifth Avenue. In one of these, an elderly little lady, wearing her black veil, rides through the military traffic calm as Shelley's cradled child while her Sudanese coachman speaks back to jeep drivers like thunder from a teacup.

Suddenly the ack-ack guns let go, and all hell breaks loose. The city seems to evaporate. The guns stop. Everything is quiet. The air is still. There is a short, uneven pause.

Then you see and feel Cairo stir again, brimming over with its own special mixture of the life of the world.

Cairo's R.A.F. airport is at Heliopolis, on the outskirts of the city. I landed there while the Nazis' Stuka dive bombers were heading for the Heliopolis airport. Searchlights were trying to pick them up. The whole immense, flat area was rimmed by beams. The sky was ablaze.

Staff cars screeched around the machine shops and hangars. Signals blinked from desert stations, pin points in the murky darkness beyond the Pyramids.

The plane I was in was loaded with Air Corps munitions from America. We flew low and headed straight into the field, blinking our coded identification lights as we came in. As we cleared the high wire enclosure and touched the apron, the ack-ack guns spoke out, angry and defiant, throwing their shells at the Nazis above. There are plenty of guns around that field, and they were blowing the roof off that part of the world.

The pilot taxied the ship towards a three-cornered sandbag pen furthest from the hangars. None of us waited very long when the ship rolled to a stop. We went out the door as fast as we could.

We ran for cover, our feet slipping back as we crunched through the loose stones. There wasn't any cover. The next thing I knew I was down in a slit trench.

I had been through bombings many times before, in Finland, England, Gibraltar, on a ship in the Mediterranean, and even—irony of ironies—by R.A.F. planes as I stood on the streets of Berlin. But these were dive bombers overhead now, and this was their target.

The first Stuka peeled off. Fifteen more, Indian-file, were getting ready to dive. The plane fell like a sash weight, tore down at us like a roaring eagle, wounded and crazy, screaming its wild and frenzied wail. The W-shaped wings, the ugly, clumsy-looking wheels that don't retract, the strange tail, sighted themselves in my eyes and consciousness for endless moments. I suppose you could close your eyes, but you don't. You just lie there. They drop fast all right, make no mistake about that.

Then something tore the air with a whine, a close, whip-like whine. All the world was that whine, brittle, sharp, vengeful.

My senses spun with the explosion. It took all air, all touch of life, twisted the earth, gripped my throat, knocked back my head like a blow in the dark, shattered my mind with its blinding fury. And with this a quick dimness came over me that might have been the haze of smoke or some state of life I had never known. I was floating in a rhythmic leisure. My shoulders seemed narrow, loose against the hard edge of the short, shallow ditch. My hands flapped senselessly. My mouth was as dry as the sandy grit in the air, burned like my eyes. My head was numb. I certainly didn't know whether I had been hit.

Then, from the edge of the field, muffled and booming like the crash of a great wave in some cave, came a bursting roar. This explosion tore suddenly forward, flung itself across the field like a wild, flaming dragon, its scorching tongues striking instantly into every pocket, every section of the east buildings. Like the billows of an inky sea, a slow pall of dead smoke sank down in a layer, and as it touched the sand a second and third burst of flame tore it suddenly upwards and far across the field. Heliopolis was on fire.

Slowly, my mind cleared. I saw a plane shot down, two thousand feet up, coming out of its dive. Something blasted it, the ack-ack or a British interceptor. The whole W-shaped contraption just blew apart in the sky. It wasn't just hit. It went to pieces like a clay pigeon. You couldn't even tell where it fell.

Fourteen other Stukas peeled off and dove, pounded the earth to pieces, rocked the moon and the universe.

Suddenly it was all over, leaving the sharp crackle of fire, and the dull, crunching sound of falling steel and mortar. The agonized cries of wounded men rose and fell like heavy breathing.

First a few dark figures ran across the field. Then in every direction men stood up from the surface of the sand, stumbled forward, some waving their arms or holding up another man, others dazed and struck dumb, clawing at themselves, bashing their fists in their eyes, throwing themselves against the ground.

Twenty minutes later I was sitting in a lovely garden in the center of Cairo, a garden as tranquil as the light of the moon. Every comfort of a good earth was in that garden. The glorious stars were there, ageless and unchanged. Light clouds, wispy and meaningless, blew on a gentle breeze that stirred the palms in a pleasant whisper. At the foot of the terrace you could hear the soft lap, lap, lap of the waters of the Nile. There wasn't another sound. Nothing but the full beauty of the desert night and the quiet voice of a good friend.

"There must be some *separate force* which is uprooting men, making men into masses," he said that night. "What is the mainspring of the war? If it's a world revolution in ideas and government, why is the world revolting now? Where is the hope that education, and the experience of the last dreadful war, would save men from self-destruction? Several hundred million people are caught in a condition as barbaric as the Seventeenth-Century Slaughters. Forgetting nations, and considering man as a whole, how did today's civilization get in such a fix?"

I had asked myself the same question everywhere I had been. I had seen the fighting start, for I was in Germany in August 1939 when the Germans attacked Poland. I had been in Germany many times before, and I was back in Berlin in the third year of the war, as late as November 1941. In less than ten months I had flown 50,000 miles, been through the continent of Europe from Finland to Spain. I had been to England twice, to Africa twice, to South America twice. In the midst of misery and suffering I had learned only this much: Some circumstance, some lopsided structure unique to this century, mocks the destiny of European fathers and sons.

"Something is lopsided, out of line in a big way, I suppose, and pressing on modern man," I said.

My friend, a great and good British soul, commanded the R.A.F. in north Africa. He lifted his eyes as a patrol plane droned in the sky. And there in his Cairo garden he associated with the war an answer I had been groping for ever since I saw the warning in the riots on Berlin's Unter den Linden in 1923.

"Modern man," he said, very quietly, "is not modern at all. He is just, momentarily, far ahead of himself. What we are really witnessing all over the world is the lopsided spectacle of phenomenal technological improvement occurring within thirty years of incredibly bad government. Actually, it is not the visible world—the world of men and things—that crumbles; it is the world of concepts, of principles, the world of *self-faith* and *integrity*, the world which governs our relationships with other human beings."

The original mistake occurred when our scientific explorers, our inventors and engineers, supplied a new world in the mechanistic network and forgot they were not supplying new men or new statesmen.

A few bright and penetrating discoverers, bursting on an unsuspecting world, gave us mobility and tools which surpassed in a few moments all the accumulated facilities of the ages. Within a single century the men of test tubes and slide rules filled Europe with an astonishing world of factories, power stations, all the mechanical panoply of the moment, without any corresponding development in the mind and spirit of man or man's leaders.

We have been on the good earth a quarter-million years. Anthropologists, worrying their hearts out over this date, place us here at about 250,000 B.C.

Somehow or other we lived through various periods for 250,000 years. No one has been able to find that throughout nearly all this time our spiritual environment or our tools altered in the slightest. Ten thousand generations of us lived without change, moved the same way, sought the same food, did the same chores, one generation after the other.

Much happened to the surface of the earth, but little happened to us. In ten thousand generations we grew no wings so that we could fly, no web feet so that we could swim, not even claws so that we could fight. We were men. We were trying to learn to think. But, looking exactly as we do today, identical with our present self, we still just stood around eating, sleeping, reproducing—and dying like flies whenever the weather turned bad.

Two hundred and forty thousand years were behind us before we even communicated with each other in writing.

By comparing the time of man with the distance around the earth you can visualize in terms of familiar distances the suddenness of our development. If you apply 250,000 years to 25,000 miles you make the round-trip circuit on the globe. For this purpose of visualization 10 years represents a mile.

Starting at New York, the time of man crosses the Atlantic, crosses all Europe, all Asia, all the Pacific, arrives back in the United States, and gets as close to New York as Chicago before we even had gumption enough to write (a little novelty the Chinese were tinkering with 10,000 years ago).

The time schedule is someplace in the Alleghenies, around Pittsburgh, Pennsylvania, before Egypt is settled. It reaches Harrisburg by the beginning of the Christian Era. It is on the New York side of Philadelphia at the Norman Conquest of England, and closer to New York than to Princeton before the Pilgrim years in new America. Man invents the steam engine on the eastern side of Newark and perfects every one of our dynamic inventions in only the last breathless stretch through the Hudson Tube under the Hudson River.

This is the Hudson Tube Age. It hardly seems a wonder that we may have lost our heads and hearts in the dizziness of our modern instant, the lightning-like flash of our latest moment in the new centuries, the meteor-like explosion of unchanged man from the ages of the earth.

In terms of environment, man's life is just starting after 10,000 unchanged generations. Yet in all seriousness people speak of the end of civilization, view the first blush of man's place on earth as the end of time. They forget that we are just beginning to stir and to adjust ourselves to the land.

That we should therefore take a static view regarding the fixedness of 400,000,000 people on the impoverished peninsula called "Europe" is obviously absurd. And that we should so far lose perspective as to contemplate Europe's future in terms of its present congestion while rich, vast areas abound elsewhere is a dull assumption.

The two great wars of our immediate split second are terrible calamities in their death, destruction, and unspeakable suffering. That we must win this war need hardly be stated. The mind and heart of any decent free man rebels against any other consideration. The powerful Axis nations are loose, and until they are hurled back and controlled we can have no other purpose in life. No

American who has seen this evil force in battle, as I have, no one who has been in wartime Germany and moved with the wretched victims of German armies all over continental Europe, could even pause to discuss the need for our final and full victory, no matter how long it takes or what its agony. I would feel a certain desecration in repeating that fact again and again in these pages.

But the awful calamity of this war is an even worse calamity if, in the process of our victory, it causes thoughtful people to lose their perspective and their hope.

Rather than be dismayed by the past, we should be encouraged by it. In our victory there is hope for our statesmen, our generals, our churchmen, and our teachers—hope for free people everywhere —if we grasp the full proportions of our day. For we are stirring at last, and this great war is not the end of anything. On the contrary, it is teaching a profound lesson and it is bringing about the coming of a new age.

"What does war, beginning from the lowest races and reaching up to mankind, signify?" asked Ralph Waldo Emerson. "Is it not manifest that it covers a great principle, which nature has deeply at heart? Nature implants with life the instinct of perpetual struggle. Yet it is but *one* instinct; the appearance of other instincts can modify and control this, turn its energies into useful and high courses."

The historian will certainly not even bother about separating World War I and World War II. He will identify them with the end of the Age of Steam, the beginning of the Age of Electricity, Oil, and Air, and the real populating of the earth, and let them go at that. He will see that they are the result, not of man's inhumanity to man, but of man's distortions within the structure flowing from the inventions of a few men, and from the liquidation of self-faith and integrity.

The human mind is slow, and so is the human temperament. They are today at least several centuries behind their tools.

The problems arising from this are concentrated in Europe. The first step in any solution of them, preliminary to any permanent peace in the world, is centered there.

The British and American governments contemplate a settlement in Europe with the defeat of Germany and Italy while the war continues against Japan. Mr. Churchill states that by making peace on the Continent while still fighting side by side in the Orient the European peace settlement will be unique in harmony and effectiveness. I hope he is right. For the settlement will require a brand of statesmanship, political courage, patience, and unselfishness, all on a plateau of idealism, that has never before appeared in the long history of Europe.

And, in justice to the American people, it will require some knowledge among us Americans regarding what the Europeans can do for themselves before we deliver further promises regarding what the United States will do for the people of the world.

I come fresh from the impact of American words on European and middle eastern minds. Therefore I am perplexed by what our leaders are saying. They talk as though the people over there were Americans and lived in America. They are not Americans, and they do not live in America.

In our deep anxiety to be helpful to the world, and to ourselves, we are making promises now and assuming superior attitudes which America and the world will deeply regret.

There is, by common consent, no better mind in Europe than António d'Oliveira Salazar, Prime Minister of Portugal, the country which is England's oldest ally. This is the secluded man, seldom seen and seldom heard, the century's most eminent international economist, a humanitarian of immense prestige throughout the world.

This is what Prime Minister Salazar told me in Lisbon not long ago: "The symptoms, which may be removed, are one thing, but the deep-seated canker which coils through Europe's economic and social life is another. The lopsidedness about which you speak multiplies crises in Europe, causes them to succeed one another with increasing intensity and creates what appears to be a permanent malaise.

"When I survey the international panorama, the ruin and impoverishment of nations, the weakness of their governments, the irresoluteness of principle, the social tension; when I see the crisis of life, the crisis of the soil, the crisis of morality, I feel that nothing can be of service to the world that does not first *re-establish the example of individual self-faith.*

"There is still in some nations a residue of ideals which should be cultivated so that they may not be lost forever. Those who still cherish such ideals are slowly disappearing. But without their inspiration it seems almost impossible to overcome the difficulties which beset us. No task on earth has such urgency now as each man's honest attempt to urge self-faith, independently and without fear. He should do no less, and he can do no more."

A few truths emerge. And the most important of these truths, as far as we are concerned, a truth which we are morally obligated to recognize in honesty to ourselves and to 400,000,000 Europeans, is this:

America can hurt Europe. I hope and pray we shall have wisdom and charity enough not to do that. But, basically, we cannot help Europe. Europe must help herself.

How this became true, why it is true, what its truth means to Americans in terms of today's conditions in Europe and the Middle East, what must be done within the United States, and what first steps can be taken by Europeans themselves before they rely on the United States, is the story born in Sir Arthur Tedder's Cairo garden.

These are human matters. This is a flesh-and-blood story. It is told in terms of my own family, not because my family contained unusual distinction or was especially important within itself, but because the broad forces of the changing world are reflected in the activities of these earlier people, their hopes and fears, their successes and failures, their lives and deaths.

Therefore this story starts in the wilderness of Ohio, one hundred forty years ago, for sometime in the future millions of Europeans must do again what millions of Americans did then.

Later, the basic changes which made the world fluid and dynamic occurred mostly in the breathless period of only a moment ago, when the grandfathers and fathers of all of us who are now forty

were alive and struggling in a pulsating America. The most fundamental changes of all history occurred in their lifetime and are
continuing in ours, for they hoped and feared, succeeded and failed,
lived and died at the very inception of the Hudson Tube Age.

As for the present and my own observation, a heavy foreboding
lies upon my heart and mind, as it does upon the hearts and minds
of millions of Americans, a strange failure to rejoice and be electrified by the mere thought that one day this war may be over. Our
souls are not lifted as they should be to thank Almighty God for
the prospect of our military victory. We are not comforted as we
should be by the idea of the defeat of our mortal enemies. What
does this mean? I can only give the answer as one American among
many who sees a Fate coming closer to his own country now as
he saw it come earlier in Europe.

For whether or not Americans of the future have any destiny
other than alternating between confusion and tyranny, between the
red and the black, between Danton and Loyola, depends primarily
upon factors which would be evident to anyone who had been in
Europe as lately as I have.

CHAPTER 2

Napoleon Had an American Problem

IN THE SAME YEAR, 1803, that Robert Fulton, living in France, and to the awe of Paris, first succeeded in propelling a boat by steam power, Napoleon faced an American problem.

The central third of the present United States belonged to his empire. On his maps in the Tuileries he called it "New France," and he did not propose to let it go to England. Furthermore, Napoleon needed money to fight England in Europe. He sold New France, five times the size of Germany, to the United States for $15,000,000.

Napoleon himself describes this act in words that are heavy with an Old World flavor: "This enlargement of its territory consolidates the power of the United States for all time. Perhaps people will reproach me when in two or three centuries the Americans become too powerful for Europe, but I cannot take so distant a possibility into my calculations in advance."

Northeast of the "Louisiana Purchase" area was a vast section of America that few white men had ever seen. No one had lived there except native Indians. No one knew the temper of the tribes or the animals, no one knew the climate or the character of the soil.

Largely unsurveyed, army scouts reported only that it was close-packed with trees and impenetrable brush. And they knew that over the mountains and through the valleys and forests, feeling your way on roads, rivers, and trails, it took two months to get there.

This was the wilderness of central Ohio.

The Wyandot Indians had undivided possession of this region.

Their villages were further north, on the Sandusky River, and their hunters came twice a year: first in the fall to procure game and later to trap fur animals. These hunters, roaming in threes or fours, ranged and trapped all over the contiguous territory. In the spring they returned to their villages with their furs, and a group of four was preparing to return when Robert Taylor, following a stream, encountered them in their camp.

He had left Albany in the spring of 1803 to develop his share of the tract given by Congress to officers and men of General Washington's victorious army.

The Wyandots were friendly and industrious, and they welcomed this white man. They helped him build his house on the clearing of their camp.

In this way Robert Taylor built the first house on the site of the present capital of Ohio, Columbus. He gave the township its present name of Truro, after the earliest seat of his family in Scotland, and Edward Livingston named the adjoining township Montgomery, in honor of the brave general who had died in their arms during the Battle of Quebec.

The winters were long and severe. Large crevices between the logs gave Robert Taylor's house plenty of ventilation, but they were stuffed with clay before the coldest weather came on. The floor was made of logs split in half, laid "with backs downward," as he recorded in our family Bible. Beds and chairs were sawed out of blocks of wood; blankets in the form of curtains broke the house into rooms. Meals were cooked at a broad fireside—venison, game birds, Indian maize, fish from the Scioto River. A hand-wrought crane swung heavy kettles on and off the crackling fire.

Robert Taylor's wife, Mehitabel, and their children followed him to Ohio to occupy the house in March 1808. She came by wagon, driving the giant team over the Allegheny range and into the western forests.

What a brave character this venture required! The wonder at such self-faith and devotion increases a hundredfold when I realize that she had then living no less than eleven children, five of whom were under twelve years of age. Under those circumstances her long, hard journey to Ohio seems appalling. She was at that time forty-one years old, and she did not die until she was ninety-four.

Together, the father, wife, and older children hewed more logs and added broad wings to the cabin. They built a lookout platform in a tall tree so that they could see a long distance when they wanted to, more for amusement than to avoid danger.

Then they began to till the soil.

Members of the Livingston family and other neighbors came to their tracts from Albany, and they were all blessed by the fact that the Wyandots did not engage in the War of 1812 but remained at peace with this isolated little community.

When Mehitabel made her way west to occupy the house she brought cattle and hogs from Chillicothe. The family tended the stock well. To get it to market Robert Taylor made an arrangement with a neighbor by the name of Reynolds to build a flatboat and a landing near the old Hebron trail (now called Lexington Avenue, in Columbus) on Walnut Creek. By this arrangement settlers for miles around were able to kill their hogs, cure their meat during the winter, and in the spring deliver it to Reynolds' flatboat.

When the spring floods came the settlers helped Reynolds put his craft in the stream and start it on its way to New Orleans. The flatboat could make this trip once a year, going downstream in Walnut Creek into the Ohio River near Cincinnati and into the Mississippi at Cairo, Illinois. With the produce of these Truro Township settlers, Reynolds drifted a thousand miles to New Orleans. There he would sell the meat and the craft, and then he would return through the wilderness on horseback.

There was only one commercial steamboat in America, and it was on the Hudson. Robert R. Livingston, who stayed in Albany when Robert Taylor's Livingston neighbors in Ohio left Albany for the tract, and with which family our family intermarried, built the *Clermont* with Robert Fulton. Mehitabel made the maiden trip on her between Albany and New York in 1807.

Her first words to Robert Taylor when she reached Ohio were of the wonders of this boat, the frightening wonders of Robert

Fulton's and Robert Livingston's enterprise told breathlessly to the third Robert in his Ohio cabin.

The settlers at first taught their children on their knees. When they could get a teacher to come to the wilderness they built a schoolhouse, as any conscientious parents would be expected to do, and the boys and girls still worked on the farm as long as they were needed.

In the evening Mehitabel was busy at her fireside spinning wheel and loomed cotton and woolen cloth with the family and the Livingston neighbors. And late at night the rhythmic thump of the beam put the threads in the fifth or sixth yard for that day.

At this hour the howl of the big timber wolf was a melancholy sound. But the boars of the frontier days could easily and quickly rout any wolf or pack of wolves, for the Ohio boars were vicious and terrible creatures.

The most formidable of all animals in the Ohio forest, however, were the black bears. The settlers killed only a few, because the Wyandots were experts in locating "bear trees," where the bears took winter quarters. Their pelts were of great use to the Indians for clothing and their meat for food, and the Indians always found and shot the bears first. Then, as African natives might do today, they put the skull in the crook of a tree and asked the bear to forgive them.

When Robert Taylor appeared on Sunday he wore his glossy suit. Made by Mehitabel's devoted hand, wrinkled and fretted, it was the American costume, such as Lincoln wore when he first spoke at Cooper Union, New York.

Wants were few, for everyone supplied his own. A man or woman's expense, beyond what was produced at home, was seldom as much as ten dollars a year. The Reverend Peter Cartwright, the nearest minister, rejoiced in his riches by dedicating a poem to Robert Taylor when he found that he had been instrumental in adding twelve dollars to the minister's stipend of one hundred dollars per year.

My grandfather was eighteen in 1857 when his grandmother, Mehitabel, died. He wrote of this in a story of Ohio. "It now seems strange," he said, "that by this living relation I was returned to the middle of the 18th Century. She was seventeen when the Revolutionary War ended and twenty-four when Washington became president of the New Republic. Her information reached back for three generations—back to Old Ulster and the formative period of Ulstermen. She talked easily about the dreadful Siege of Londonderry and of the life and experiences of our forefathers there. I can see her now, with her white lace cap on her venerable head, her half-knit stockings in her hands, plying her needles and glancing at the large clock which stood in the hall. The spirit of self-faith and accomplishment seems to have been born in her and stayed with her even at her great age."

This was the American family unit. It thrived and prospered, not in the "good old days" but in the good, hard days. Work and the freedom to succeed were, in turn, its inalienable duty and right.

These Americans lived in the thought of self-faith and personal initiative. It never occurred to them that there was any rightful place for man on earth except as he himself supplied it under the rules of Almighty God. They were individuals, and they would never have been content to be anything else.

"We are ourselves alone," the American man and woman said. "Treat us as such."

Like thousands of others, when my grandfather's time came he pioneered in another direction. In his generation he contributed his minute share to the mechanistic network. Grandfather built a wagonworks in Columbus.

Only since 1835 had use of the iron plow gradually spread. It was as late as the time when my grandfather built his Columbus wagonworks that even horse-drawn mowing machines were used on farms anywhere in the world.

Grandfather saw his small enterprise fail when he went off to the Civil War, but he started it again with our family savings when he came back.

He made good wagons and sold them cheaply. As more and more Ohio farmers bought them and his business grew, the iron foundry where he purchased his forgings grew too. So did the mill which supplied lumber.

One of his neighbors began making paint, and Grandfather bought it for his wagons. With this demand to count on, the paint man began selling his product throughout the state. Now there were four small industries in Columbus instead of one.

Every farmer who could use a wagon could use a buggy. As soon as Grandfather could afford additional tools he made buggies. This cut production costs and cut the price of both the wagon and the buggy, and the factory grew in a very important way.

Grandfather's second son, my uncle, was married to the daughter of the Governor of Ohio. Grandfather never could understand what the governor meant in political speeches to the people, and he often told the governor so. He could never see that office-holders supported life, any more than a nozzle on a hose supplies water.

He used to say that he could see how politicians would get along all right with their promises and their oratory as long as others were willing to work and were able to do so in a successful way. But at the same time he wondered where the people and the politicians themselves would get off if everybody got something and nobody supplied anything. In this respect Grandfather was a hopeless reactionary.

In these conversations the governor, without batting an eye, would say that he really wanted to act wisely but that people voted for what a man promised instead of for the man himself. He would present this answer as though it were justification for getting in office and keeping power rather than a confession that this made politics a private business of its own.

This so infuriated my grandfather that he asked his youngest son, my other uncle, to run for Congress. Everybody in Columbus knew and liked my Uncle Ned. Grandfather told him to promise nothing.

In his first speech Uncle Ned announced that, if sent to Washington, he would regard his election as his constituents' mandate to use his own judgment and not theirs. He conceived this as the true spirit of *representative* government and in accord with the earliest purposes of a republic. Then, if the community he represented in the House of Representatives did not like his record, he suggested that they throw him out at the next election. But while he was on the job he would do the job as he thought best, and not on the basis of bewildering voices from "the folks back home." "That only leads to pressure groups," he said, "and government by pressure groups is the least democratic government of all. Government by appointment or by special blocs, loud and howling, is not American democracy.

"The politician who is afraid to have a mind of his own and does not want to base his own political life on his own convictions, but, instead, tries to puzzle out the weights and counterweights of organized groups before he can make up his mind about anything, is not a democratic statesman. He is merely a paid agent. And he is an agent, furthermore, of whatever group is the most indispensable at any moment, and of whatever group is the most articulately greedy."

The governor smiled at this sensible and honorable appeal. "Ned will never make it," he said the night of that first speech in the Columbus Opera House. Uncle Ned was elected overwhelmingly.

"The boy seems to have more confidence in the people than you have," Grandfather told the governor. "Plain people aren't as foolish as you think. It's just that we have poor choices. This is the greatest country in the world, and ours are the finest people on earth. You politicians just don't realize it. Actually, you're cynical about our people and you don't trust us to support you when you tell us the truth and ask us to make sacrifices. If you don't trust us how can you expect us to trust you? Well, you can't—and we don't. But that's not our fault, it's yours."

Uncle Ned went to Congress, and Grandfather was very happy about this whole affair. And he was proud that Uncle Ned never pussyfooted after he got there and was, nevertheless, sent back term after term until he finally retired to look after Grandfather's affairs when the fine old gentleman died.

For his oldest son, my father, Grandfather had other advice. "I want you to go in business for yourself," he said. "Use your head and your hands and build something, anything, of your own. Get into the coal business if you can. This is the day of steam. But in any case make your own way. That's your privilege and your best guarantee of happiness in life."

Steamboats had left the Hudson and spread to all the world. Steamers from Duluth brought iron ore 500 miles from Lake Superior down to the steel mills at the mouth of the Chicago River. First a trickle, this traffic was growing in 1886.

Father thought he might start a sound business if he could build a coal hopper dock near Chicago.

Couldn't empty iron ore steamers take aboard coal from Illinois's bituminous fields, after they had dumped their ore, and carry coal north instead of returning empty?

Coal was badly needed in the northern lake communities to warm homes and run new factories which were developing, but it was now delivered by rail, and the long haul made it very expensive.

Father believed the freight cost of the ore to the steel mills could be cut this way while the cost of the coal, in turn, could be reduced to all who bought it in the Minnesota-Wisconsin territory. At the same time, the steamers' revenue would be nearly doubled by hauling pay loads both ways.

So much for his idea as a whole. He realized that it was sound and could have important results, but it presented a great many difficulties.

What could a man with only an idea offer the vessel captains? He had no facilities, and the ore vessels were owned by dozens of individual captains and proprietors, as hidebound and heavy-fisted a crowd as anyone could imagine. Each fought for his place in the great ore race when the ice broke and navigation opened. Each ran his ship under his own particular arrangement with an ore pit owner. And although it was fresh water that swamped his bows in stormy weather, each lake captain had all the sea sailor's instinct for indifference to anything except his ship and his crew. Each was suspicious of most men who did not live on water and of nearly everything that did not float.

Father had no steamers, he had no dock, he had no coal, he had no customers, and as a young man of twenty-one he had no credit. He had just an idea.

But when he talked this idea over with Grandfather, the old gentleman said that was enough. "You know this is a good thing," he said, "and someday it will be done. Go to it. Keep your own counsel, keep your promises, hew to the line, and finally, if you're sure you're right, go ahead. It'll be a problem all along the line. But the tough things are the only things worth doing anyway."

The old gentleman took him to the bank in Columbus, and Father borrowed three hundred dollars on his personal note. The bank gave him the money in gold coin. He bought a ticket that day to Chicago.

CHAPTER 3

Duluth's Dogs Bark in Accra

FATHER WAS a large man. He stood well over six feet—six feet three, to be exact. He weighed two hundred forty pounds, yet he was lean from head to toe, trim and hard. His shoulders were broad, his arms were heavy, and he stood very straight without seeming stiff or military. You could see that his strength was prodigious, and his powerfulness itself seemed to emphasize the appeal of his easy and friendly manner, the kindness in his blue eyes, and the warmth of his smile.

There was nothing ponderous about him—the way he moved, the way he spoke, or the way he laughed. When you talked with him there was something about the frank way he looked at you, his whole bearing, which made you feel that he would be easy to get along with and that he was ready to do his part.

He was slow to anger, absolutely free of pettiness. "I don't like grudges," Father used to say. "They are sad things and an awful waste of time."

I don't think anyone could have spent ten minutes with him without coming to the conclusion that he was a forthright and cool-headed man.

Father decided that his first step should be to work his way aboard an ore steamer to Duluth, make the trip his coal would make, and see the shipping situation with his own eyes before he said or did anything.

Signing aboard a vessel for the trip up the Lakes was no trouble at all. The *Charles Hutchinson* was unloading at a pier. The famous *Onaka* had been launched in the Cuyahoga at Cleveland in 1882, four years earlier, and set the pattern for the permanent type on the Lakes. These new ships, built especially for this run, were among the largest ships afloat on any lake or sea. The *Charles Hutchinson* followed the *Onaka* pattern. She was 300 feet long, shallow-bottomed, and had a good prow for ice-breaking—useful until the Lakes froze in too tight. Her wheelhouse and bridge stood far forward, at the very tip of the bow. Her engines and crew quarters were aft, clustered at the base of her high, black funnel. The flat hundred-yard expanse of ore hatches in the middle of the boat, separating the clusters of superstructure at each end, made the *Charles Hutchinson* look as though she had been stretched out like a toy boat made of taffy.

The captain of the *Charles Hutchinson* was a hot-headed, red-headed Irishman named Christopher Whalen who knew the lake traffic better than he knew his own back yard and who ran his ship with an iron hand. He was a stocky man, square off the deck. His head was round and set close on his shoulders. His face bristled with whiskers, and his orders sounded like the roar of a bull.

"A very strong man," the dockmen said.

"I can see it," said Father.

Father soon found that the captain could outwork any of the dock loaders, or anybody aboard. Father decided to outwork Whalen. He never did this, but the captain liked the try, and finally, when Father began to ask him questions about his dock idea, the captain was only too glad to give the answers.

"Coal is better than coming home leery [empty]," Whalen agreed. "Any ore boat on the Lakes would be glad to haul it. But make your dock a good one so we can come in easy and load up fast or it won't be worth our while."

Whalen told Father to get busy at Waukegan, Illinois. Some of the ore ships went to Milwaukee and others to Chicago, and as the port of Waukegan was between the two, in Illinois just south of the Wisconsin border, it would be the ideal place.

On the return trip from Duluth, loaded with ore, Whalen put in at Waukegan and let this young Ohioan off there. Father went ashore and for fifty dollars in his Columbus gold coin bought an option on a piece of water-front property, started a search of the titles, and measured the distance to the shore-line railroad. Whalen picked him up a week later on the *Charles Hutchinson's* northern trip, and he sailed north again.

This time Father stayed in Duluth, went to the boom towns of Minnesota and Wisconsin.

In the century before 1886, 15,000,000 Europeans moved to the American colonies and the United States. But the great rush started that year. In a spillover from the fantastic growth of population on the European continent, 10,000,000 Europeans came to the United States between 1886 and 1900, hundreds of thousands settling in our Great Lakes country.

"They were a good-natured crowd," I have heard my father say. "They just liked to hit each other over the head. There was a fellow named Karl. He had a chest like a gorilla. Somebody bet him a dollar he wouldn't wrestle a bear. Karl took the dollar. And the bear took Karl."

Everything was growing—Duluth grew, Ashland grew, Marquette grew. Father often quoted the saying of the times: "The four toughest places in the world are Hibbing, Hayward, Hurley, and Hell." He believed it. Every town had its duckboard sidewalks, with the sprinkling of red dust that was the mark of iron. The town of Florence had a half-acre dance hall and barroom, and Wakefield was famous for its barrel house, where whisky was sold only by the barrel or bottle and a burlesque theater opened from the rear of the big saloon. Another saloon in Wakefield featured a red-capped monkey, which was trained to steal wallets and watches and did very well at this until it knocked over a lamp. Wakefield burned to the ground.

At Negaunee the men moved a cemetery to strike into the black magnetic rock. The main street of Hurley had only one building that was not a saloon, dance hall, or gambling room. This was the Hurley jail. There wasn't a hospital in northern Wisconsin or Michigan; there wasn't a minister, a doctor, or an undertaker in the whole Gogebic country. Hungry dogs fought in the dark streets at night.

Today the marvels of Wisconsin or Minnesota must stir any American who sees them.

A few months ago I heard hungry dogs bark in a dark street on a continent which can someday be a new America for trapped Europeans.

I was in Accra, seaport capital of the British Gold Coast.

The dust of iron ore gave way in Accra to the smell of cacao, but the whole place was right out of Father's Duluth–Lake Superior days, and I felt as Father must have felt as he came down the gangplank of the *Charles Hutchinson* fifty-six years ago.

When Father reached Duluth he made a list of the largest coal buyers in the territory.

One by one, he showed these buyers that if they would support his dock project they would save half the rail rate from Chicago to Duluth. One by one, he got their agreement to buy their coal from him at this saving if he could deliver it.

Before Father left Duluth he had agreements to buy more coal than his projected dock would handle. His idea was now in a very snug position. But it was still only an idea—and an option.

He still had no coal, and it was beginning to look as though he was not going to get any. The largest mineowners in southern Illinois simply were not interested. There was no reason why the mineowners should upset their good railroad business, and when Father went down there to see them the owners made this painfully plain.

He had the Duluth agreements to buy coal, he had the site and the plans for the Waukegan dock, he had a bank's loan contingent on getting the coal, and yet he had nothing. "You know this is a good thing," his father had said, "and someday it will be done." He went from mine to mine in the coal field—and ended up empty-handed.

"We dig what coal we can," each told him, "and sell it at the mine. We aren't affected by the Minnesota freight rate."

Father was just about at the end of his rope.

Nobody had said much about the newer field at Coal City, up near Joliet, only forty-five miles from Chicago. It was "a sort of wildcat operation," just getting under way. But a Welshman named Billy Harkess had come in there and put down some shafts, and Father heard about him from a machinery salesman in Streator. "He's a newcomer," the salesman said, "but he has worked the pits in Wales and he knows more about coal mining than any two men in this district."

The next morning Father was talking with Billy Harkess in Coal City. They were partners through the last day of my father's life.

Billy Harkess was putting down his mines, but he didn't have anyone to buy his coal. Father had the market.

The dock was built in Waukegan, and spurs were run to it from the railroad. Father lived in near-by Milwaukee until it was finished and the coal was falling from its hoppers. Then he lived between Duluth, Waukegan, and Coal City, with Chicago as his head-quarters.

The first ship loaded at his Waukegan dock came in under the hand of Whalen. "You built her well," he said. "She's worth our while. I'll spread the news to the skippers."

"That isn't enough," my father said. "We need a man who knows the Lakes." Chris Whalen went to work for the company. With a Welshman at the mines, an Irishman on the Lakes, and an Ulsterman all around and in the center, they had their team. Father was launched in business.

The first hero of the American labor movement worked in this mine.

John Mitchell became president of the United Mine Workers. This is the office that John L. Lewis holds today in the union which Mitchell pioneered.

Born in 1870 in Braidwood, Illinois, a mile from Coal City, John Mitchell grew to be the canniest, most fearless and dynamic figure in the whole American labor scene. There is a monument to him in Scranton's Court House Square, and the United Mine Workers still make an annual pilgrimage to this spot each October 29.

In the early days of his career, after he launched out as an organizer, Mitchell would come to a mine with his coat slung over his shoulder, his sleeves rolled up. His black hair lay down over his high forehead. Keen brown eyes in a swarthy face misled many into mistaking him for an Italian. Mitchell was Irish.

Those were tough days, tough as any in the history of our country, and coal mines were tough places. When the quitting whistle blew and the miners came up Mitchell would stand on a freight-car coupling or a pile of ties and gather the men around him. Then he would start to talk. He had a remarkable voice, and as he spoke you could see the thoughts of his listeners follow every word. The men would lean forward, their hands grasping their picks, their heads nodding in agreement. Their faces were as black with coal dust as their grimy clothes. This stranger could have told these men anything, but the fact is he told them the truth. He was organizing his union literally from the ground up. Of the 300,000 miners in the bituminous fields, less than 10,000 were members of the United Mine Workers.

The miners' women would listen too, a little frightened, their eyes less intense, their lips parted. They would shush their children when they moved or, if that failed, give them a half-tender slap and send them off to play in the shade. Sometimes a woman's hand reached out and lay possessively on the arm of the man beside her. "Be careful," the hand's pressure would say. "Don't listen like that. Don't look at him that way." But all men listened to John Mitchell, and among those who did was my father.

Father agreed completely, absolutely, with two thirds of what Mitchell said. He disagreed violently with the balance. On this third of his program, Father fought Mitchell all his life. On the two thirds he was Mitchell's most important supporter. And in all he was Mitchell's dearest friend.

Mitchell's biographers always point to the remarkable open-mindedness of these two men, their mutual respect.

And today, when the words "collective bargaining" sound like an advanced idea, it is interesting to realize that the first collective-bargaining agreement ever signed between any coal operator and a labor union was signed over forty years ago between my father and John Mitchell.

It created a sensation and caused Father many difficult hours with other coal operators. But Father believed in collective bargaining—believed in it thoroughly. It was part of the two thirds in which he went along with Mitchell. But it was not a cure-all then any more than it is now.

Father challenged this union leader any time he saw fit. He fought against Mitchell as of a Monday, sided with Mitchell as of a Tuesday. There was one famous occasion when the central Illinois strikes were on. The miners were holding a meeting in the Masonic Hall at Braidwood. Alone, Father strode into the hall while Mitchell was speaking. He was as mad as any man alive, and he showed it. With a thousand miners packed in there, he mounted the platform, the only man in the room not carrying a union card, and all but called Mitchell's last statement a lie. Mitchell sat still, angry and flushed, the hard-set muscles showing along the line of his jaw. But he let Father have his say.

A miner in the front row hurled a chair. As it hit Father square on the shoulder the miner sprang to the platform. Mitchell jumped up. Father whirled around. They made a dive for the man together. Mitchell and Father threw that man out on his head. And, instead of a riot, the crowd began to laugh.

This was the American way.

If this were an account of genius it would not be important. Geniuses are few. The importance in the review of these careers is that they were *commonplace*.

Business enterprise in our nation never consisted of such noticeable titans as the Rockefellers, Vanderbilts, Hills, and Morgans any more than New York consists of skyscrapers. The skyscrapers are a noticeable feature, but they are not the city.

There had never been a monopoly in America on brains, good health, and education, and with these you could get along in this remarkable country. This fact—that a man could get along—was the chief incentive for every alert American. It was the chance to test himself, do what he wanted to do most, and make the best mark he could, that gave Americans their strength and gave America its place in the world.

That some should succeed more than others is natural and elementary. But it is not true that those who succeed do so at the expense of others. Exactly the reverse is the case. How could it be otherwise? Anyone with the slightest experience knows that men succeed by being fair, trustworthy, and co-operative; they bring others along with them, start countless careers in the wake of their own, help when they can, and in this way earn loyalty.

The primary factor in American life is our own self-faith. Out of self-faith, out of a clear vision and an unshakable confidence in his heart, the American man believes that he can stand up to the world of his times, whatever his times may be, refuses to be dissuaded or discouraged. In short, he doesn't quit. He drives steadily on, until he learns a trade or a profession, or founds a business, or develops his land and his future. Sometimes he founds a fortune and a legend. America abounds with such men. Their credit is character. Their funds are faith and hard work. Their purpose is the American way of life.

Surely there are greedy men and vicious men, as mean as snakes, and as cunning. But they are parasites on the American scene, as they are in any community where they appear. What thoughtful person would say that such scavengers limit the progress of life and that therefore the politicians should be our keepers?

A state of 130,000,000 Americans is not the sum of these millions of people. It is only the form of their organization. These millions are citizens of the State, of course, but that is a single matter. The State exists for the sake of man, and no man for the sake of the State. Each man lives, tries, loves and hates, dreams, thinks, and works for the most part outside the province of the State. His being is flesh and blood, and his citizenship represents only a fraction of his being. First, he is a creature of God and belongs to his Maker, to himself, his family, their cares and hopes. He belongs to his own religious sect, his profession, his business associates, his land, his vessel, the infinite variety of relationships in his community. He is not the building material of the national socialist, not an atom or a cell. He is an individual; he is an end, and not a means. The State is a means, not an end.

The handling of a state is as artificial as the making of a flower bed. A gardener tends to a bed and speaks of it as such. But the bed remains an artificial arrangement of flowers, as the State remains an artificial arrangement of men. The gardener can speak of the bed as blooming, smelling, or fading. Actually the bed does not bloom, smell, or fade. Only the flowers bloom, smell, or fade. Only the flowers live.

CHAPTER 4

The Hudson Tube Age Begins

BY THE EARLY YEARS of the century Father's interests were wide, but his heart remained in the Coal City operation. Nothing was too good for that mine. Father knew every inch of the vein underground, every piece of machinery in the tipple.

Matt Keefer always had tended to the mules, tough little Shetland mules, a cross between ordinary jacks and pure-blood Shetland ponies which Father imported from Scotland as an American experiment. Any man who worked at Coal City could write his own ticket when the time came to quit, and Matt Keefer's time was near. He had trouble with his eyes and was slowly going blind. He was all through, but Father simply couldn't tell him so.

Father bought a farm near the tipple as a surprise for Matt Keefer —built a house on it, barns and all—and just kept off the subject of Matt's eyes until the gift was ready.

On the day that everything was in apple-pie order, Father took him by the arm and walked down the road. They stopped in front of the gate, where Matt's two sons were waiting. Father whirled this big mule skinner around and grabbed him by his tremendous shoulders. "Matt, you're the best damn muleman in all the world," he said, "but you're a farmer now. I never had a better friend, God bless you." Great, hulking Matt Keefer cried like a baby.

"This is my wonderland," Father used to say when other interests tried to buy the Coal City mine. "Here's where I got my start. I own this mine with Billy Harkess. Billy and I will never sell it." They never did.

29

Father went back there often, and sometimes he took me with him. These were always great adventures for a city boy who occasionally had a chance to wear his Indian suit and shoot at hawks with his slingshot. There was no limit to the interesting things to do, and there was nothing in Chicago that half compared with them. I loved to go to Coal City.

A buggy would meet Father at the station, and I would pile in on his knee. If it was raining the countryside and the roads would be a sea of mud. The horse would tug at the traces and lunge so hard I had to hang on for dear life.

I remember Father's telling me not to be afraid. I can hear him now: "Never be afraid, boy. Don't worry too much about yourself and about getting hurt. People who go through life being very cautious miss a great deal. Take your chances whenever you have to. It's better luck, you'll see more, and you'll probably live as long anyway."

In Billy Harkess' house I could play with the dogs and the cat, and see the cream separator work on the porch. I can see every corner of that home—the blazing logs in the fireplace, a canary bird that sang beautifully, wall mottoes worked in colored worsteds: "Peace Be Unto This Household." There was a melodeon in the corner by some house plants, a rag carpet on the floor, and Billy Harkess had a split rocker where he sat and rocked, smoked his pipe, and told me marvelous stories of the time when he was a little boy in Wales. And Father would tell me some bear stories, and about the "secret place the elephants go," and about the fight Billy's big dog had with a wolf, and the one about the deer he killed near the tipple of the shaft.

At lunchtime we ate a big dinner. I sat next to Father, a thick book under me to raise my head above my plate, and Billy Harkess asked the blessing that contained not one word about poverty but was a plea to the Almighty that all of us might be properly grateful for the benefits and blessings that had reached us. Then the meal, home-produced, home-cooked, and home-consumed, and no chef ever concocted finer food. Finally, hickory nuts were cracked and eaten and a bag of red apples was laid aside. Sometimes I was given a large cake of maple sugar, and once at this moment Billy Harkess gave me his wonderful staghorn-handled jackknife, which was my most treasured possession and served me for long years.

No automobile in the barn, no radio or talking machine in the living room, no furnace in the basement, no gas or water or electric lights, no bathroom, no cement walks, no mail delivery or street lights, no airplanes buzzing overhead, not even a neighbor nearer than half a mile towards the mine; but hospitality, contentment, consideration, self-faith and integrity, and a determination to do one's duty and make the best of things—these were everywhere.

If Father and Billy were busy talking I could go out in the barn and slide down the hay chute, or climb up on top of the silo and see the whole country for miles. But the best thing of all was the endless wonder of the mines themselves.

The first time I ever went underground I went down into the darkness in a barrel. This was a new mine at Coal City; only the shaft and the main entry were finished. The elevator, called the cage, had not been installed. The hoisting engine lifted the workers up and down one at a time in a large wooden barrel. Dropping fast, it swayed and twisted in the slimy shaft, banged from one side to the other all the way down.

Father got into the barrel first, reached over, and lifted me in. The cable swung the barrel out over the center of the dark shaft, twisting us around and around as it dangled there. All I could see below was blackness and a tiny light at the bottom. The engineman threw his lever.

We started to drop. In an instant the white-blue of the sky, every sight, was gone. Father held me tight in his arms. My heart was beating like a trip hammer. My little world of time and space and the things I knew and could see had suddenly been whisked away, as though some giant hand had snatched it from around me. I had left the world for the first time in my life. Many times afterward, once frozen and blinded at night in a plane over the North Sea, and again tied down on ammunition boxes in a sandstorm over Egypt, the feeling of that childhood moment came back. The world was this. The only reality was what my fingers could touch. All else had been a dream, and this was not. All else had ceased to exist. This was really the world, always had been, and always would be.

But my father was there. I felt him in the darkness. We were dropping very fast in the rush of air. As the cage shot down in the darkness, banging hard against the wet, black walls, I could hardly catch my breath.

"Don't be afraid, son," he said.

The speed of the cage diminished. A pressure came in my ears, and I swallowed hard. A second later the black wall of the shaft before me suddenly gave way and we came to a stop at the bottom of the mine. Father lifted me out of the barrel. I was as bewildered as a boy could be; I just stood there, clung to Father's hand, and wondered what could possibly happen next.

The low, black roof, closely beamed with timbers, stretched back into the darkness. Thin tongues of yellow flames, spurting from the diggers' pit lamps, marked men working in the distance but did not disclose them. It was as quiet as a mausoleum; I could hear only the steady trinkle of the mine seepage, water dropping on loose rock, and Father's breathing near me. A mine is echoless, for sound, like light, is absorbed by the blotter-like walls of the tunnels.

Father called out, "H-e-l-l-o, John. H-e-l-l-o, John." Then he lit a kerosene torch, the flame blown forward by the downcoming current of air from the shaft behind us. He took a better grip of my hand in the dark and told me to follow him. Stooping low, the shale roof pressing down on us and the walls of coal pressing in on us in the darkness, Father led the way along the tunnel towards the yellow dots of light.

I could walk straight up, and this was very much easier. As we got further into the mine the air grew thick with a mist of fine coal dust. The mud was deep and very heavy. Two lights ahead appeared larger than the others, and from their jerky motion I knew the men were coming towards us before I could hear their feet thumping over the ties on the work track. The little lights bobbed closer, grew larger. Suddenly I heard a voice, a flat, eerie sound in the heavy air: "H-e-l-l-o."

Then below the lights I could see the body of a man, stripped to the waist, a black coating of dust that was moist with gleaming streaks of sweat. The other light was on the head of an animal. He was leading a mule.

"Look out for gas," the miner said to Father, not even seeing me behind him in the darkness. "There's a bit here up high."

He lifted his lamp slowly to the jagged roof. A quick, blue flame suddenly extended from the lamp and puffed gently at him as he took his hand away.

I was so astonished I could not speak.

How was I to know, as I stood there in my copper-toed boots, transfixed by all the mysterious things that were happening to me deep in the earth, that I and all the world stood on the threshold of the most quickening and bewildering era in the entire history of mankind? How was I to know that the small force of that puff of gas was no more startling and strange to me than were the forces which would seize and transfix adults too wherever they stood on earth that day? How was I to know that the suddenness of the quick, blue flame was no more abrupt than a new comet which had come in the sky with the turn of this twentieth century?

The things I could see and touch and feel, as I stood there in my copper-toed boots, were my world. Such was the world of adults too. Darkness covered me, as it covered them. Here in this tunnel men moved slowly, used picks as ancient as the discovery of metal itself. Men moved slowly in the world, used tools that would soon make way for the miracles of electricity and air. Coal supported me in my boots. Coal supported the world, made nations what they were, bound them into a system in which coal was the anchor and to which the chain of a century was being broken.

The modern world was growing in a headlong rush. The comet's tail was in the sky. The Hudson Tube Age was beginning.

Year by year mechanical things, and the systems that kept them operating, gained ground on the fundamentals of life. Year by year life itself became more subservient to this rotation. First more and more men, then more and more women, caught in the momentum of the mechanistic network, reached up and grabbed the comet's tail, enrolled in the task of hanging on. More and more men and women constantly devoted the energies of their lives, not to their own development, but to their development through the mechanistic network.

Like steam in relation to the coal and water from which it is made, the mechanistic network grew to be the real ruler of the men and tools which bound it together. Both labor and capital succumbed to the mechanistic network in serving it and in obtaining its benefits. For the overwhelming fact is that the mechanistic network became, as does steam from coal and water, *a separate force*.

As late as a century ago—a mere instant in the time of man— there were no basic industries. There were, instead, basic occupations, and they had not changed since the first day of civilization. There were three: those of the farmer, the shepherd, and the builder. These corresponded to the three basic physical needs of man—food, clothing, and shelter—which are the foundation of all society.

These are still the three basic physical needs of man, yet today we speak of the basic industries instead of the basic occupations. Actually, we devote ourselves to the mechanistic network, at the expense of the occupations. The basic industries are not basic for men and women. They are basic for the mechanistic network.

The length, breadth, and thickness of our lives changed into coal, steel, and chemicals. Separating ourselves from the good earth, we accumulated weight to a fantastic degree—our clothes and the factories that made them, our food and the slaughterhouses and plants that processed it, our refrigeration and the artificial-ice plants and electric iceboxes that kept us cool, our warmth and light and the central furnaces and power systems that supplied each in its turn, our writing and calculations and the amazing devices that did them, our speech and the heavy system of transfer which carried a metallic voice, our reading and the newspaper presses and magazine plants and bookbinding establishments that supplied it, our recreation and the ball parks that offered it, our amusement and the studios that delivered it. Notice how the weight shifted, even for warmaking. In Napoleon's day each soldier in battle was supported by one worker. In the Kaiser's day of World War I, a century later, it still took only five men in workshops to support a man in the trenches. Now, a moment later in World War II, it requires fifteen men in the mechanistic network at home to maintain one man under arms.

All over the world, men and women entered a network, relating themselves to each other in undreamed-of manners and with a sudden speed, accumulating additional weight around themselves for the purpose of transportation—more steel rails that carried their trains, millions and millions of automobiles and the highway systems, fueling systems, rubber systems, and credit systems that maintained them; airplanes and weather bureaus, landing fields and ticket offices; subways that rushed man underground, bus lines that roared and tossed over the hills and valleys; escalators and doors with electric eyes, elevators to whirl anyone a thousand feet in the air and deposit him there on a marble floor.

For all this network in its myriad complications man was only the partial consumer. For every pound of weight and every ounce of energy that finally reached him, and of which he was conscious, countless times as much weight and energy were necessary to maintain the network itself. As a consumer man received much from all this. But what was his place as a producer for himself? Each man's place was negligible—so negligible that it was like one straw in a gigantic and unsettled haystack. The product of his own labor did not apply to his own life at all, could support him in no way whatever. Man produced as a slender straw in a haystack, and he lived in a matted forest. Each man had been a tree himself for 10,000 generations. Then, in the twinkling of an eye, each became the straw.

For the mechanistic network represented an uprooting, in which man's struggle to sustain himself and his family was changed from a personal matter into a structural matter. The system which built up modern life, refined the substance of life, transported it, gave a new nature to everything. It made us more leisurely but more vulnerable.

Electricity and oil effected the ultimate transition. The dynamo and the copper streams of power systems, petroleum and explosive fuel, revised and accelerated the mechanistic network within itself, and uprooted the whole network from the anchor of coal.

All the technical developments of the Hudson Tube Age gravitated in the direction of creating and intertwining the mass everywhere: mass production, mass requirements, mass thinking, mass feeling, mass living. Mass armies.

The whole network is appropriate only to mass production for the mass demand of human masses. And these human masses, steadily growing more uniform, solidify themselves as both mass producers and mass consumers. In fact, the rotation is such that *it is difficult to see whether production occurs for the demand of consumption or consumption is controlled by the demand for production.*

Our own government's policy, for example, is so terribly confused by this rotation that many in authority discuss the matter as though they had been inspired into deciding which came first, the hen or the egg. Actually, one of the most elevated men in our government, without batting an eye, states that Americans do not ride around in 27,000,000 automobiles because they are prosperous —they are prosperous because they ride around in 27,000,000 automobiles!

Be that as it may, it is the mechanistic network, with its slumps and booms, purchases, horsepower, kilowatts, credits and loans, paper money and bank credit, personal and industrial machinery, communication and transportation, which now holds the real supremacy of the world and its inhabitants. Now civilized life is chiefly shaped and conditioned by this network, the workableness of which ebbs and flows in relation to mass habits, mass fears, and mass values.

A new superworld exists. Its forces, not those of nature or of nations, are shaping the destiny of man. *This superworld is the mechanistic network en masse.*

It is supranational, supraracial, and supraideological in its action and its effect. The action of the mass builds up a curious human solidarity in an atmosphere of predestination. The society within its momentum thinks, and must think, along predestined lines. I do not believe that any true philosophical mind can question this point for a moment.

The atoms of all this action are human beings, each of whom understands reasonably well his individual task and his general relation to those nearest him. Each has a piece of the jigsaw puzzle under his eye. But the size of the puzzle is so vast that when put together it is difficult for any human eye to realize the immensity of the picture as a whole, which is uselessly oversimplified by tallying any detail. Its over-all significance is lost.

Surely, we do not realize that a billion of us have conferred almost mystical powers on the mechanistic mass and that it has actually succeeded in mechanizing us, its so-called owners, to the point where we are bewildered by the complexity and determinism in which we find ourselves involved.

Jung long ago observed that Rome, at the beginning of the Christian Era, boasted three slaves to every two freemen. Then he went on to describe how this slavery influenced the freemen. "Every Roman," observed Jung, "was surrounded by slaves. Slaves and their psychology flooded ancient Italy, and a Roman became inwardly, and, of course, unwittingly, a slave. Living constantly in the atmosphere of slaves, he became infected through the subconscious. No one can shield himself from such influences."

The people of modern Europe, in our day, hardly realize how they have been infected by the almost mystical powers of the mechanistic network en masse. And surely we of the rest of the mass realize it even less.

When immense populations spend the whole of their working life doing something whose purpose they do not understand, handling things from mysterious sources, and delivering them to unknown outlets, they are very likely to acquire an attitude which makes them feel that the use and purpose of life itself is not only mysterious but totally beyond their grasp as individuals.

Great populations, regardless of nationality or race, and with little in common, begin to show a certain resemblance. They organize politically for what are really mechanical ends, and they themselves form what you could call a social network which has many similarities to the flow of mechanical life and constantly grows more like it. There is a certain spiritual interbreeding between the people and the mass. In a larger sense, the detached mass itself determines the nature of their political souls.

Yet Thomas Edison himself was not able to draw any human deduction from this. "It is hard," he once wrote, "to understand where everything comes from, where it is going, and why." If this was hard for Edison, imagine how hard it was for the rest of us. The answer is that we just did not know anything was happening to us, mentally, spiritually, and emotionally.

We did not know that we had created a miracle in the history of man—the miracle of doing more while thinking less.

CHAPTER 5

Woodrow Wilson Lived on S Street

Harvard's charlie brickley drop-kicked a football across the street to Yale's Jack Gates, perched on the balcony of the New York Stock Exchange. The Armistice was signed.

So the new era of peace began. That is what the Armistice meant. The Armistice meant peace.

But it did not last long. Even as our doughboys returned from camps and from overseas—just as they will return from the four corners of the world after World War II—even as peace became a reality instead of a dream, the nation still had the mind of a nation at war.

Step by step America had learned to strike down; not to argue or modify, but to strike. We had struck down the Kaiser. Soon we would have to strike down Woodrow Wilson.

Apparently we no sooner rid ourselves of old enemies than we acquired new ones.

As for my own thoughts about Woodrow Wilson: As a boy, Father had taken me to see Mr. Wilson at the White House. That was enough. I had shaken hands with the President of the United States, talked with him. The very school I went to and even my wondrous pony, Dinah, were known to the President of the United States. Sometime he might even say, "Yes, that boy has a pony and a dog too, and he is very much in favor of going to baseball games."

Further, and along more practical lines, when I asked the President whether it was true that he had his own special box at the Washington ball park and could go there every day if he wished, he told me this was true but that he didn't spend as much time in this box as he really should and arranged for me to see the ball game in it the next day.

Mr. Wilson was very superstitious about the number 13. He thought it lucky. (He timed the *George Washington* to arrive at Brest on Friday the thirteenth. He emphasized the importance of Article Thirteen in the League Covenant. He put in twice thirteen clauses, and announced its completion on the thirteenth of the month. His name had thirteen letters.) The President wrote the number on a piece of paper along with his name and gave it to me as a souvenir.

"I hope this brings you good luck, my boy," he said, "and keeps you from falling off your pony."

About Woodrow Wilson there could be no question at all. Woodrow Wilson was the greatest, the finest man in the world; anybody ought to know that.

But, now, in these later years, people talked as though he had ruined our country. What kind of world was this, anyway?

America was sick and tired of the whole European situation, wanted nothing to do with it. Our people didn't intend to be elevated by words of new sacrifices. They had made plenty of sacrifices already. Gone was the lift from high phrases, gone was any American confidence that the nations of Europe would ever learn their lesson. The tension of war was relaxing, the bubble of idealism had been pricked. Some Americans were tired of applauding the French; others had their own ideas about the English and the English treatment of the Irish question. Many were just fed up with "our noble Allies" in general, thought we had fought the war to save our own hides and that the talk about making the world safe for democracy was hypocritical.

The winds were shifting. Human nature was continuing its oldest and saddest habits. It was turning to "realism" exactly as it has turned at the end of every war in history, and exactly as it will turn again after World War II unless our wartime managers are exceedingly modest, careful, and restrained in what they do and say in the meanwhile. For by immodest promises and visionary plans many of our World War II leaders hurt grievously the case for America's place in the postwar world and immensely increase the already too great possibility that America will wash her hands of everything outside the twelve-mile limit, good or bad, at the earliest possible moment.

In 1918 the cons began to speak freely, where only the pros had spoken before. Millions listened, and did not know what to think, just as millions are listening now and are bewildered. They knew only that something was wrong somewhere, just as millions know that something is wrong today.

By the time I entered the University of Virginia in 1920 there were still men who wanted our country to take a place beside the continental nations and be involved in the European system, and possibly they were right. But the point is that their voices were small, and their plans were hopelessly mixed. Europe let herself down, and in the 1920 era the process was painfully evident.

No prudent man should blame America today for "letting Europe down," if that is what we did, after World War I. It is a fanciful and totally unjustified criticism. And any man who makes it should, in fairness and duty, speak first about what Europe did to itself, and then about what Europe did to us. In such talk about our place in the world and how we "let Europe down" last time there is the implication that the United States was largely responsible for the debauch in postwar Europe. This false idea would be bad enough as an injustice, but it is even worse than an injustice. It paves the way for the assumption that after World War II the United States can stabilize Europe if we finally use the powers for peace which have been contained in our great country all the time and "were not used before." That is a dangerous contention. And it oversimplifies even history itself to prove its point. For in our postwar service to the world and to ourselves we shall have to limit our commitments so that we can do our task properly, and we need to be warned that it will take great patience to succeed in even this rather than be told that we must do something anywhere in the world because we "failed" to do everything in Europe in the past.

International history has no bright page, but ours is the brightest of all. No American serves his country or tells the truth who tarnishes it with the word "slacker."

The leaders of the meek of the earth in Europe were as blind as the pet owl in Merlin's hair to the first rudiments of maintaining American relations. Regardless of the virtues in the Allied people themselves, all that the American people could see was the plain and fancy politics of their leaders. Once more the light of the meek of Europe could not shine through the darkness above.

Referring to the homecoming of one of America's most able journalists, F. P. A. wrote in his "Conning Tower" column: "Back from a trip abroad, Louis Fischer says that Europe has no goal. It will probably be charged against America that we stole the goal posts."

As for our country: In the last analysis it is the people who make the peace, and the fact is that, as soon as Mr. Wilson began to reduce his words to specific proposals, the people did not agree with him, just as they will presumably disagree with Mr. Roosevelt.

My father again took me to call on Woodrow Wilson only nine months before he died. This was in 1923.

For three years after his defeat Woodrow Wilson lived in a large, pleasant house on S Street in Washington. We went to see him there. It was late afternoon, a lovely day in June. He sat in a big chair by a fireplace in a bright, high-ceilinged room. A large clock ticked on the mantel, a French clock that might have come from Versailles. Someone was humming softly in the distance. I think it was one of the servants working in the hall, for I heard a door slam, and then there wasn't a sound in the house. Nothing but the clock ticking, as though measuring off each minute with great care.

It was quite shady where Mr. Wilson sat; the sun could not get at him, but it made the rest of the world bright and let him see out into the secluded street and hear the few footsteps that sounded on the pavement as they passed the quiet door.

"You must excuse my not rising," he said to Father. "I am really quite lame." Mr. Wilson's face was much fuller than I remembered it in the White House, and it seemed to me that there was a strangeness in his expression. His cheeks and forehead looked moist. He was now almost bald.

Mr. Wilson had a small tray on his lap, and a bowl of soup. He drank his soup and pushed the tray away, lying back in his chair very quietly until a servant had removed it and left us alone.

His hands were folded in his lap as he talked to Father and me, and he did not move his head. Only his eyes followed us as he spoke. They were keen and challenging, bright as a fire-flash, and as alive and vivid as though they burned with every thought in his mind. He was not feeble. Often his right arm struck the air in a weird and menacing gesture, then struck again and again as though he would be done with his enemies forever.

Now his voice was full of bitterness, and his words were charged with hate. His gray eyes flashed. "I want some scalps," he said to Father time after time, "and when I am well I am going to get them."

It made me catch my breath, and feel strange all over, to look at this poor man. Now I couldn't remember him as I had seen him before. I really felt terribly sorry we had come.

Five years earlier he had written:

My Fellow Countrymen; The armistice was signed this morning. Everything for which America fought has been accomplished. It will now be our fortunate duty to assist by example, by sober, friendly counsel, and by material aid in the establishment of just democracy throughout the world.

All over Europe there were countless millions of men and women for whom Woodrow Wilson had spoken as a messiah. These were the meek of the earth, who had no greed, no malice, no scheme; who wanted only to earn their bread, to protect their families and their children, to live their humble lives and worship their God. But even before World War I it was too late. *If it had not been already too late there would have been no war.*

The day after my visit with Woodrow Wilson I sailed for Europe.

I landed in Liverpool, traveled through the England of 1923, and saw a violent throwback from the war even more pronounced than our own. There had been a rush to forget the war as soon as possible. Those who fought in it, and my own younger generation, led the rush.

The scene was a long way from *Mr. Britling Sees It Through*. And there was something about it which seemed strangely disquieting. Whatever it was, it did not contain any thought of the congestion in Europe, on the Continent or in England.

In Bond Street photographers' shops you saw photographs of young women in court dresses, or of young men who might accompany the Prince of Wales on his projected inspection of backward Africa. Paul Whiteman, at the Savoy, led the best jazz band in London. He was introducing "Yes, We Have No Bananas" to enchanted Britain. No one had occasion to listen to the "Horst Wessel Lied" that drifted across the Rhine:

> Die Strasse frei den braunen Bataillonen;
> Die Strasse frei den Sturmabteilungsmann!
> Es schant auf uns voll Hoffnung Millionen;
> Der Tag für Freiheit und für Brot bricht an.

> (*Make free the way for our brave brown battalions;*
> *For gallant storm troops sweep the broad road clear!*
> *On us are fixed the longing hopes of millions;*
> *The day for freedom and for bread draws near.*)

"Yes, We Have No Bananas" set England's postwar tempo.

Important medals of the war were worn by men who were now hotel doormen. Cut-rate excursions were advertised to the battlefields in France—Reims, Chemin des Dames, Hill 108—places described like tours from Cairo to the Pyramids and the Sphinx: great but final tokens of a time and condition forever past.

A London–Brussels air route was just opening. Until 1923 the British Imperial Airways had not flown to Belgium. These were early days in postwar aviation, but I wanted to fly, and I had been invited on the inaugural trip by an English friend, Captain Walter Hinchliffe, the wartime ace, who was to pilot the plane. He had lost one eye, and his black patch was as familiar in England as Floyd

Gibbons' patch was to us. Hinchliffe was a good friend and a marvelous companion, who finally met his death at sea in an early attempt to fly the Atlantic east to west.

The party set out from Croydon with a good deal of fanfare. The ship was a new De Havilland, with a top speed of about ninety-five miles an hour. We rolled across the field to the strains of a regimental band, then Hinchliffe pulled the stick and we took the air.

Although this was only twenty years ago, even this most advanced type of airplane was clumsy and sprawling. It looked like Gracie Fields's "Biggest Aspidistra in the World." Its immense canvas wings all but flapped when it flew.

In those days, for reasons I never understood, European pilots liked to fly low. We zoomed over the English countryside, hardly above the treetops, as isolated dispatch planes and single warplanes on missions fly low over the Egyptian desert today. When we sighted the Channel, Hinchliffe put the De Havilland high, so that he could "glide to the other side" if anything went wrong. Down again when we were over France, and on across the poppy fields of Flanders. We flew low over the battered forts of Liége and Namur, the first bastions blasted when the gray German armies tore up "the scrap of paper."

Only eighteen years later I was to fly as low over the wrecked bastions of the Maginot Line, weedy and abandoned, see pillboxes which seemed ironically small, gaping steel and concrete sentries like the fort at Beaufort that looked as ineffectual as the painted cannon on a vaudeville backdrop. Then I was moving nearly three hundred miles an hour in the air, and battle on the ground had been as different. *Blitzkrieg*, and the next German menace, this time called "Nazism," had overwhelmed France in thirty-nine days.

But on the lovely August morning when I landed in Brussels only a few men were thinking about three-hundred-mile-an-hour airplanes, and nobody was thinking about *Blitzkriegs*. Hinchliffe and I were thinking about a good glass of beer, and the Belgians were thinking about the Ruhr.

We walked into the lobby of the Palace Hotel. There was a

dispatch from the New York *Times* on the bulletin board near the reception desk:

PRESIDENT HARDING DIES SUDDENLY; STROKE OF APOPLEXY; CALVIN COOLIDGE IS PRESIDENT OF UNITED STATES

"He was quite a different man from Woodrow Wilson, wasn't he?" Hinchliffe asked me as we stood in the Brussels lobby.

I mentioned that there was no more accurate way of gauging America's postwar public mind than by the speeches of Warren Gamaliel Harding.

Wilson talked of and for the world. Harding, commonplace and easy, stuck to his own front porch—mentally and physically. He was old-fashioned, amenable, simple to understand; "America's present need," Harding said, "is not heroics but healing, not nostrums but *normalcy* . . . not surgery but serenity." Postwar America tore the rafters down in cheering for this, just as it will again after World War II unless our wartime political leaders speak with restraint and care in wartime promises to the world.

The Harding-type vote was not a momentary surge away from Wilsonianism on the impact of the war's end. After three years in the White House, when Warren Harding died on August 2, 1923, the dispatch from the New York *Times* to Brussels described how the special train bearing his body was slowed at every station from San Francisco to Washington by thousands of men and women. The crowds of mourners were so dense that the train was nearly a day late. "It is believed," said the dispatch, "to be the most remarkable demonstration in American history of affection, respect, and reverence for the dead." This may sound strange today. But it did not sound strange then.

The Belgians and French were furious over England's and Italy's refusal to participate in the occupation of the Ruhr mines. "This Franco-Belgian action . . . is not a sanction authorized by the Treaty," Britain's August note said. The British had washed their hands of the continental problem of enforcing reparations. The Italians, technically as associated as the British, did likewise.

Each country had its own fish to fry, and each politician had his own job to hold.

Belgium and France, torn to shreds by the Hun, and tragically unique among the Allies and enemies alike in that they were the actual battleground of the war, had no patience with the crafty Germans in this stalling operation. And, when the German Government stopped paying its indemnities, the Franco-Belgian troops were prepared to enforce compliance. The German people cheered for every German politician, including Hitler, who objected to this policing. The result, as always, was passive resistance by the policed population.

France was the greatest military power in the world, maintaining the greatest peacetime establishment in history:

	France	Germany
Infantry regiments	223	21
Cavalry "	86	18
Artillery "	104	7
Engineer battalions	56	7
Tank "	19	None
Heavy artillery groups	282	None
Air squadrons	135	None
Balloon companies	18	None
Regulars under arms	650,700	99,191

Yet the policing idea, even on a limited scale in western Germany, was an utter and devastating failure. *It has never been possible, and it will never be possible, for a victor to police a highly developed nation, and especially an industrialized nation.*

No nation resents anything so bitterly as the presence of foreign troops on its soil, whatever the purpose, "police" or other, and whatever the cause, and in a thousand ways the Germans nearly drove the French and Belgians crazy. As the Franco-Belgian troops "policed" the Rhineland, all German factions initiated a boycott behind signs in hotels, restaurants, and shops. Some signs were red. Others were black. In either case they said the same thing: "French and Belgians Will Not Be Served Here."

Every worker showed up for work from two to three hours late in the morning. The Ruhr miners went down in their shafts, but they did not lift their picks. The whole country soldiered on the job, and every local politician, like Hitler, who shouted against policing had an issue supplied him on a silver platter. What local demagogue would overlook the opportunity to thunder against policing? His appeal is automatic, it is universally effective.

Whoever promises "joint policing" as a post-World War II operation for Americans in Europe promises a preposterous nightmare.

Our American citizens and our soldiers deserve a better victory than that in this war.

CHAPTER 6

Europe, an Impoverished Peninsula

THE EUROPE OF 1923 had changed little when I returned there in 1928. The feelings and problems of my own generation abroad had changed even less. Europe just looked better in the newspapers. It was only the statesmen who were in the headlines.

Their rosy words of 1928 made pleasant reading in the United States and contributed to the losses of all Americans who invested in German loans and securities.

The largesse of the outside world, chiefly the savings of the American public, was Germany's meat and drink. And the Germans drank it like swashbuckling buckeens until they left America, and every other country which trusted them, holding the bucket.

The whole prelude to Hitler was in the hands of conservative, traditionalist Germans, and openhanded Americans gave them the greatest free spree in history—to the sorrow of the American people and the ultimate sorrow of the gullible world.

This is what our dollars meant to our war enemy:

Germany's Industrial Production		*Germany's Foreign Borrowings*
1925	63.0	$500,000,000
1926	81.2	700,000,000
1927	96.0	660,000,000
1928	100.0	600,000,000

In these four years alone the United States gave Germany nearly a billion dollars more than the entire prewar debt of our nation. If we had paid it to ourselves, instead, we should have written the slate clean of our own prewar indebtedness and have paid off nearly a billion dollars of our war indebtedness besides.

No wonder wondrous Dr. Hjalmar Horace Greeley Schacht had honey in his mouth on his visits to America. Is this the America that let Europe down? Is this Uncle Shylock? None on earth are as free with their lives or their savings as the American people. But if the Germans ever really thanked us we should know, like the boys who painted Tom Sawyer's fence for him, how valuable and fantastically liberal we are. And we would probably not do it again.

The Secretary of State, Mr. Kellogg, had forwarded the Locarno powers a plan for the renunciation of war. It was a wholesome and honorable statement on the most elementary moral plane, and if this simple agreement did not work what contract could?

At once the German politicians rushed into print. The Germans fairly tripped over American newsmen in their eagerness to speak. Their conveniences of red tape and delay were cast to the four winds. Platitudes stumbled over platitudes. The "official spokesmen" were rudely hurled from the ventriloquists' knees, and the Great Germans themselves revealed their voices and bowed their words onto the breakfast tables of the world.

Since the whole thing required only renunciation of aggressive war and involved no sanctions or penalties, this clamor of approval was foolproof.

The pact was promptly signed by the continental powers on August 27, 1928, at a ceremony which I witnessed in Paris.

Over all the years, working or on holidays, from one end of the Continent to the other, I always enjoyed Europe. Except for the Nazis, I liked the people enormously. I found it easy to get along with the European temperament. I never felt any restraint abroad, or any sense of distance. I never had the feeling of being far from home.

Rich sounds cling in my mind, clear as the moments that bore them: sounds that recall friendly voices, revive the clatters and stillnesses of cities and countrysides I love, sounds that bring back the shouts of kind people, echoing across Swiss lakes or out of the snows in the mountains, sounds that replay the music of Bayreuth,

Paris, and the Mediterranean shore, or seem to be the Viennese stationmaster's whistle or the clack of wooden shoes on the flagstones at Marken, or to give again the round, full note of Spanish bells, speaking the summons of a church to its faithful.

Yet, under these, like the dull thud of the miners' powder blasts under the surface in Father's mines, I always heard a dull thud under Europe. I heard it through the whole postwar era. The sound grew and swelled with each visit, and as I saw each country time and again the cumulative effect was inescapable.

Structures like the European civilization do not pass away in a red blaze—they wear away in a hazy mist. It would be as difficult to state when this process began as to announce the date of the decline of Rome. But certainly both World War I and this war are symptoms and not causes of the transformation.

War itself could not hurl the Continent into new Dark Ages in this or any other generation. The idea of collapse as the result of war is too deep-set in the public mind to be dislodged by the roaring facts of history, and I suppose this is natural. But the chapter and verse of history cry "No." No civilization of importance has ever been destroyed by war, and those which have been permanently reduced by battle were already so prostrate from other causes that war simply delivered the *coup de grâce*.

The millennium-long role of Europe was as an appendage of Asia, impoverished in both resources and climate. Until our rich, new continent relieved the pressure the Europeans were in the larger sense fighting a rear-guard action against the expanding peoples of the Mongol East.

Western civilization described a semicircle. Beginning in Egypt, curving northeast by way of Mesopotamia and Turkey and the Aegean Islands, it followed its course westward until it reached the European peninsula.

It reached there through centuries crowded with wars, and it fertilized itself on the European peninsula in its own blood. Europe was conceived in war, lived in war, and actually grew in war.

European history is the saga of an immense and shifting struggle between the leading countries and those that hoped to succeed them. This is so elementary, so irrefutable, that it is astounding how words and phrases have obscured it at regular intervals for nearly five hundred years.

Spain took over the great Italian commercial republics and the sea lanes of Portugal. As soon as she had these, Spain and Portugal were no longer, from Spain's viewpoint, "enemies." However, Holland was growing. The Dutch Republic, a midget in this battle royal, did amazingly well. But after the Dutch acquired valuable sections of the Spanish world, France and England sprang into the Dutch corner to relieve the Hollanders of most of their gains. Then France and England battled for these Dutch gains, and for everything else in sight. This time it took a good many years of costly warfare.

England won, and she held the balance of power in the world for over a century.

This was a great boon to the world, for England established the principle of working towards self-government. This was unique in the history of large empireship, and, although the process was slow, it was as constant as the great diversity of England's problem would permit. There had never been such an important and valuable stabilizing force in the world as the British Empire.

For the glory of England does not lie in her flag, but in the justice and quiet independence of her average citizen. There has never been a good cause, no matter how distant, which has not found Englishmen among its courageous champions. If his country fails in its duty or its honesty, the Englishman stands and says so, and the government he attacks will respect him. It will, in fact, protect him against the very politicians whom he so often criticizes and whom he frequently surpasses in courage and intelligence.

New America supplied the Europeans with a secure new breeding ground and at the same time revived the wealth of the European peninsula.

Europe stirred from centuries of stagnation. America, and the conquests in Mexico, Peru, Africa, and Asia, gave the Europeans new strength in their continent, new channels of trade through which impoverished Europe could take advantage of its technological superiority over the rest of the world. Europeans could thrive under the umbrella of the mercantile system of exploitation, founded on the exchange of steam-made goods for raw materials.

Charles V pioneered this program. Then the alert Queen Bess made it the principle of British economic life. In behalf of France the Bourbons cast this country's lot in the same direction, and the renowned Colbert, Louis XIV's Minister of Finance, became the Messiah of Mercantilism.

Cromwell's foreign policy was the mercantile system in the raw, but whatever the time and whatever the country the system was always the same. As for the effect on the far-off heathen, a colony became a land of honey to be drained for the folks back home. Asia, America, and Africa were raw-material pools, monopolized for the most part by whatever country staked out its claim and maintained its "rights" of possession.

But Napoleon left victorious England with heavy debts, and the English population had tightened up their island, changing it from a place in which the English could live into an island on which many must starve. The only recourse was to import foodstuffs, and then and there England became a food-importing nation in a larger way each year. The only way in which England could pay for food and meet her unfavorable trade balance was to export goods. She had no forests for the exportation of timber. She had no iron for the exportation of ore. She had no fields from which to export anything. She had no herds (just as she has hardly any oil today, and no water power with which to make electricity). She had only coal—and Watt's steam engine. As she drew her belt tighter, England plunked hard for industrialization. She hitched her national life to Watt's invention.

The influence of this blessing upon the social and political structure, the life and future of England, staggers anyone's imagination. This moment was literally a miracle outside the ordinary course of history. What would have happened if several quiet men had not already thought out the matter of other machinery and if England had not found at hand at this moment the invention of a penetrating spirit?

But, from 1066, it has always been the miracle of all history that the English could do so much with so little. This has been due to the spirit of the people, the nature of the Britisher, the intelligence and sense of balance of the British man and British woman, which has always been there as it is there today.

Both England's distress and England's salvation through the steam engine had a profound effect on Europe and the world. England took new life.

In less than twenty years—within a period approximately as brief as the sensational development of modern Russia—England sprang forward. Towards the end of these twenty years first France and then Germany felt the sparks of British invention and followed in England's wake. Man and new machinery were acting and reacting.

In this period, first in England, next in Germany, and then in France, the population on the European peninsula swelled like a sail in a new wind. Between 1800 and 1835 England's population increased 57 per cent, *the most striking birth-rate increase in all history* and one of the outstanding phenomena in the career of man. At the same time Germany's population increased 26 per cent, France's 21 per cent.

English landholders, furthermore, were moving into towns, beckoned there by the royal scepter of the mercantile system. In England, in percentage of total population, industrialization reached a degree of urbanization by 1820 which even Germany did not reach until 1900.

In this way England became the world's vendor of finished products, and the world became purveyor to England of raw material for machine and human consumption. England's chief market was the Continent itself. Over 60 per cent of England's exports went to the continent of Europe in 1820. But by 1860 the Continent had developed so much manufacturing within itself that it could absorb only 38 per cent of British trade, and England made up the slack by violent expansion into the world markets, while France, Belgium, and Germany steadily took over England's place as purveyors on the continent of Europe.

From 1875 to 1900 Europe gave consideration to modernizing

its fringes, its Mediterranean and Balkan outskirts in particular. But natural poorness, the political and financial confusion, and the social systems preserved since the Middle Ages repelled all advances. The capital of Europe turned to more fertile fields, to the younger countries overseas.

The countries of the Continent, with England, stepped up their attention to the outside world with great competitive force and struck out vigorously to add to their colonial outposts in the English pattern.

France became a colonial nation with "rights" in Algeria, Madagascar, Annam, and Tongking. In her typical atmosphere in inevitableness, heavy-handed Germany discovered that she had "rights" in Africa's Cameroons and in New Guinea and the scattered islands of the Pacific. When the spears of the Negus plugged Italy's suction pipe in Abyssinia the Italians dispossessed the Turks holding Tripoli.

But England remained the center of gravity in the mechanistic mass.

"Steam," said Emerson, "is an Englishman." And so it was. Low-cost collieries served British factories at home and shipped British coal overseas. British steam-driven merchant vessels carried British steam-made goods. Coaling ports in the vital military crossroads of the sea lanes enabled the British Navy to protect this commerce. Britannia ruled the waves, but under the sufferance of King Coal.

To a lesser degree the pattern throughout Europe had been the same. Modern Europe was founded on coal. *It had, and has, only one abundant natural resource: coal.* Actually the protruding axis of the whirling mechanistic sphere was grounded deep in the earth, deep in the coal mines of Europe.

The increased output of coal is the measure of Europe's fantastic speed in development. In 1800 the world's coal output was about 12,000,000 tons per year. By 1850 it was 85,000,000; by 1870 it was 243,000,000. Europe was producing 200,000,000 tons of this total output in 1870, and 130,000,000 tons was concentrated in the adjacent island of England alone.

In England, also, liquid iron was purified of the phosphorus which makes it useless, and this added the decisive step in the march of modern metallurgy and gave English steel its dominant position along with English coal.

In another burst of energy and ambition, Europeans set out in earnest to conquer distances and to build. And, again, they multiplied fantastically as they did so. This multiplication was the greatest of the phenomena leading up to the Hudson Tube Age.

From 1875 to 1900—a mere twenty-five years, two and one half miles on the map of man's time on earth—Europe's population increased from 239,000,000 to 316,000,000. Exclusive of Russia, there were 77,000,000 new souls on the European peninsula. Then and there, Europe suffered a basic distortion of population from which it has never recovered; for, later on, the sustenance of this excess population was to disappear.

From 1875 to 1900 English railways increased 40 per cent, French and German railways an average of 120 per cent, and throughout the world from 150,000 miles to 490,000 miles. In fifteen years alone nearly $23,000,000,000 was invested in steam railways.

The Suez Canal sped the changes in world shipping. Sails were furled, and steamships dominated the markets of the world. The volume of trade in England, Germany, and France rose from $6,000,000,000 in 1875 to $8,500,000,000 in 1900. The British mercantile marine grew from 1,000,000,000 gross registered tons to 7,500,000,000, an increase of 520 per cent. The number of steamers in the world increased from 820 in 1860 to 1,230 in 1900.

(By the outbreak of World War I England still maintained well over a billion dollars' surplus from her shipping trade to invest in other enterprises. Later, before World War II, this had shrunk to such a degree that when England entered World War II the balance was less than $150,000,000 a year.)

Gradually Europe's opportunism outopportuned itself. Technological Europe committed suicide. Seeing better profits through cheaper labor, Europe entered a program of transferring part of its modern machinery to the backward countries themselves. It is doubtful whether Europe could have maintained its original monopoly for longer than it did; but, in any case, when Europe delivered her technology and skill to the backward world, Europe deprived itself of the advantage on which it had lived in the mechanistic structure. Europe folded up its own umbrella. Europe's antiquated mercantile system, filtering all through the network of the superworld, rolled over and died. Its demise left 60,000,000 of Europe's 400,000,000 population dependent on government aid in one form or another for half of the present century.

At the same time King Coal lost his hold on the mechanistic network as a whole. Throughout its growth he had lent at least a certain fixedness, a certain restraint, to the whirling mass. Now the anchor was pulled up. The protruding axis was suddenly jerked free of the ground by the network's new taste for electricity and oil.

Basic elements within the sphere were not only changing because of the death of the mercantile system, but the sphere itself was released from the localities where coal was abundant and began to revolve in the new and unfixed fields of electricity and oil.

The superworld began to roam.

Europe was faced once more with the realities of its meager resources, its small and dwindling assets, its fundamental characteristic of being utterly unable to sustain itself.

In this way, to the sadness of the world, the European peninsula began to retrace its steps, descend again to its historic position as an appendage of Asia—and a pauperized, congested appendage at that.

World War I obscured this temporarily, but, while it was obscuring it through mobilization and regulation, at the same time it destroyed the last vestige of industrial stability. The shock of peace on an unsound economy did the rest. Peace, not war, revealed the hopelessness of Europe's plight.

When peace came Europeans tried to find their way back into industry and trade. It wasn't there then, and it will never be there again in sufficient volume to support them.

Europe had been falling off rapidly as a food-producing area ever since 1914, but after that war the fall-off became violent. Not only did the curve of Europe's food imports turn up, but the nature of these imports changed. Europe never recovered, in the best postwar years, even her prewar deficiency.

After the last war Europe bought less wheat but more flour, less raw rice but more polished rice; she bred fewer cattle but bought instead ready-cut beef and mutton from South America, Australia, and New Zealand; she produced less milk and bought more evaporated milk in cans; she produced less butter and cheese and imported more frozen butter from Siberia; her hens gave fewer eggs, and she bought egg yolk instead.

Europe's annual imports between the two wars increased roughly as follows: grain and flour from 36,000,000,000 to 79,000,000,000 pounds; meat from 300,000,000 to 5,512,000,000 pounds; milk from 8,000,000 to 106,000,000 gallons; butter from 128,000,000 to 298,-000,000 pounds; cheese from 220,000,000 to 320,000,000 pounds; eggs from 13,000,000 to 88,000,000 pounds.

England's imports of finished manufactured articles increased 70 per cent. England, thanks to her banking and to foreign investments which she had then but which she has lost in World War II, was in a position to pay for this drain on her national economy and have a stable currency longer. But the continental countries were not. Work fell off everywhere. Incomes shrank, unemployment rose. Europe was a self-sacked city. *Sixty million people in Europe received unemployment allowances in one form or another for twenty years.*

In failing government economies there is a scarcity of everything except money.

Throughout Europe each country was swamped and smothered in the crazy quilt of the whole: kings and soviets, dictatorships and democracies, revolving pin-wheel cabinets and stationary regencies, social-worker adventurists, college professors, saddle makers, Marxists, and wearers of the old school tie.

The first World War increased Europe's nations from twenty-five to thirty-five and supplied 6800 miles of new boundaries to defend. It is careless to look at Germany's career and say that "bad times" there made Hitler possible. The conditions that "made" Hitler covered Europe as a whole. The most fantastic coups had

already occurred in countries all around Hitler and had preceded
Hitler in Germany: in Russia, Italy, Hungary, Austria, Poland, and
especially in Germany's former ally, Asiatic Turkey, where the
British and French had been intriguing against each other and
Mustafa Kemal Pasha had rallied a youth movement in the Milli
Mücadele, "The National Struggle."

Hitler came late.

"The National Socialist plan promises you Strength through
Joy," he said. "We shall banish want. We shall banish fear. The
essence of National Socialism is human welfare. There must be
cheap Volkswagen for workers to ride in, broad Reich Autobahns
for the Volkswagen. National Socialism is the Revolution of the
Common Man. Rooted in a fuller life for every German from childhood to old age, National Socialism means a new day of abundance
at home and a Better World Order abroad."

CHAPTER 7

The Idea Spreads to America

W<small>HEN</small> governments go bad in a large area, anything can happen. For the mechanistic sphere, with all its mass action, *communicates* its political venoms.

This is why, since the mass forces took hold and the mechanistic sphere began to roam, occasions of economic and political crisis have multiplied. And this is why there have been fewer crises affecting only one country, confined to a single nation.

The mass forces have presented mankind, therefore, with a new kind of crisis, the LONG-DISTANCE CRISIS IN GOVERNMENT IDEAS, which advances and spreads in the saturating way that a tide fills all crannies of a cave.

This is reflected in the amazing similarity of political movements all over the world, all in a direction away from individual self-faith and national integrity and each in the hands of men who ride the forces of discontent in the way most practical for their special locality.

Therefore the brew of bad government has blended between nations, boiling to higher and higher levels as one moral value after another has been sacrificed to meet a general pattern of financial, social, and political expediency. And the tragedy of the world is that our own country, which should have repudiated this process with every act and every deed of its national life, took its place in the pattern along with the rest.

Instead of dedicating our nation to arresting the swing away from self-faith, our national socialists actually accelerated it.

Communism is the red. Fascism is the black. We are shepherded into a blending. We are both reddish and blackish. We are a brown. For the fundamentals of the government idea brought forward in our country were already prepared in a combination of the polyglot doctrines of Europe. *Our government became Europeanized.*

In the name of a strong personality, our national socialists practiced in wider and wider measures a strange mixture of sheer opportunism, emotional economics, and reckless adventure along with a hardheaded political program of making the labor unions and farmers of our nation so dependent on *special* favors from them that they could control the votes of these two groups and thus maintain themselves in power indefinitely.

In this, they performed a profound disservice. For one of the political venoms communicated from abroad is that even America now wonders whether democracy will work. *We are losing faith in our own system at home while we battle the system of our mortal enemy abroad.*

The depression itself was not a direct reflection on the American principle of self-faith and the fundamentals of American government.

In the worst months of the depression it seemed obvious that the closer we stuck to the fundamental truths—economic, political, and social—the quicker and more certain our recovery would be. The real danger was that we would lose our heads and go off on some tangent when our basic problem was to keep our heads and undo our mistakes one by one.

As with all, things were very difficult for me during these years. I had to meet my problems the same way that all others had to meet theirs—by working harder than ever before, by developing new products in the paper company I ultimately founded, and by protecting my savings as best I could.

Two Douglas airplanes had flown around the world—the first aircraft of any nation to circumnavigate the globe. They carried United States Army Air Service fliers. I was convinced that these ships were the best planes in the world, and I had bought a third interest in the Douglas Aircraft Company at Santa Monica, California. I had all confidence in this company, and it turned out to be justified, but I had to sweat through it. There was nothing else to do.

I seldom left my office, and it did not seem possible to keep up with one disaster after another. Sometimes I didn't know whether I was coming or going, and I could see myself and my friends age in front of my very eyes. We were all up against it, and we were all up against it together.

Otto Schnering's immense confectionery company in Chicago went into the hands of a creditors' committee, owing me nearly all the money I had in the world. But every man who ever knew Otto Schnering trusted him. I had known him all my life.

"Harry," he said, "we can't collect the accounts due from our customers now. We can't pay your bills now. I know what this means to you, and I won't let you down. If everybody will wait and is willing to help I can see this awful time through." His whole life centered on this task. His courage never faltered, and his word never weakened. He fought like a tiger to keep his business—and his honor. He did both. He paid every cent he owed. And through his self-faith and integrity his company retained its place as the largest candy manufacturer in the industry.

In all these trials and bewilderments it never occurred to him that the depression was proof that our nation was weak and that free enterprise had failed in America. He knew that neither of these contentions was true. He did not think that any American had the right to lose confidence in himself or his country at a time like this, and of course his common sense rebelled at the assumption that we had become the greatest nation in the world by doing everything wrong.

I felt the same innate protest against the suggestion that we had reached our peak, that henceforth we could not have a national life of our own but must, instead, adjust ourselves to the qualities of a governmentalized civilization. I thought this a cynical and mischievous contention, and I resented it as un-American.

I felt it just as untrue to believe that the depression had stabilized us at a low level as it had been to believe that the Coolidge prosperity had stabilized us at a high level. And, in any case, by the summer of 1932 it was clear to anyone who traveled around our country that we were on our way up. The real bet for the future of our nation and the future of the world was that we make the grade soberly. The Europeanized national socialists, however, were sure to scrap the good things with the bad in the process of their national socialism.

All my life I had been steeped in the cause of liberalism. And, for a number of years, I had been urging certain economic modifications in American and British technical periodicals. About this time I was invited to lecture before the Economics and Political Science departments of a large New York university. In a question period afterwards a student remarked: "I disagree with nearly everything you have said, sir. But, you see, I'm a liberal."

The term "liberal" had grown so out of hand that an honest use of it was impossible. I stopped saying I was a liberal. I have refrained ever since from saying I am a liberal. I answer that I am an American and let it go at that.

National socialists stole the liberal label and falsified the concept.

It is typical of national socialism that it calls itself liberal when it is, in fact, reactionary. It is reactionary because it turns back the course of man's advance to the liberal social order which it seeks to overthrow. Its enemies are Chatham and Burke, Fox and Pitt, Palmerston and Cobden, Bright and Gladstone, and, on our side of the Atlantic, Washington and Franklin, Jefferson, Madison, Clay, Webster, Lincoln. Where in all history can be found a group of names like these, and in what teachings have there been more fruitful influences in the thoughts and institutions of mankind?

Instead, there had been various sorts of incompetents, like Karl Marx, preaching the doctrine of national socialism for the better part of a hundred years. But they were not listened to until the sudden growth and distortion of the mechanistic network, when new industrial, social, and economic problems began to face us with such force and in such a bewildering manner that, separated from the good earth, we hesitated to act in terms of what had, since the early immigrations to America, been the fundamental, underlying convictions of free people.

The great mass beliefs in a society of individuals, centering around Jeffersonian concepts of "individualism," "inalienable rights," "natural prerogatives," "freedom of contract," and similar conceptions, were appropriate to the task of instilling personal attitudes and habits favorable to all of us. It was only when the distortions within the mechanistic network diluted the power of these beliefs over the minds and hearts of discouraged Americans that the national socialists had their chance. History will never forgive them for having used their opportunity in abusive ways which led to weakness and cleverness when mankind all over the world had so much at stake in an American example of sobriety, stability, and integrity. It was against this new and saddening background here at home that I saw the wartime world abroad.

If our national socialists were honest with us, and with the world we seek to help, they would agree that it is moral principles, and moral principles alone, by which any individual's accomplishments should be limited. But they are herd-minded, and they have a special interest in the advancement of national socialism.

The State is both useful and dangerous. But the fundamental lie of national socialism is that it professes to be the sum of the State's citizens. It is really only the instrument of a few.

But our situation is temporary.

The changed world, with its problems of the mechanistic network, its lopsided development, its faster pace, its departure from old ways and the simple life of Billy Harkess' time, has never outstripped the American spirit.

The destiny of our country is within our people. The things within us that make us Americans can never change, please God.

CHAPTER 8

The Nazi Pigs Were in the Pasture

IN MANY MATTERS, the job of war correspondent has advantages.

I think I was the luckiest person I know in that my business interests turned out well enough for me to take advantage of the opportunity to devote a large part of my time as foreign correspondent for the North American Newspaper Alliance, owned by fifty American newspapers, and that my economic background gave me some basis for it.

Being a correspondent is printer's ink mixed with dynamite, however, and I saw the dynamite blow up in Germany in August 1939.

I arrived in Berlin directly from the United States. Once more I went all over Germany. The date was August 1. This time these strange Teutons were on the threshold of war. It was the very last moment before the march into Poland. The bars were down, and the Nazi pigs were in the pasture.

In the middle of August I made an air trip from Berlin to Scandinavia and back to Germany. I flew to Copenhagen. The Danes were nervous but reasonably hopeful. They reflected the German view. "The English will not die for Danzig," they said.

Woodrow Wilson had voted with Clemenceau that Danzig be handed to Poland. This gave Hitler capital to work on, for Wilson had refused a plebiscite. Lloyd George had insisted that Danzig remain in Germany. The solution, like most political solutions, pleased no one and settled nothing. Danzig was neither retained by the Germans nor given to the Poles.

I flew from Copenhagen to Stockholm. The larger interests in Sweden were fearful of war at any moment. They knew the basic German forces, and they respected the British far more than did the Danes. They saw the world picture.

Like the sociologist Pareto commenting on Aristotle, the most important man I saw in Sweden pointed out that views are often dimmed by much talk about how people ought to behave instead of discovering first how people do behave. The Swedes knew how the Germans behave.

On my return to Berlin, I headed west across Germany by automobile. I drove a German car to the Rhineland border and then drove two hundred miles down through the fortifications of Hitler's West Wall to Baden-Baden, near the Swiss border. Germany was ready in the east and ready in the west. The fat was in the fire.

Alexander Kirk, United States chargé d'affaires, America's top man in Germany in the absence of an ambassador, stood out like a star because he predicted that there would be war by fall and had been saying this all summer. He saw the boomerang in any appeasement, recognized the cruel and explosive force in German momentum. If ever anyone kept his head while others in Berlin's diplomatic colony were losing theirs, that man was Kirk.

Kirk, a bachelor, lived in a beautiful house in Grunwald-Brahmstrasse which he leased from an Argentinean. Each day, after leaving the Embassy, he worked there around the clock.

"It's war this time," Kirk told me. "The Germans want what they want without war. But if anything stands in their way they will fight at the drop of a hat. Make no mistake about that. They're going into Poland by September first, and the war will occur by then."

He had been reporting this consistently and emphatically to Secretary of State Hull and Under Secretary Sumner Welles. Even more important, these men, able, wise, and honest, the best international minds of this period, believed in the soundness of Kirk's reports from the time Kirk first decided that war was inevitable. Kirk saw nothing but a red herring in the "success" of Munich.

Actually, the war was sixteen years overdue. From the time I had seen the torches in the Unter den Linden in Germany and heard the marching feet of men of my own age in Italy, the war was on. Europe had temporized with dictator aggression for sixteen years to the very day. The peace of World War I was buried at Corfu with the first Fascist reassertion of power. Ending, after five short years, the lull in aggression since November 11, 1918, the Italians of my generation—cocky, loud, eager for trouble—bombed and occupied Corfu on August 31, 1923.

The war started on August 31, 1923, not on August 31, 1939.

And when Hitler thought he had neutralized Russia, the other great force in Europe, by his German-Russian Non-Aggression Pact, the deck was clear for action in the full arena.

In Berlin I had seen some of the Russian negotiators and a number of the Germans involved in the commercial treaty, but the final spadework on the non-aggression deal that made World War II feasible was done far away. Later, in Turkey, I was to find that the deal was actually made near Istanbul in a fishing cove in the Sea of Marmara.

I was in Baden-Baden on August 23 when news of the Hitler-Stalin Non-Aggression Pact burst from the Berlin radio: "His Excellency, Herr von Ribbentrop, is flying to Moscow with thirty-two experts of the German Reich. His Excellency, the Russian Commissar for Foreign Affairs, is waiting even now at the Moscow airfield. An agreement will be signed at once."

I was having coffee in my sitting room with a German who had traveled the world. He was no party man, not a Nazi. He was the best of what we think of as "a good German." Yet he jumped to his feet and shouted his pent-up feelings: "Now we have nothing to fear from Stalin," he said. "Now we can take Poland and settle that score." His whole nature responded to the electrical words. This quiet man's eyes flashed. His tone was eager, his breath came quickly. His Germany was busy doing something, and he was German. "What can England do to help Poland? This means peace," he said, as he paced up and down the floor. "England must stand by. She cannot interfere. Look at the map! Look at the map!"

To the German's dismay, I booked passage through the Deutsche Bank in Berlin on the first boat out of Europe. It was the *Nieuw Amsterdam*, sailing the next night from Rotterdam.

"Ribbentrop's sister says there will be no war with England," the German kept repeating. "I know the English very well. You are foolish to leave Germany."

The *Nieuw Amsterdam* docked in New York the morning England declared war.

By fighting when she did, England rushed the Germans' hands by at least five years and upset the whole fundamental sequence on which Germany intended to operate.

We could not have looked forward to winning this war had Hitler been able to complete his original strategy, which was to seize, organize, and exploit the Continent *before* he attacked en masse. He would have liked to fight the present war five years from now, with his Germanic Europe job and his continental Pax Germanica behind him, if others then resisted an Axis-dominated world.

Praise and glory to England and France. Without England's having fought when she did, and France's final willingness to risk death and destruction in the forefront, there would have been no future for free men anywhere on earth.

In October 1941 the "short war" was still going on—and I was going back to Germany and once more through Europe.

It was plain that time was running out fast for anyone going abroad a few weeks before Pearl Harbor. And I was to go a long way—from New York to Finland, and down through the Continent to Sweden, Germany, France, Switzerland, Spain, Gibraltar, and Portugal, and finally to England.

The first problem was to get from New York to Helsinki to visit the President of Finland. In order to do this I had to pass through Germany, and that meant the problem of how to do so on the eve of Pearl Harbor.

I ran into trouble right off the bat. Von Ribbentrop's Foreign Office in Berlin refused my transit visa through Germany the day before my clipper flew from New York. "The Foreign Office in

Berlin raises some question about the advisability of your going to Finland at this time," the German Embassy in Washington notified me at the last minute. "We must refuse you transit."

I flew to England, then across the North Sea in a plane at night, and over the Skagerrak and on to Sweden. As the whole trip developed, step by step, it involved 21,000 miles by air, and I found myself the last American to get in and out of Germany before the United States entered the war.

Except for five assorted Nazis, such as Grossadmiral Erich H. A. Raeder, sea-lord member of Hitler's Cabinet Council, every important leader I went to see in Berlin was a conservative, traditional German.

I certainly would not have gone into Germany when I did to find out more about the Nazis. Anyone who had seen them there since 1923 should know all he needed to know about this collection of hoodlums. And, in any case, who does not realize that they are America's mortal enemies? Therefore, it seems a little absurd at this late date to find so much written about the threat of the Nazis to free men. If there was ever an evident and banal subject this is it.

German refugees, especially the more sophisticated and brittle ones, offend America's intelligence and belabor the obvious when they tell us to beware the Nazis. We need no warning against Nazis. The Nazis are liars, thieves, murderers, and egomaniacs. No man in his right senses, American or European, would trust them as far as he could throw an anvil. We are at war with them, and we will never stop fighting the Nazis until the whole Nazi hierarchy is pounded to pieces, from Hitler down. There is not the slightest chance of England's or America's making "peace" with the Nazis. In the words of Winston Churchill, our idea is to "beat them to the ground."

Accordingly, the Nazis have lost their chance to fool the world. But the Germans, including some German refugees in our country who intend to return to Germany as soon as the war is over, know all this. And the Germans now are mending their fences. Another crowd stands on the threshold of creating the same situation that

Germans have created before, doing the same thing they did after World War I.

To find out what they were up to, I went to Germany to see "good Germans." I knew them and had seen them operate for eighteen years.

The beliefs of the so-called conservatives whom I saw in Germany from 1923 forward—Junkers, industrialists, diplomats, scholars, generals; Hugo Stinnes, Fritz Thyssen, Dr. Rudolf Havenstein, president of the Reichsbank, Dr. Hjalmar Schacht, Heinrich Brüning, Wilhelm Cuno, chairman of the Hamburg-Amerika Line, Albert Vögler, director-general of the United Steel Works, Felix Deutsche, chairman of Allgemeine Elektrizitäts Gesellschaft, the world-wide electrical trust, Helmuth Wohlthat, who carried on the loan conversations with Hudson in London in 1939, conservative army leaders like Brauchitsch, and all the others—had not changed in the intervening years.

These men—those now dead and those still alive—and the traditional Germans in general did not believe that Germany lost the last war. I am convinced that their attitude will remain absolutely unchanged at the end of this war.

I suggest that our next danger from Germany centers in the traditionalists. I believe that, along with certain German refugees in the United States, they are keeping us so busy thinking about the Nazis that we are fully prepared to make the dreadful mistake of believing we have eliminated the German problem when we have eliminated the Nazis. This would be a fateful error.

When we get rid of the Nazis we shall not have got rid of the German problem.

The German people as a whole stand committed on the record.

The Germans, fathers and sons, believe that their race is inherently superior to every other race and the German is the superior of all other people. This is a racial concept. It is not their estimate of Germany as a nation. It isn't directly related to Hitler, or the German Army, or what German soldiers are able to accomplish. It isn't related to losing a war, and, as a matter of fact, it is hardly embellished by winning a war. It is related to their blood.

They are strange people, these Germans. At least they have been in history, and at least I have always found them so.

In our generous American spirit, we just think too well of all people to blame the Germans as we should. That's what gets us in so much trouble. In international affairs we're openhearted, open-minded, and open-handed. The Germans are exactly the reverse, and so are most Europeans.

If you ask Bill Jones, from Atlanta, Pasadena, New York, or anyplace else in our marvelous land, whether he knows Tom Smith, he will say instinctively, "Yes, I know him. He was in my office the other day. Nice fellow."

"What!" you say in surprise. "Tom Smith is a convicted murderer and thief!"

"Is that so!" Bill Jones will reply. And then he will say a very significant thing, in the American spirit. "I'm sorry to hear it."

This is not a European reaction, and it is emphatically not a German reaction. The German mind would speculate on how efficiently Jones was caught, and how prompt his punishment. Then he would relate the incident to its place in the State: "There has been much of that lately."

He seldom uses the words "honor," "duty," and "talent" alone. It is always "German honor," "German duty," "German talent."

It is such differences as these which make us babes in arms when dealing with the mentality of the German people. We give them benefits of the doubt to which they have never been entitled by their history or performance.

Many ordinary Germans in Germany are unconscious of their attempts to camouflage this, for the German never sees himself as others see him. Though the party men are not, the so-called ordinary Germans are the most disarming crowd in the world.

As everyone who has been to Germany knows, the good German will be scrupulously honest in personal dealings, adore his family, educate them well, and carefully bring each child to adulthood. He will enjoy music and a glass of beer, lead a gentle life, give you whatever he can if he likes you. He will live up to every standard of decency, and he will be restrained by his conscience in all he does. *But the German has a blind spot.* It is a blind spot that has cost and is costing the world untold misery and suffering. He believes that the German race-nation has an inherent right to mastery, and whenever his country has the strength to demonstrate his belief he abandons tolerance, moderation, respect for the rights of the weak, justice, and the first rules of morality in favor of a Greater Germany.

Representing the top-flight traditionalist Germans and referring to them chiefly because they are known to so many Americans, you could not have better examples of this than Fritz Thyssen, Dr. Hjalmar Schacht, or Dr. Hans Heinrich Dieckhoff, last German Ambassador to the United States.

I was in the Foreign Office in Berlin with Dr. Dieckhoff on Armistice Day 1941. Naturally, it was no holiday in Germany. Everything was going full blast. The Foreign Office people were plainly resentful because Ribbentrop, always as close as he could get to the *Führer's* coattails, was seldom in Berlin. Dr. Dieckhoff spoke for Ribbentrop at the Wilhelmstrasse. Dr. Dieckhoff was popular in America and continually referred to himself as "still the German Ambassador to your country."

The Foreign Office is unexpectedly small. The building itself sits back off the Wilhelmstrasse on three sides of a bare cobblestone court, the front side consisting of a fence along the street. Sentries pace up and down before the tall gates, and two guards in dull-green battle dress and oversized helmets stand at toy-soldier attention in front of their cubicles. Ribbentrop's own section is the right wing as you come into the courtyard. A small white door leads directly from the court into his suite, which is on the ground floor and gives you the feeling of entering a maisonette.

Inside, the Virginia country house style of the exterior is forgotten, and you burst into streamlined modernism: overhead light tubes, square-cut furniture, blended colors, interiors and upholsteries like those of the new cars on our railroads. The hallway is narrow, the ceilings are rather low, and none of the rooms, including Ribbentrop's office, are large. You get the impression that everything is being done very close to the vest. Everyone I saw around Ribbentrop's office could speak English, and, like Ribbentrop, they spoke it without reluctance.

Dr. Dieckhoff sat me down in a chair on the other side of his desk in his room adjoining Ribbentrop's and, crossing his arms, fixed me with eyes hard under his beetling brows. His round face was pudgy, and he had something of a jowl. His business suit was a tailor's dream. His knuckles had little dimples, and his skin was very pink. Altogether, he looked extremely well fed, and no doubt he was. These bureaucrats live on the fat of the land.

"Why are you in Germany?" he rasped.

The question was abrupt enough.

"I'm just passing through," I replied. "I have an appointment in Vichy to interview Pétain. This Office was kind enough to honor the request of the Finnish Government that I be allowed to pass." I knew that he knew all about it, but that's the way these Germans are, and I've never found it feasible to do anything except answer their questions and not remind them that they know the answers anyway. They all have a Gestapo complex.

"I know all about it," he said.

Accordingly, we were ready to talk.

"How are things in America?" he asked.

"We grow stronger every day," I said.

Dr. Dieckhoff smiled. It was a very patronizing smile, and it would have made any American a little mad. He went on at great length to explain the sweetness and light of Germany's international intentions, threw in a few pat words about encirclement and such trash, and finally asked me whether I thought America was "ready to declare war on Germany."

I told him I did not know, but asked if it didn't seem obvious that Germany would hardly take a chance on this happening. I asked him if it were not about as sure a bet as any man could make that Hitler would declare war on us before we declared war on him. Wouldn't he try to beat the gun whenever it proved evident that we were set to declare war on him, thereby avoiding the appearance of being on the defensive in the eyes of the German people and, instead, once more appearing as the patient, peaceful man who had stood by until declaring war was the only right and proper thing to do, just as he had done in the case of Poland?

Dieckhoff kept walking around the office, agitated and blustering. Like the fat boy in Pickwick, now you saw him and now you didn't.

The variety of ways in which Dieckhoff protested and said "no" added up to a complete and simple "yes." And, as far as my judgment was concerned, they added up to a "yes" at any moment. I was to leave Germany by December 1. As I sat there I knew this was going to be a tight squeak. Actually, I knew the Germans might declare war on the United States any minute. If they did I would be in Germany for a very long time.

"Do you think Stalin expected you to attack him when you did?" I asked.

"No. There had been no previous demands, no negotiations. Our attack was a complete surprise to the Russians. But that was unfortunate for Germany, as it turned out. The main Russian armies were not at the front, not in position. When our blitz forces advanced we gained the ground, took our objectives, and encircled some troops. But we did not cut off or destroy any important quantity of Russian forces. Had the main Russian forces been in position we would have cut through and around the Russian Army as we did the French Army in France. We would be in Moscow today. Our own element of surprise cost us quick victory."

"It's hard to see why you attacked Russia anyway when you did," I said.

"Stalin was going to break the Non-Aggression Pact and attack us in the spring."

"Do you really believe that?"

"Yes. Ours is a defensive war. If the *Führer* had not marched when he did Stalin would be in Berlin next spring. Russia had 28,000 tanks and a larger air force than our *Luftwaffe*."

Dieckhoff frowned, as though he could hear the buzz of Russian planes in his ears and see the flash of Russian bayonets at his door. "Russia has great military strength," he said.

"Do you have to go to war with everybody who has military

strength?" I asked. "Stalin had everything to gain by staying out of war. Why would Russia attack you?"

"Russia opposes Germany's destiny."

"Who doesn't?" I asked.

Dieckhoff did not answer. He just pouted.

"If Russia is so strong, how do you account for her army's bad showing against Finland in the Russo-Finnish War, the winter war of 1939–40?"

"First, the Finns are terrific fighters, and they were fighting in their own woods, on their own land. Second, there was a great deal of faking by the Russians for the purpose of camouflage. They wanted to fool everybody, and they did. Russia wanted to look weaker than she was. They fooled the British General Staff observers. They even fooled our observers. We admit that. They fooled everybody but the Japanese observers. Both the Russians and the Japs know how to hide their strength. It takes a thief to catch a thief."

"You've mixed me up, Herr Dieckhoff. Japan is your Axis partner, and you call her a thief."

"*Ach*, you know I didn't mean that." Dieckhoff smiled.

"Germany did pretty well in hiding her strength too."

"On the contrary, Germany showed her strength at Munich. Germany used her strength to ask for peace."

It seemed to me it was now my turn to smile.

"But the *Führer* made a mistake at Munich," Dieckhoff went on. This was interesting. I had never before heard a German official say that Hitler ever made a mistake.

"The *Führer* himself suffered *a great disappointment in himself* the very day after the pact was signed. He confessed this to all of us. The *Führer* was sad after Munich, sad and self-angry. I was surprised, Mr. Taylor, surprised."

"What could he have wanted at Munich that he didn't get?"

"The *Führer* felt he should have attacked, and not held the Munich meeting at all. He has told me himself that he made a mistake in listening to advice. 'Chamberlain won this meeting,' the *Führer* himself told me. 'I should never have come.' Munich gave the British time, and with it the chance to somewhat balance Germany's strength. The morning the *Führer* returned here after the Munich meeting he swore to us that if he could ever again be as much stronger than England he would not be talked out of German victory a second time. He would attack."

"Of course he obtained that new ratio of strength when he signed the Non-Aggression Pact with Russia."

"Yes. By removing the threat of Russia we gained more in military power than England had been able to accumulate in the year between Munich and August 1939. Once the pact was signed, there was no possibility the *Führer* would make the mistake of Munich again. *There was never any chance of a second Munich*, as far as we were concerned."

"All this sounds pretty aggressive for a peaceful nation, doesn't it?"

"No. Germany wants peace."

I suppose we could have gone around and around in the same circle forever. My experience has been that this is what happens always when you trace an important German's arguments step by step. Like the Egyptian serpent, the argument swallows itself.

When Dieckhoff went to lunch he suggested that I walk with him, and we left the office together. Now, walking down the Wilhelmstrasse, Dieckhoff spoke for the conservatives. He was out in the open air. Didn't I realize what was going on? This war could not last indefinitely. The day must come when England and Germany would be friends. Surely, with the United States in the war, this prospect would be complicated, not only by the added strength of American arms, but by the necessity for dealing with America as well as England when the time came for peace. (Implicit in this statement was the assumption that Germany would lose the war when America entered it.) "Germany certainly has no interests whatever which are opposed to those of the United States. Or to England either," remarked Dieckhoff. My, no! None—except victory.

I had heard this in earlier years from Herr Fritz Thyssen, messiah of the German conservatives, steel king, self-styled "philanthropist," family man, gentle little wizard of the original Nazi moneybags. Thyssen answered me then, and Dieckhoff answered me now:

"Germany's destiny is very important." He spoke as a true German.

We reached Dieckhoff's house. I preferred not to go in, and we stood talking in front of his door.

"The *Führer* has had an important place in German life. He brought orderliness. Hitler is a great man. But we did not want war."

"Did you want Austria?"

"Austria is a German state."

"Did you want Czechoslovakia?"

"Czechoslovakia was a monstrosity of the League."

"Did you want Poland?"

"Now, Mr. Taylor, you have been in Poland. You know as well as I do that the Poles are an inferior race."

"Do you think the Norwegians, the Danes, and the Dutch, Belgians, and French are inferior races?"

"We were being encircled. We were going to be attacked. Germany's flank, Germany's flank."

We were off on the same old German merry-go-round. Perched on their wooden horse of Purity, they simply cannot break the monotonous rhythm of their contradictions and tell the simple truths, namely, that Germans would like to rule the world and that if they can at any time in history summon enough strength to do so, they will.

"Who was going to attack you after the Russian Non-Aggression Pact?" I asked.

"England and France, of course. England rearmed immediately after Munich."

"Rearmed? Don't you think she should have had a reasonable army and air force, when she had none? You know she wasn't rearming to attack. You know you did not expect that England would even fight for Poland, a year later. With Germany banking on the fact that England would avoid war at any cost, isn't it a little paradoxical to explain German action on the ground that Germany was to be attacked?"

"You never know, in Europe."

"What about France?"

"*France is a decadent nation.* What could you expect of a people who ruled themselves as France did? France is living in her past glories. France is finished."

"With a lost war Hitler is finished too."

"Germany wants peace."

"That means, it seems to me, that if you can win the war with Hitler you will keep Hitler, but if you lose the war you will throw him overboard."

"Hitler would not face defeat."

"Do you think, if he were licked, and knew it, that he would commit suicide?"

Dieckhoff did not answer.

"What happens if Germany loses this war?" I asked.

"Germany would recover from this awful war as best she could. You say Thyssen told you the world will discover that the German people can wait, *with better results*, than any race in the history of man. He was right."

"But that was in 1928, midway between these two wars."

"Germany will always be ready to wait," he said.

"And with better results?"

"Yes. Germany's destiny is very important."

"And Hitler would think of that when he committed suicide?"

"Hitler will always think of Germany's destiny. He would have failed, but he could not add to his failure by weakening Germany further if his battle is lost."

"Then the rock-bottom fact is that if the war gets too tough, and it is clear a year or so in advance that Germany will ultimately lose, you are convinced that German strength must be maintained and that you must go into an armistice period with a strong force still intact?"

"*If Germany is to be saved for her destiny,*" Dieckhoff said, "*the war must not be fought to the bitter end.*"

I did just what you would have done. I looked at this German and wondered once again at the uncanny shrewdness of this greedy nation in throwing itself on the mercy of a gentle world.

Many of the German conservatives, industrial leaders, bankers, scholars, diplomats, soldiers, know America well. Sometimes they seem to know us even better than we know ourselves, perhaps in the way England's Drinkwater, in his detachment, excelled Americans in writing of the qualities of Abraham Lincoln.

When these German traditionalists see the end, foresee Germany's defeat clearly and without question as a matter of six months or a year, GERMANY WILL NOT FIGHT IT OUT.

At this point all the logistics calculations go out the window, along with all the estimates for the probable length of the war. For they are based on the full and final defeat of Germany's military machine, entrenched on the Continent, and Germany does not propose to bleed to death.

The top policy makers of Great Britain are convinced of this, including Mr. Churchill. One of the most important figures in wartime England, a member of the War Cabinet of the Empire, expressed it to me, in fact, in approximately the words I have used here.

CHAPTER 9

This Life Is New

To REPORT on the position of Africa in the war and its relation to the postwar world I went abroad again as soon as I could manage to get off after my return from Germany, Finland, Sweden, France, Spain, Portugal, and England.

Events were spinning fast in the ancient lands, from the African hump to the Nile and from there to the Golden Horn of the Bosporus. Dakar and Casablanca were smoldering, Lake Chad was boiling, and the southern rim of the Mediterranean, the lake in the Europe-Africa land mass, was on fire.

Rommel's torch lit the sands. The flames lapped around the great bend of the lake's shore in the Middle East and flickered at the borders of Turkey.

Beyond Africa, my destination was Turkey. I was sent to see the Prime Minister of Turkey in Ankara and to visit the General Staff of the Turkish Army. Round trip, I was scheduled for another 30,000 miles by air.

Five of us made the start for Cairo: Brigadier General Patrick W. Timberlake, air combat officer, taking his post as Chief of the Army Air Forces Bomber Command in the Middle East; Colonel Louis J. Compton, Chief of the British Empire Section of our Military Intelligence, and Captain Charles H. Hiser, his signal officer; British Colonel Reginald R. M. Mayhew, British Royal Artillery Ordnance Corps expert returning to the Egyptian desert after consultations in Washington.

This was a war trip, yet in the entire history of fundamental science there has never been a moment when so many avenues for peaceful development have opened before the eyes of a distracted world.

The invention of the steam engine did not appear in news accounts which met the eyes of a world distracted by the Napoleonic Wars. Adam Smith wrote the *Wealth of Nations* while Watt was experimenting with the steam engine; he referred to it in his writings as a "fire engine" and dismissed it as such. Yet Watt's invention alone was a thousand times more important to the human race than Napoleon or the Napoleonic Wars, and, as a matter of fact, the simultaneous invention of the steam engine saved the world from much of the pauperism created by those disasters.

Now the next era's new tool is in the making. The airplane is coming of age. It was born of hard work and long hypothesis, and with every step in its development we shall have taken one more step towards the Age of Air. It can open vast new areas of the earth. New streams of development in all hemispheres will one day flow from this new river of transportation and communication: new lands, new soil, new life. Inherent in this invention itself, thought of so keenly for the winning of this war, is the greatest single contribution to future peace and a better world.

Our peacetime output of new locomotive horsepower averaged 40,000 horsepower units per month. We are now producing 20,000,000 new horsepower units per month in airplane engines—500 times our peacetime locomotive construction. This new horsepower will be disbursed all over the world, expanding the area of population.

The air contains the dynamics necessary for release from the tensions and distortions of the mechanistic structure through attracting attention to vast open lands.

Steam went to the shores of such lands, but it stopped there under the exploitation tactics of the mercantile system. Air can go inland and develop free lives there for trapped Europeans as our ancestors developed free lives in America.

Already, under the impetus of this war, American minds and materials are winging civilization to the vast riches, to the broad, diversified lands, and especially to Africa, the neglected political domain of the United Nations.

Already, underneath the surface of the war, the congested hopelessness of the surplus population in Europe contrasts with the breath-taking openness of Africa, Canada, Australia.

What of this Africa, unfixed in its destiny? It, alone, is an awesome thing for the trapped Europeans to contemplate.

Our Clipper flew from La Guardia Field to Miami and a Caribbean base. With berths ripped out and the whole ship gutted, I slept as best I could. There is plenty of room on a wartime Clipper, because the limit is on weight, and the weight does not fill the space. The crates are stowed and roped everywhere, but there is always space on top of them, or you can sleep in the aisles. We were carrying munitions for our fighter planes, giant bomber wheels and tires, electrical parts, storage batteries, carburetors, airplane superchargers, medical supplies and surgical instruments, mosquito netting, all kinds of boxes and cases of delicate replacements for American machines in Egypt and India.

By now it seemed this plane was geared to a race with Rommel. From the Caribbean air base I telephoned the editor of a local newspaper. The only news he had was bad news—and later on, when we took off, it was the last report we were to get which was not totally contradictory and confusing. In central Africa you might just as well rely on native drum signals and voodoo practitioners. You simply don't know what is happening beyond your nose. It is practically impossible to send a personal telegram and equally hard to receive one. Radio reception is poor, and news broadcasts reach central Africa as fuzzy as the tail of Mary's lamb. As for filing news dispatches from there, wiring out each dispatch is a career in itself—and a short cut to bankruptcy.

The harbor was a mass of ships.

The green mountains of the curving shore seemed to nestle around these ships and hover over them in gentle care. The sea glistened, the same azure-blue sea I loved to fish in at Bimini. There were beautiful stretches of beach, a sparkle in the waves that broke on the sand and welcomed each other, in little eddies, to this friendly shore.

Ships of all sizes, solid and abrupt as islands, stood sheer out of

the surface of the water. The lines had been formed. Patrol planes
from Waller Field hovered lazily overhead. Destroyers cut great
swaths in the water and circled the alignment, like cavalry officers
riding inspection around their troops before the march.

Little boats darted back and forth from the shore, throwing
spray and looking very fussy. Gulls circled the tops of the masts.
A cruiser, gray and solemn, stood at the head of the line. Before
long now it would give the signal. These ships and their men would
start for the war.

All the centuries from Moses to Napoleon and from Napoleon to
this breathless age, and all the zones from the man-cradle of Turkey
to some new Texas county had united in the assembly of this force.
The industry, science, art, geography, commerce, and mind of the
whole human race were accumulated in this interlacing of the ten
thousand threads which Necessity wove into its production. But
only to one who had never been in this war would it be exciting.
After nearly four years I see no adventure in war. I haven't seen
any since the day it started. I see none today. Overseas, anyone will
tell you there is none.

The suffering and agony, the dangers of mutilation, remain the
most awful trials through which civilized men can pass.

You have adventures. But war itself is not an adventure. Most
of its acts are without personal meaning. Even the war's progress is
veiled if you are at the front. A soldier knows his own little strip of
action intimately, knows his own airfield or his particular sector;
but its effect on the pattern is more lost on the man on the spot
than it is on those at home. The first thing a soldier asks when he
comes out of action is, "How's the battle coming?" Then he wants
news of the war.

From the instant you leave our shores you are on another planet,
a separate planet, a life which only a few of our gentle people
know. This is the world of indescribable shocks and the terror of
noise and confusion. This is the world of aching hunger and thirst
and a curious numbness that comes at night before you fall asleep.
This is the world where men who wanted nothing but to be left
alone, to work honestly, and to make their way in peace have

been torn from their families, hurled into every kind of misery and pain, their lives and the lives of countless others bashed in and twisted like the wreck of a derailed train. This is the world of blood and sweat and tears. This is the world, and this is the hour.

It is an hour of pagan frightfulness, where the right of self-determination is silent in the rumble of Axis tanks, where the shining hope of free men is a bright target in the gun sights of roaring Axis planes, where all that is gentle and good and modest will perish from the earth if these powerful and ruthless people can have their way. What is to stop them? Nothing but force, in this hour or any other hour, until they and all they stand for are halted in their tracks—once and for all.

Before we left the Caribbean base we saw the cruiser give the signal. The gray lines of force started to move.

The ceiling was low; our Clipper headed southeast. British Guiana, Dutch Guiana, French Guiana, Brazil—we never stopped until we reached the mouth of the Amazon in the eerie light of the morning. We landed, as I had landed many times before, at Belém. The ship was refueled in the river, while we had breakfast on a barge offshore with a Brazilian official who was a friend of Colonel Compton.

In an hour we were in the air again, over the jungles and winding rivers of one of the richest countries on earth. Vast stretches of fertile loam, great high plateaus for grazing and for crops, untouched wealth at every turn—95 per cent of it lying closer to the Old World than to us. In its varying climates, I had seen it like this all over South America, down to the Argentine archipelago. Water power in the mountains, loam in the valleys, the fantastic tablelands of the pampas, so flat that even from the air you could see no ridge or hillock in all the vastness that stretched to the horizon.

We made our next landing on the inlet at Natal. From this point, 5,000 miles from New York and 1700 miles from Africa, we started across the Atlantic.

We tried to get under way at seven in the evening. The take-off in the L-shaped basin was long and risky. We had a heavy load—

84,500 pounds—and a bad cross wind pinned us to the choppy water. We made three tries. On the third try we went to the far end of the inlet. We turned and waited before we started our run.

A launch came out from the shore and set a lane of buoy beacon lights, talking with our plane over radiotelephone as each light was plotted in the course. A larger launch rode at anchor near the end of the run, ready to shoot a rocket, a brilliant white flare. Our pilot would have full vision when he needed it most.

With propellers idling and the water lapping the side of the hull, the Clipper turned into the course. Then we started the rush that should free us to fly the ocean beyond. Our wings' floodlights lit the matted trees and sparkled on the churning water. The violent body of our charging ship hurled the surface into furious spray as we banked deep at the treacherous bend, faster into the straight-away. Our wings tilted at an angle, one tip skimming the water, then leveled off as we made the final try. The rocket flare exploded, lit the water like day, lit the heavens and the hills that lay ahead. The plane quivered with its full power, trembled for an instant, and at last shook off the sticky hold of the water on its keel. We were in the air, climbing into the haze of the sky over the Atlantic.

Dull red circles glowed under the flanges of the cowlings, and short stabs of flame, trailing a wake through the blue light, came from the four engines. It seemed to me that I could hear a note of vengeance in these motors as we headed for Africa and the battle in the desert. They roared a deep blast of American power, seemed to answer the guttural voice of the weird, dark little man I had heard declare war on the United States over the radio from Berlin.

A dairyman from Neenah, Wisconsin, sat at the radio earphones; a lawyer from Seattle climbed along the catwalk inside the giant wing to make adjustments on the number-four engine, as he was taught in the schools of the United States Army Air Corps. A clear-eyed, two-fisted, tough-minded ex-salesman from Virginia was at the controls. These men and this machine, turned suddenly from peace, were at war.

What is most precious in men seldom shows itself, seldom finds an issue, in ordinary life. Only a part of man reaches any other man's or woman's consciousness, and what is most precious scarcely enters into action except in prayer and is perhaps only perceived by God. Always and everywhere salvation is torture, deliverance means torture, and peace lies in sacrifice. This great principle of Christianity and of patriotism remains still the highest solution of the inner life. Only in it is there any peace of conscience for the man or the nation, and without this peace there is no peace.

We seek distractions, we wander away, we sometimes consider that America as a whole may still escape the test, and yet there is no help for it—we must come back to it in the end.

We climbed into an overcast sky. The ocean mist mixed with the jungle vapors behind us. The clouds over the sea were gray and ugly. It was dark as doom, and there wasn't a break-through to the stars above. We came down low, close on the angry, frothing Atlantic. The propellers charged the blasts of heavy air, tore through them with the fitfulness of horses straining up a hill. Tossing hard in close quarters is a curious feeling when you are in utter blackness over the Atlantic.

The haze turned to light fog as we flew close over the long, rolling waves. Then, as the night wore on the fog lifted and we climbed steadily higher in the clear and quiet heaven. I mounted the aluminum ladder midship to the Paraglass blister, the astrohatch, on the top side of the plane. The sky above and the sea below blended into a circle of azure light, so that there was no end to this blue, no break in this union of ageless elements.

It was a magnificent night. The heaven was blue and high and clear. There was a great glory in this sky—the stars in a fragile, sparkling mass, the vast tapestry of celestial needle point behind them, radiant as a weave of silver, thrown with gusto and great assurance from one horizon to the other; the light of the moon in a long shaft of gentle light, touching the water in ruffles like the most delicate blanket of an eastern king.

And against all this the foremost stars stood out so clearly, suspended as they are over a desert, each alone and each alive, each in its place like a jewel in a velvet box, suggesting that you compare it with the others. "It is a quiet task I have," this one seems to say, "but I am always here for you to see. Your friends see me now. I can unite you, for I am fixed and certain and visible, no matter how far apart you are, and I look the same to you both. It is only miles that separate anyone under me. I am a friendly matter, a universal thing. I was here when you were born, and I shall be here when you die. It was Orion you saw over the housetops at Coal City. There is Orion. Your father was alive then, and you were a small boy. He pointed out Orion. 'That is Orion, son,' he said. 'You can always tell Orion.' "

And under the stars the water speaks. The sea, veined with green and drab, has the serious look of labor. It is about its business, making its clouds, gathering its floods for the tide, heaping up its sands, visiting its shores. "I am the sea. I am not distant. I am not remote. My touch extends to the shore of your home. But I am a tedious matter. I am restless. I have not learned the quiet lessons of the stars, and I gain so little by my anxiousness, my strains. I am a reservoir of mystery and action. No one knows me fully, and I am a changeable thing, a wasteful thing, under these stars. Mine is not a quiet task. I am bold and expansive, powerful beyond all words. But I have no memory, no past, no future. My name is Confusion. Leaving old worlds, both old worlds and new I touch but do not view. Look back to the stars. They see all, and through all time."

The ephemeral perceives the eternal. What does it matter how brief all sight by men in motion, how brief the span of men in motion, seeing that the generations, the centuries, the worlds themselves are but occupied forever with the unceasing reproduction of the motion of life in all its hundred thousand modes and variations which mobilize the universal symphony? The motif is always the same: time and motion. The universe represents the infinite wealth of the Spirit seeking to exhaust nature's possibilities and the goodness of the Creator, who wishes to share with the created all that lies dormant within the limbo of Omnipotence.

To contemplate and try, to receive and give back, to have uttered one's note and moved one's grain of sand, is all which is expected from such as we are.

It hardly seemed a moment since I had flown the South Atlantic westward, from Portuguese West Africa to Brazil. The night was just like this. And this night, too, lying on the floor of the Clipper, the power of its engines vibrating through the metal under me and pounding in my ears, the same throbbings seemed to speak in endless revolution:

"The world is just starting. This life is new. The world is just starting. This life is new." The reorganization of nature is not a simple thing. Nature is equivalent to the heaven I see above. On our one satellite—one of the least of the myriad of systems—we vegetate. The notion that men are ready for this life is a sad fallacy. But that we shall fit ourselves to it is not a wishful dream.

We liberated ourselves from the emotional delusion which supported the medieval persecutions within the machinery of the Church. This was accompanied by pain and suffering, education, migration, and the broad action of vital life for centuries of time. Similarly, we shall free ourselves from the distortions of this day.

This life is new. This evolution towards a truly human status, this repopulation of the world and the real enlightenment of man, must be gradual and painful, and we who live at the moment are seeing it in sorrow. But we advance as this plane advances.

The time lag in our lopsided development is being shortened by the forces of this latest war. War and peace resolve themselves into a mercury of development. This day is the end of nothing. All history teaches men to put trust in ideas and not in circumstances. God's time is not more distant. God's time is closer now than ever before.

CHAPTER 10

Europeans Stop the Clock in Africa

AT DAWN we saw the coast, a profile strangely scalloped, as though some giant had taken bites, and one especially big bite, out of an ordinary shore line.

Soon the long "power drag," close on the water, suspended. The blur of green-and-brown landscape fixed itself into trees, crags, gullies, weather-beaten hills, all in quick succession as we skimmed close to the water. Sharp, metallic noises on our keel, like the quick playing of a hose on a tin roof. Then the grip of the water spray. In a driving rain we landed on an immense inlet in Liberia.

The Clipper run was over. The giant forty-two-ton Boeing flying boats surrender their burden at this important base to United States army land planes, which carry it across Africa and along the Nile.

Pat, Jimmy, Charlie, Reggie, and I came ashore in a launch. We sloshed our way over the rocks on the jetty to a grass hut at the edge of a large new compound which was under construction.

Here on the western side of the great African hump, close to the point where the continent curves in so abruptly, we were 6,849 air miles from New York. Yet we were still further from Cairo than Miami, Florida, is from Juneau, Alaska.

Africa, the richest of all continents, is a land mass 5,000 miles long and as much as 4600 miles wide.

The great continent on the underside of Europe's Mediterranean lake has an area of 11,000,000 square miles, half again the size of the North American continent from the Arctic Ocean to Panama. It has every temperature and every climate known in all ages as favor-able to the development of man.

The great mass of Africa lies in the tropics, but in vast belts some distance above and below the equator and for vast areas in the northwestern and southern extremities temperate climates exist. There is nothing orthodox about Africa in any respect, and there is certainly nothing orthodox about its climate. It is impossible to exaggerate the climatic variations on this great land mass, and it is chiefly the *Beau Geste*-type movies and stories of the *Trader Horn* sort that have given the public the impression of Africa as a land of either burning sand or sweltering jungle. Africa is everything. Not only does Africa contain every climate, but there are endless variations and paradoxes from one end of the continent to the other. You can ski close to the line of the equator on the slopes of Mount Kenya, and you can find perfect winter-resort climate, like that of Florida, at the tip of South Africa, the point nearest the Antarctic Ocean.

The continent divides itself into four broad sections:

(1) The northern section, with the great Sahara Desert, the immensely fertile sections at various coastal points, and the garden-like area of the Egyptian Nile.

(2) The northwest section of central Africa, extending from the Atlantic coast to the edge of the Abyssinian plateau and south into the Congo. This is a series of highland blocks interposed between wide basins.

(3) The eastern highland area, dominated by large blocks of elevated plateaus and giant crags the area of the Great Lakes, whose feature is the African phenomenon of the Albertine Rift. This rift is an enormous gash 2,000 or more miles in length which splits the center of Africa. It is the backbone of the Albertine Rift valley system, part of which is below sea level.

(4) The southern lobe of Africa, which is a broad, high basin occupied by the Zambezi and Limpopo river systems and the four high plateaus of Angola, Southern Rhodesia, southeast Africa, and South Africa.

Once the greater part of central Africa was covered by a high forest, and evidences supplied by Roman explorers suggest that this forest once stretched across the continent almost as far as Khartoum. This area is much smaller today, and the forest growth is very different, but the timber area is still half the size of the United States.

The continent has more nearly some of everything than any other continent, and it has more of everything than any place on earth.

Africa is, of course, the center of the world's gold supply. Much more gold still remains in African rock than is buried in the ground under Fort Knox. Southern Africa alone has contributed 41.9 per cent of all the gold dug in any place in this world in the present century. And by the outbreak of World War II, the area of the Union of South Africa alone had delivered $6,000,000,000 in this metal. From its first development until World War II, the African Rand paid foreign holders over $1,000,000,000 in dividends.

In the Hudson Tube Age of hydroelectric development the water-power potentialities of Africa lead the world, for in Africa's turbulent rivers, cascades, and great waterfalls is represented more hydroelectric energy than there is in Europe, Asia, and North America combined. Nearly 200,000,000 horsepower has already been surveyed. Europe is using all her potential horsepower, and it is only 57,000,000.

In the Katanga region alone the copper deposits are ten times the size of the Lake Superior fields and far more accessible today than the Wisconsin-Minnesota deposits were when the *Charles Hutchinson* steamed to Duluth.

In this land mass is most of the world's bauxite, a raw material which, combined with hydroelectric power, makes aluminum. It has chromite, immense deposits of manganese and sulphur, and diamonds beyond all dreams. Over half the world's supply of uranium, the source of radium, is found in Africa. It has mercury, potash, magnesite, and it has every one of the so-called strategic and rare metals except cadmium. There is no possible limit to the development of rubber on this continent, or of cotton.

Unlike South America, which is a conglomeration of twenty-three separate and autonomous republics over which no country in Europe has any control, and over which the United States has none, the immense continent of Africa is in the hands of the United Nations. Exclusive of enemy territory, England, France, Belgium, and the Union of South Africa control all of Africa. The only other European nations represented in any way are neutral Spain and Portugal: Spain in Rio de Oro and the tiny area of Spanish Morocco, and Portugal in Mozambique (Portuguese East Africa), Angola (Portuguese West Africa), and Portuguese Guinea.

Vast, rich, and fabulous Africa, the continent of the Age of Air, is available to our European friends, the European units of the United Nations.

Yet no country has even taken the trouble to count its African population. "At one time the population of the Congo was guessed at about 40 million," reports Lord Hailey, writing officially on this matter. "Shortly before 1910 it was taken to be 15,500,000; in 1933, however, the administration accepted 9,272,558. The population of Nigeria was put at 20 million. It was put down in 1906 to 7 million, and returned to 11,500,000 in 1931. The population of Kenya was estimated at 4 million up to 1916, but a count in 1917 put it at 2,848,700."

The *Statesman's Year-book* at one time gives the French figure for the population of French Equatorial Africa as 15,000,000, and another time as 5,000,000. The official *Principes de Coalition* of the Législation Coloniale (the latest official figure) gives it as 3,124,173.

The *Statistical Year-Book of the League of Nations* for December 31, 1934, the latest in this record, gives the total population of the continent as 145,045,000, going out of its way to state at the same time that it may be as low as 138,100,000 or as high as 163,-300,000, depending on the accuracy of the European governments' figures on their colonies.

Meanwhile, according to the official 1,837-page report made by the British Committee of the African Research Survey (Oxford University Press, 1938; directed by Lord Hailey under the auspices of the Royal Institute of International Affairs), everyone is missing the forest for the trees.

For there is nothing new about European settlements on the African continent, and nothing new about European neglect of this land. The Europeans have been settled there much longer than there have been white men in America. They were entrenched in Africa nearly a hundred years before the *Mayflower* came to Plymouth. Only the German colonies, lost at Versailles, date as late as the twentieth century.

During this entire period, for the full span of time that parallels our development of America, the European activity in Africa softened but never changed. From the very beginning until now, it has been the same old story of exploitation without development.

The tale of the Europeans' career in behalf of the Gold Coast is typical.

In contrast with the saga of our own land, the story of this rich European possession on the underside of Africa is told in the ruins of fortress castles, built along its shore by Dutchmen, Danes, Brandenburgers, Portuguese, and Englishmen. They are the gravestones of the mercantile system, which is dead but not buried.

Mercantile transactions date back to 1551, 122 years before Joliet and Marquette, reaching the Great Lakes of America, made the first commercial transaction in Chicago. In 1551 Captain Thomas Wyndham carried back to Bristol, England, from Accra, a cargo of melegueta pepper and a quantity of gold panned in the Volta River. The Gold Coast reached its prime in 1600; it looked then as our Lake Superior country looked in 1900, and it has stayed that way ever since.

The Dutch seized the area from the Portuguese in 1642. The Danes contested the Dutch there, and then they both contested the British. It was a number-one item in the spoils system for over two hundred years, but nearly a century ago it fell entirely into British hands. The fighting stopped, and so did the clock. The crown colony was frozen in its place in the whole European mercantile system. In this connection the high light of the century was the official visit of the Prince of Wales and the governing people eighteen years ago. Nothing had happened there before, and little has happened there since.

The English group stepped ashore near Accra in the early afternoon of April 9, 1925. At this moment nearly a million destitute coal miners in England, victims of oil, electricity, and the death of the mercantile system, were in the midst of a terrible strike, which was soon to be followed in sympathy by two and a half million other trade-union workers in the British Isles.

Yet the official report of the royal party's visit to the Gold Coast, written on its return to London, shows only perplexity about what the party saw in the rich, open land to the south:

"To the newcomer the first surprise accompanies the discovery that those Englishmen and women who are there do not want to leave. . . . They resent any suggestion that it is a good country to live out of. They take unusual pride in the development of their province and frequently betray a liking for their work and for the native."

I suggest that anyone seriously interested in the history and future of Europe, and who does not see possibilities in Africa, read that twice.

Colonial office administrators in Europe's governments at home— British, Belgian, or French—are close to the bottom of the ladder in government rank and have always hamstrung and plagued the local administrators.

Although better organized, even at that, than the French or Belgians in colonial setup, Britain alone has nineteen official administrations in Africa, and countless subadministrations. These confound each other in a bewildering array of dependencies and subdependencies, customs unions and subcustoms unions, mandates and affiliated groupings, separate and separated colonies, wheels within wheels, cogs within cogs, contradictions within contradictions. The entire crazy quilt, all in the hands of three European members of the United Nations, is a patchwork of customs barriers, double duties, conflicting laws, and blushworthy concessions in the hands of the boys back home.

In varying degrees, it is the same story all over Africa. Public services, government-owned or private concessions, operate at outrageously high rates and in a flagrantly inefficient manner. The whole continent, except for the independent Union of South Africa, which means the whole continent controlled by Europe, is tied up in a mesh of red tape and exploitation. Every healthy principle of reducing costs to increase commerce simply does not fit into the plan of the European governmental and business offices.

The charges are terrific for standard utilities, and even then they are exceedingly poor. The Kenya and Uganda Railway, for instance, is a government monopoly. Joining Nairobi and Mombasa, it operates at a monopoly rate twelve times our equivalent American charge per mile. All the rest of the rich area is shut out from reasonable development because the railroad monopoly prohibits all commercial trucking. The limited, archaic telegraph and telephone service in important communities stifles all contact; and, as for cable and wireless, it costs a king's ransom for merchants to reach the outside world.

How long the European states of the United Nations will continue to hamstring and restrain the general development of their African colonies I do not know. But with all the unsolvable problems they face, the British Cabinet and the chiefs of the governments in exile cannot indefinitely by-pass that fabulous land.

The world has too much at stake.

Yet, wherever such facts as these are applicable in the British Empire, it is a distortion—and a dangerous one—to take such facts and use them as arguments against the British Empire *as such*.

Considering its scope, the British Commonwealth of Nations is the most remarkable political achievement in history. It has overcome more tyranny, supplied more safety, removed more fear, taught more justice, and given more freedom to more people than any other institution on earth. It is not only worth preserving, in the interests of all free men, but unless Britain preserves her so-called empire there will be no freedom for millions upon millions who are now as free as they can safely be.

There is one great democracy which should dedicate itself to the stability of the British Empire, and that is America. To say that this means we are fighting to "preserve the British Empire" is the most rank kind of distortion. But without the British Empire we are fighting for an unworkable world, as far as free men are concerned, and for a world spotted with Fascists in one place and Communists in another. That is not going to be a peaceful world, which is the first thing we must fight for. That is a world in which there is no end to war.

Talking about colonial freedom is one thing. Supplying it is quite another. Furthermore, 80 per cent of the colonials of the world could not, or would not, use their freedom to maintain freedom. Eighty per cent of the world's people simply are not ready for what we are talking about.

We have no real experience in governing colonial natives. We don't know the first thing about it, and, judging by our most recent demonstration in Puerto Rico, we are very slow to learn. For a country whose own cities and counties are in the most deplorable condition in the history of the United States, with vastly rich areas like Boston, Detroit, and Philadelphia facing financial crises in spite of maximum employment and maximum taxes, our government planners go far afield in solving colonial problems for the world.

The word "free" itself carries certain insincerities, because it is so meaningless. Freedom is a combination of things. It is miserably appropriated in the mouths of politicians, because they imply that it is their own special field whereas the real accomplishments have been due to quiet men, scientists and scholars, teachers of the truth, churchmen who delivered the word of God and the mercy of Christianity.

Faraday transformed mechanical energy into electricity through induction. When an English politician asked him whether it would be useful to mankind, Faraday replied, "I think some day you will be able to tax it." Taxes, however, are not the achievement. Faraday achieved freedom from darkness, and a thousand other blessings, for rich and poor. Doctors give freedom from death itself as they save lives through the development of medicine and surgery. Against such contributions the words and phrases of the political speechmakers are small indeed. They take great airs to themselves to which they are not entitled on the record.

CHAPTER 11

Europeans Can Make This Contribution

N**ATIVES, WOMEN AND MEN,** ferried the Clipper cargo ashore in skiffs. The little boats bucked in the water like ponies, flanked both sides of the temporary jetty. Balancing the items on their heads, chattering like birds in an aviary, the natives paraded the cargo from the jetty to the grass hut and checked it in, piece by piece, with the American soldiers in charge. Then they started into the jungle to the United States army airport.

It is two miles by a jungle path from the headquarters hut to the airfield. It is over 800 miles from the airfield to Accra. It took our cargo about the same length of time to cover each distance.

While a jungle road was being built, every pound of freight flown from the United States went over that path on the heads of natives.

Nothing was too awkward or heavy, especially for the girls. Straight as arrows, sedate as peacocks, three women balanced a giant bomber wheel flat on their heads and sauntered along, emitting their strange "cha-cha-cha" like overgrown katydids. The whole unloading operation was done with amazing speed, the natives chirping away at each other, gesticulating with their hands and feet, some young and lithe, others as old and as wrinkled as dried black prunes.

Most African natives are pitiably anxious to please the white man. If you ask, "Is the airfield this way?" the native's reaction is, "Does the white man wish me to say yes?" He doesn't know what you are saying, and it hardly occurs to him to guess from any sign you make. He will lean forward, eager and perplexed, with an expres-

sion of intense interest combined with pained confusion. He thinks
you want agreement, and he will smile broadly, show his teeth, and
bob his head up and down as merrily as a minstrel. Point in the
other direction, and he will do the same thing.

This special congeniality makes it a little tough to find your way
around, what with eight hundred different native languages here
and there. But, like Ohio's Wyandots, Africa's natives can't be
ruled out for not wanting to be friendly. They are remarkable
mimics, and imitating strangers to the merriment of each other is a
wholesale outdoor sport.

The five of us followed the natives and the freight down the
trail, oozing our way through the mud towards higher ground.
You could see hardly a patch of sky through the matted trees. The
path had been hacked through twining, swinging lianas as strong as
coils of heavy wire. We came to a growth of strangler figs, the
small vines which circle tree trunks and press tighter, as a cobra
presses, until the vine strands cut through and fell the tree itself.

In the driving rain Pat Timberlake kept asking me to take a
movie shot of this temporary route. Brigadier General Timberlake,
six feet three and built like an Indian wrestler, is a great combat
flier, one of the best in the Army Air Corps. He handles big bomber
formations as a ringmaster handles ponies. He can and does fly anything, any time, any place. His touch on the controls is as light as
the touch of a baby on a toy balloon. At West Point, in 1923 he
beat the Navy, when the score was 10–14 against the Army, by
catching a forward pass. But he is not a good man with a camera.
I handed him mine, and he dropped it in the mud.

It is hard to clean a camera on a jungle path while you walk in
the rain. An accident like this can be very tiresome. But I finally
got the lens presentable again by lagging behind. I heard a voice.
It was Jimmy Compton coming back. "I ought to have a picture
of this route for G-2," he said. Colonel Compton is a spectacularly
alert intelligence officer. He handles codebooks and maps with the
deftness of a cardsharp. His fingers are as sensitive as Fritz Kreisler's. But he is not a good man with a camera. As I handed him mine
he dropped it in the mud.

Pat, Jimmy, and I swung on a rope suspension bridge. The three women were edging the bomber wheel across. This was no time to give the ladies a lift. Step by step they eased forward, for the bridge was only wide enough to walk Indian file. They steadied the wheel with their hands, never looking down and only now and then touching the vine ropes at the side.

"This is a good place for women with feet like cats," Jimmy said.

"Rather than anything, I'd like to have a picture of this," Reggie said to me. "To show our people in the Middle East, you know." Colonel Mayhew is a fine British officer, a scholar and a gentleman. He has an affection for artillery and tanks; he practically strokes the nose of a tank as Buffalo Bill stroked the nose of Soldier Boy. He handles guns as though they were made of china. He is nimble and very quick to see what he is doing. But he is not a good man with a camera. I handed him mine. Yes, he dropped it in the mud.

Our plane was a Douglas C-53, a modified DC-3, standard on the Army's skyways overseas. It is stripped inside to the skin of the ship, the floor reinforced. A narrow aluminum bench protrudes from each side of the fuselage, for this type is rigged to carry parachute troops. A shallow dent and a wide canvas safety belt mark each place. Red and green signal lights for the jumps are fastened by the door.

In parachute-attack work the commander-pilot, signaling from the cockpit, flashes the red light as he nears the area of descent. The paratroopers, facing each other in the "seats," get busy, give their equipment a final check. The jumpmaster crouches by the door.

At his command, when the light flashes on, they stand in line and face the tail. Each man clips his rip cord to an overhead wire which runs the length of the cabin. When they jump, paratroopers do not pull their rip cords. Very long, and held to the wire, the rip cord opens the parachute after the man clears the plane, detaches itself automatically from the parachute, and dangles idly from the ship.

When such planes are heavily loaded with cargo, as ours was, and space is needed, the narrow bench on each side is folded down to give the fuselage more width, and you sit or lie down on the cargo boxes as best you can.

"Twenty-eight men can leave this ship in twenty-eight seconds," Pat said as we thumped along on the boxes of ammunition and bomb-fuses stacked in the aisle, "but if we get a bad landing five men sitting on this stuff are going to break a record."

Pat knew that we were in for a night landing at Accra. The weather over the jungles is fickle, except in the rainy season, when it is always terrible. It just keeps raining in sheets, as it did when we took off from the Liberian base, and, once in the air, the downpour mixes with the jungle vapors in a blanket of haze and water. Further across Africa the problem is the wind and the sand; here it is the rain and the fog, and no place to land if you are off your course.

But we were not off our course. We were skirting the Ivory Coast and the seaport Abidjan.

Next to Casablanca and Dakar, Abidjan is the most strategic spot in West Africa.

Under the direction of Admiral Darlan, the Vichy French there completed the jungle railroad, curling through the interior of the Ivory Coast, through French Guinea and Senegal, directly to Dakar. Halfway along this line, at Bamako, on the banks of the Niger River, there is a junction which gives the French railway system the shape of a Y. At Bamako the other branch swings north for a thousand miles. Rails connect Abidjan with Casablanca, tie Casablanca to the whole interior. The system links Abidjan, Dakar, and Casablanca with Tangier, across the Strait of Gibraltar from Spain, with Oran, Algiers, and even the central Mediterranean city of Tunis. The Nazis extended the line beyond Tunis and Sfax and carried it into their main base at Tripoli. It's a nice setup, developed since the war.

German tankers, flying whatever country's flag was best for the occasion, put in to Abidjan, took fuel supplies, and then stood out to sea where they could easily transfer their liquid cargo at night. The arrangement was perfect for submarines, and this is where Nazi U-boats in the South Atlantic got their fuel.

One lubricant which they got was peanut oil, squeezed from the bulging supply of African kernels grown in this area. This peanut oil lubricated U-boat propellers in our sea lanes around the Dark Continent, lubricated death to Russian ships in the distant Baltic, lubricated the undersea patrol between Sicily and Tripoli which struck at all British convoys there. It flowed in Nazi hulls as German submarine captains gazed at the silhouette of New York's sky line.

The seaport of Accra, capital of the British Gold Coast Colony, nestles among the Akwapim hills halfway in on the underside of the great African hump. It is the world's largest port for cocoa; one out of every two pieces of chocolate you eat has been in Accra.

Our landing at the Accra airfield proved easy. The guide lights at the United States army airport flashed on to bring us in, a frazzled and mysterious-looking splotch of strange white beams in the black mat of jungle below. We came in like a dove lighting on a feather bed.

We spent the night in the army barracks at the airfield, an immense, wire-enclosed clearing cut out of the solid green mass, ten miles back in the jungle from the harbor town. Brigadier General Shepler W. Fitzgerald of our Air Corps makes his headquarters here as head of the Army's African transport system. Accra is the nucleus of the whole operation.

"Pan American Airways blasted out three square miles here," General Fitzgerald told me. "They used enough dynamite to bore a hole to China. After you finish knocking down trees, thick as pickets on a fence, you get an education in how to pull thousands of stumps out of jungle mud. Every native in this section of the Gold Coast has had his hand on a stump on this field. Then the underbrush grows back while you are looking at it, unless you go down to the roots. Then you are ready to start your drainage. Until you get the field set, of course, nothing can come in by air. You couldn't even land a toy balloon. That meant oxen and flivvers from Accra. But there weren't any flivvers to speak of, so we had to bring trucks over from home, convoyed by a corvette. As soon as materials could be flown in, the biggest headaches were behind Pan American. They built this field in two months."

Every tool I saw at work on our airfields across Africa had to be brought from the United States: grading machines, trucks, tractors, picks and shovels, even the dynamite itself and the caps to set it off. Portable houses, barracks by the shipload, commissaries, street-paving equipment, hospitals complete to the last piece of gauze, dentist's chairs, barber's supplies, refrigerators, kitchens, power plants, sometimes big enough for a city the size of Duluth, runway-lighting equipment and powerful radio stations—all these things came from our country. Thousands of tons of steel, machinery, plate glass, mosquito netting, rope, lumber, nails, wire, paint, and chemicals came with them, shipped in by boat.

It all was born in the U. S. A.

Modern barracks, cement walks, paved roads, electricity everywhere. Good beds, good food, and a good hospital. Machine shops, plane-repair hangars, a wireless station that reaches ships at sea and into the Egyptian desert. Specialists on all kinds of motors, ground crews who can maintain any kind of plane, pilots who know how to fly them any place and in any kind of weather. This compound in Africa is as American as The Star-Spangled Banner.

There had never been a single water closet in Accra, home of 65,000 Europeans and natives. In June 1942, America's Pan American Airways-Africa, Ltd., installed the first water closet ever used. The company shipped twenty-five from the United States and installed them as ordinary equipment for American employees. While I was there the Governor of the Gold Coast colony, a British lord, bought one from the airport manager for his official residence, Government House.

"We have needed this for some time," he said. The house was built in 1886.

The only progress which Africa itself has made, in fact, has been in the face of dull and obstructionist European administration or rank exploitation on the part of the special European interests. Africa's position today is no test whatever of what it should be or could be under enlightened and constructive circumstances.

Europe's mercantile system was based on exploitation and on concessions to favored sons at home. Government inertia and special privilege have not changed at all as the system rolled over and slowly but surely died. The Europeans have neither economic policy nor purpose in Africa today other than exploitation, differing hardly at all from their ancient attitude towards the gold-bearing coasts of the world.

The so-called "have" countries of Europe stupefy and ignore the most important "have" that they have, and starve on a peninsula of Asia while they do it.

At the same time that the Europeans are congested on the European peninsula and create pressures there which involve the United States, they are lackadaisical and inert about their neighboring continent, where they have the first instrument for relief in the deterioration of the mechanistic network. They have space.

No one can tell what is under Africa's surface or latent in its 11,000,000 square miles. But two things are certain. One is that Africa contains the greatest potential for economic change in white civilization in this century. And the other is that something must be done about it.

All this might be none of our business, and these observations would certainly be impertinent coming from an American, were it not for the fact that, as America helps her friends in the war and her friends help her, she is certainly entitled to an estimate of how her friends can first help themselves after it is over.

Africa is the best hope of Europe. And as political action is notoriously ineffective, it is nothing short of a miracle to observe that here is one problem of vast importance to the coming world which European statesmen can really solve.

Europe cannot be rebuilt on the impossible Europe of the past. It will be ten times the problem after this war that it was before. The specter of Dante's she-wolf looms, more lean and hungry than ever, with "all ill-greed defiled," stalking through a multiplication of the destitute Welsh coal miners whose work has been washed away by water and oil, the stricken lacemakers of Belgium whose product is now made so cheaply on Belgian machines in India, Japan, and elsewhere, the impoverished steelworkers of Europe who must compete with Stalin's plant at Magnitogorsk, all in the condition of post-Civil War Spain.

The facilities on which Europeans depend do not operate on good will and charity, or even on the need of the individual man or his nation. The Europeans are dependent, as will be their children and their grandchildren, on the productive system.

That system, in turn, operates only under the umbrella of industrial preference, and it has lost that preference forever. Without it millions have no place, removed as they are from the good earth.

To them, caught in the circumstances of this day, "Necessity's sharp pinch" is a steel vise. It is inflexible. There is no give to it. Men cannot help themselves, and they cannot help others. They cannot be saved by "freedom from want" programs like the Beveridge Report in England. In principle such approaches are only deficit-financed state insurance for a "fuller life," based on an expanding economy which will not expand. They represent only "perpetual motion" treatment of a problem which is profoundly social and is hemmed in by past shiftings of population and work and by disasters of shifting markets as elemental as the dust storms of a few years ago which ravaged our Middle West.

No postwar conference, no second postwar plan, should, under the artificial claim that we let Europe down the last time, put responsibility on the citizens of the United States while Europe remains overcrowded to the extent of something like 60,000,000 people.

I was at Málaga, Spain, a mile or so out of town. This is one of the loveliest spots in the world, the glorious hills rising from the Mediterranean, the sky a blazing chrome-yellow and the sea the color of a bright sapphire, the snow on the mountains in the distance and the sound of the breakers on the rocky shore.

There was a house close by the road, a plain house, but bright and whitewashed, with horseshoe windows in the walls and flower boxes under them and by the sides of the door.

I was trying to find something to eat. I found it there. I did not have to knock on the door. It was open. I could see easily into the single room. A woman was working over a fire, stirring a heavy black pot.

She was bending very low, but she lifted her head as my shadow fell into the room through the small doorway, and her eyes roamed all over me as I stood on the sill.

Her hair was gray; she wore a lace scarf. Her frame was so tiny and frail that it seemed as though she might blow away if there were any wind at all, and the way she clutched her bodice with one hand while she stirred the pot with the other added to the impression.

She did not stop stirring as I asked her for something to eat. She just nodded in the pleasant way that country people have with strangers anywhere in Spain.

She gave me a cup of black lentils. That is all the food I had for three days in southern Spain

"I am very fortunate," she said. She meant that, because she lived on the outskirts of town, the typhus had not reached her. She meant that she had a roof, two or three chairs, a few earthenware pots, a bed with straw pallets. I saw thousands of other people not far away who lived in hillside caves and lived on only spinach and grasses.

Are such people Communists? Yes, they are—if the Fascists are in. Are such people Fascists? Yes, they are—if the Communists are in. Will their lives change if they are given a dole of food? No, they will not. Some day these men must feed themselves and work productively to live, must earn at least the necessities with which to support themselves.

If a man out of a job jumps off a pier, a lifeguard can jump in and save him, pull him back up on the pier. But he is the same man, only more wet and more tired. He is still out of a job. The lifeguard cannot feed him indefinitely.

"It is not to die, or even to die of hunger, that makes a man wretched," wrote Carlyle. "But it is to live miserable we know not why; to work sore and yet gain nothing; to be heartworn, weary, yet isolated, unrelated." To live miserable we know not why, to have the dread of hunger, to work sore and yet gain nothing—this is the essence of poverty, and this is the essence of postwar Europe. For just as Spain was the proving ground for Stuka dive bombers, the 88-millimeter mobile gun, and other armaments of World War II, so is it the mirror of the conditions, the tensions, the bitternesses, the impoverishments of the era to follow throughout the Continent as a whole.

Europe's only hope is a second, gigantic migration.

Europeans have ample opportunity to give themselves permanent relief if they have the courage to face the truth and to act.

We all know so well the rewards of a willingness to move that we forget it shaped our destiny. And we forget, in the disillusionment of today's awful moment, that the same spirit can shape the destiny of countless millions of Europeans in the future.

Whether or not each man's chance proves feasible, whether or not he succeeds, is a relative question. *The history of the world is the history of immigrants who did.*

Immigration is history's road to peace, and through it there can be new Americas for today's trapped Europeans, with far more than our forebears had here.

Already, in the course of war, America is contributing the groundwork for this, a circumstance in Europe's favor which has never before occurred in the history of the world.

Free of all charges, America's materials of civilization, the fundamental installations for the Europeans' development of vast new lands, are being installed in the colonies of our European friends—in Africa, which belongs to England, France, and Belgium; in Canada, Australia, New Zealand, which are dominions of the British Empire; in Newfoundland, Bermuda, Trinidad, the Bahamas, and the West Indies, which are crown colonies of England; in cold Iceland and warm Greenland, which belong to Denmark; in India. The list is long, and it is growing. And our contribution is on a scale so large that neither the American people nor the people of Europe have any idea of its size.

The United States is performing in central Africa alone more public works than all European states would do in the next hundred years. Great airfields that can take the largest planes of the future, harbors dredged for ships of the line, cantonments and sanitation systems built with the most modern equipment. Electric-light and powerhouses that can be the nucleus of immense networks, ready to give life and motion where it never existed before. Radio towers, so powerful that all the earth is a neighbor, reach out like fingers beckoning to a tired Europe.

American docks, breakwaters, and piers, bridges and thousand-mile roads, aqueducts and viaducts, railways and telegraph lines, things without end that would have seemed like a dream world to Robert and Mehitabel Taylor, or, even a century later, to my father in the Lake Superior country, or to the richest man then alive—all these things are being built to remain in European colonies.

Is it too much to require, in exchange, that the Europeans do away with their autocratic concessions and restrictions and open up their fabulous lands to the free men of the world?

In Africa and elsewhere the Europeans can at least and at last make this contribution towards the peace of the world.

As for the British, on whom the leading role depends, that this is a friendly contention and not an unfriendly one is best expressed by the Manchester *Guardian* itself:

"What we can do and ought to do is remove those obstacles which our follies have erected and our inertia maintains. . . . The past, with its mixture of paternalism and repression, has plainly had its day."

In the political view, I know there are questions. "How should we give land to citizens who apply and to the refugees? British Colonies are one thing. But British Dominions would not receive people from Europe, including Britishers. Our own Dominions control their own legislation. We would have to get them to change it." Somebody will have to change something. America can't change everything, and she certainly cannot be expected to change British regulations in British colonies and the legislation of British dominions. No particle of Europe's problem is easy. It would be easy, instead, for Europe to keep on failing to solve her problems—at home and overseas. And the Europeans, from Sir Montagu Norman on down to Harold Laski, will keep on failing to solve European problems if we make it easy enough for them to turn to us. But, basically, we cannot solve them. Europe must help herself. The destiny of the Europeans is within themselves, and so is the destiny of their world-wide system of colonial land.

For the British and French, aside from Africa, the truly great Dominion of Canada alone could solve their population problems if the Europeans were sufficiently determined to help themselves within the confines of *their own land system.* Canada has a vast area of 3,694,000 square miles, stretching from the Atlantic to the Pacific, its population first drawn from France and then from England.

"Will men leave their homes?" Millions of Europeans have no homes. Other millions have homes but no hope. These millions see no future where they are any more than our forefathers saw a future in Europe when they freed themselves from the religious distortions of their day. For the fundamental fact of immigration, the history of immigration, is that it ebbs and flows like the tide. It lies dormant; then it moves. Again it lies dormant; then it moves. The reasons for such movements are various and colorful. And they are constant, for men are shifting all the time. That is why it is a dull assumption to look at the congestion on the impoverished European peninsula and say, "People will not move." "People want to stay where they are." "You can bomb out a town and people will come right back again." Life looks like that only if you stand too close to it. It really isn't like that, you know, in its true perspective— the perspective which includes the dimensions of time and accumulation.

The voyages of our earliest ancestors from Europe to the new world in America were the most obvious kind of migration. But Robert and Mehitabel Taylor's taking of a new life in the Ohio wilderness was also migration. My father migrated when he left Columbus, and all his roots there, and took up a new life on the Great Lakes.

The story of migrations is the story of small movements which accumulate as the result of small events. As the small migrations accumulate, the great waves of migration appear to be dormant. But when the accumulations have taken place, *events occur.* And with these events, such as World Wars I and II, the next great wave of migration breaks out again, and man populates the earth.

Yet the chances are overwhelming that, if Americans are not exceedingly watchful, we shall find the Europeans knocking at the doors of the United States and urging us to let them in here.

It hardly seems conceivable that we should be so dull and thoughtless as to permit this. But there are many indications that it can happen and that Africa, the other colonies, and the dominions will be passed over by the Europeans, preserved in very much their present state, while arguments will be advanced, presumably along so-called humanitarian lines, to obtain immigration to the United States. You can close your eyes and practically hear foreign voices saying now, "America was built up that way. It would be a good thing." "It would be wise *in the self-interest of America.*" In fact many Britons will already tell you that the solution of England's unsustainable population is for many English immigrants to come to the United States *because they do not expect Canada to change her policy and let them in there!*

We ourselves have invited all such coming clamor by our visionary talk about what we are going to do for everybody after the war. Surely the Europeans will not permit us to forget that. And equally surely the Europeans will not develop their own areas, as earlier Europeans developed America, if they can enter the America we have developed.

Shortly before we entered the war the incipient stages of this paradoxical imposition were already apparent. We were being asked to admit to Puerto Rico refugees from Spain and France, and of course the United States had been asked consistently to receive quantities of refugees from Germany.

First, all refugees are not good refugees. Europe was very glad to get rid of many of these people, some of whom exasperated everyone abroad with their infatuation for thinking and talking and not working. Others had been ceaseless troublemakers wherever they were, castigating all who disagreed with them and assuming a superiority to which they somehow claimed title by virtue of the fact that Europe was old and wise and they were Europeans.

This is the brittle and sophisticated fringe of European immigration; and, while it is unimportant in numbers, it is nevertheless composed of such persistent schemers—already so vocal in telling us what is wrong with our country—that we might as well be ready for their bombardment in favor of changing our immigration laws and the length of our visitors' permits, which so many of them already abuse.

Second, we should not take any immigrants at all. *We are doing other welfare services.* We are doing them on a scale so vast that our gifts are nearly beyond enumeration.

We should not receive refugees in exchange.

CHAPTER 12

The Farmer at the Zoo

THE GOLD COAST is the center for American wings in central Africa. The name of a Gold Coast port enjoyed priority on Germany's African bombing list, and the *Luftwaffe* tried to hit it several times with Focke-Wulfs based far to the north.

But long-range bombing can be militarily expensive—and it can be disappointing unless fairly continuous. For example, mass bombing of Germany from England cannot be limitless or independent. It takes a big slice of the total war effort and must be allocated as one element of the invasion program of which it is a part.

Using dollars only as symbols for war materials, war labor, and war time, money values can express at least the size of the picture which is so oversimplified in much that we read.

The average bomber we fly over Germany costs $200,000. Training and equipping each crew member is represented by $25,000: a total of $175,000 symbolizing the war effort involved in providing each seven-man crew. This means $375,000 per bomber over Germany, plus each bomber's share of materials, labor, and inventory in the vast ground and supply organization and not including such items as bombs and gasoline used in its operation. (Each 1,000-plane raid requires from 40,000 to 60,000 drums of aviation fuel. The planes use approximately one million gallons of gasoline each trip.)

The final military effect depends on the constancy of the raids, so that the raids become a barrage, for a bomber is really a *flying artillery platform*. Each raid is a salvo. Assume ninety raids, ninety salvos, for each barrage operation. Even if losses are held down to 5 per cent, each barrage of ninety salvos requires allocation for the loss of 4500 bombers and 31,500 trained airmen. This means a war drain (in "flying artillery" losses alone) symbolized by $1,677,500,-000. That's how big the problem is. The results have to be *related to the ground forces of the army* to capitalize on them sufficiently to justify the expenditure.

"You'll escort some new fighters, show them the way to Lake Chad, when you leave in the morning," General Fitzgerald told me when we turned in.

At dawn the fighters were lined up on the field, waiting. And at dawn I met the brave father of a good friend.

In Berlin, two weeks before Pearl Harbor, I got in a mess with the Gestapo. I was stranded in the Gestapo headquarters in Prinz Albrecht Strasse while a pig-eared nabob named Offenbach got very ugly about a pass that the American Embassy had obtained for me but which the Gestapo would not approve. One thing led to another in this Nazi jail, and then they began to close it up for the night, with me detained inside. I don't know how long I should have been there if it hadn't been for F. H. Cunningham, Jr., from our Embassy, who charged in to release me and bulldozed the Gestapo official into letting me go. The officer who came up to me at the field in Accra was Cunningham's father, a colonel in our army.

"You knew my boy in Berlin," he said. "His mother and I were always worried about him while he was there."

I told him that sounded a little like the steeple jack who sat on top of a flag pole and worried about aviators in the sky, for the father's mission was as tough as any in Africa. He was based at Brazzaville, the capital of the Fighting French in French Equatorial Africa, on the edge of the Belgian Congo, over a thousand miles to the south.

The African war began in what is now Colonel Cunningham's stamping ground. After the fall of France General Charles de Gaulle, operating from London, sent six officers—all he could spare —to this area. They went into the teeming basin of the Congo River, won first the allegiance of remote and distant French military and civil administrators in that vast back country, and gained pledges of resistance to the Axis. They went the rounds, stealthily —the Gabon territory, Middle Congo, Ubangi-Shari, Chad. Then the six Fighting French officers were ready to tackle the Vichy French capital at Brazzaville.

They came down the Congo, announced themselves to Vichy's Governor General Husson, and asked him to declare himself for Fighting France then and there and to pledge resistance to Hitler.

The officers gave Husson until midnight to come under their command. They received his answer at 11:40 P.M. "*Non!*" In one of the most remarkable Commando operations of the war they quietly gagged General Husson, wrapped him in a French army blanket, and carried him aboard his own private river launch. At the point of revolvers the six officers took over the craft and headed out into the murky, swirling current of the Congo.

They piloted it without lights across the broad river to Léopold-ville and landed on the friendly Belgian bank. There they threw Vichy General Husson into the local jail and picked up Fighting French General Larminat, who was waiting for them. Slipping back across the river, the French Commando officers installed him in General Husson's house as the new governor general.

General Larminat declared French Equatorial Africa—an area of nearly a million square miles, stretching two thirds the diagonal of the continent—as Fighting French. The strategic region, bordering the Belgian Congo, Anglo-Egyptian Sudan, Nigeria, and, on the far north, Libya, was opened for use by the United Nations.

As American liaison officer with the Fighting French at their Brazzaville capital, Colonel Cunningham serves his country single-handed and unafraid in one of the most dismal swamp areas on earth. Yet, in typical Cunningham fashion, the last thing he said to me as I got in the plane was, "Good luck, and be careful. Take care of yourself."

The fighter ships, tuned up, stood in lines of three. "We shouldn't have any trouble. Everything looks fine," one of the pilots said to me.

His name was Richard Day, and he lived in Massachusetts.

These planes were going to Egypt, and they were painted a delicate pink. During strafing or bombing in the blur of early daylight they need the most protection on the ground, and this color was chosen by McClelland Barclay's camouflage group in Washington as hardest to see in the dawn's sandy haze. They look like sissies over the jungle, but they pack a terrific wallop.

As each man flies alone in a single-seater, without instruments for difficult cross-country flying, the pilots need an escort to find their way. We took off first, and the fighters followed us up in threes.

Purring like beautiful kittens, strong and fast as Indian braves, this American cavalcade wheeled over the field and turned out to sea. We had to circle out over water, around Vichy's Dahomey territory, before we could take up our course northeast.

America's air development spreads out all over central and southern Africa, but the cross-Africa route strikes northeast from Accra and covers nearly a thousand miles to the upper section of the British crown colony of Nigeria. From Nigeria, it follows due east into the big-game country of central Africa around Fort Lamy, near Lake Chad. Then it strikes further east into the rolling desert of the Anglo-Egyptian Sudan to Khartoum. Over all, it is pointing from Accra to Khartoum, towards the Abyssinian border and at the conflux of the White and Blue Niles.

The route splits at Khartoum. A plane going to Cairo does a left-face there, flies a thousand miles north along the Nile to Egypt. Planes for India go straight ahead. They fly to an army transport base which the British took back from the Italians, and then along the shore of what used to be called Arabia until they cross the gulf and reach Karachi, India.

The main destination of our convoy was therefore Khartoum, where the fighter formations split. We, however, were to convoy them only as far as Fort Lamy. They would lie over there a short time, and we had to go on at once.

Approaching the shore line of the British crown colony of Nigeria, we led the squadron inland towards the heart of the continent. We flew near the course of the Benue River, over land rich with palm oil, cassava, Guinea corn, yams, and all the ordinary crops of the good earth, over hedged or fenced roads, over fields cultivated in as orderly a way as the rolling fields of Ohio. These natives had tended to the soil.

The entire valley is a native co-operative farming area, originated and maintained by natives and cultivated on a profit-sharing basis. Further, the most successful agricultural establishment in Africa is not a European development at all but a co-operative native enterprise.

This is an organization of 25,000 native coffee planters on the slopes of snow-capped Mount Kilimanjaro. The Kilimanjaro Natives' Co-operative Union tends to its own business and employs an English secretary to market its coffee under its orders. These people are experts in irrigation and raise some of the best coffee in Africa.

Native villages were everywhere. The main native city in the northern section has a population of nearly 100,000. This is the ancient city of Kano, covering seven square miles on an open plain, contained within the giant circle of a famous wall.

This was near elephant country. Elephants' ideal environment is underbrush. But they are remarkably adaptable and can live anywhere, in mountain ranges, on plains, in semi-desert arid sections, or in wet jungles. Elephants are exceptional wild animals, and our soldiers in Africa consider them by all means the most interesting.

The African elephant will eat anything green, dig holes in a dry river bed and find water where men have failed to discover it, travel fifty miles a day through dense jungle, sometimes smash his way through the trees, sometimes slip through like a noiseless phantom. Tamed and in harness, he hauls three tons or more on a road—a job for twenty oxen.

Often found eleven feet tall around Lake Chad, and weighing fifteen thousand pounds—as much as six Ford sedans—his feet do not stick in the bottomless mud. They expand as he puts down his weight and contract with the shift of his body, so that he is able to lift them out. His life begins at forty, and he can live a hundred

and fifty years. With ridiculously small eyes that can hardly see
and ridiculously large ears that can hardly hear, he has a fantastically keen sense of smell. If it's true that an elephant never forgets
anything, that must be the way he remembers it.

Elephant trails crisscross this area. If you see an elephant, which
we did not, the good old soul might be going anywhere, for these
lumbering playboys migrate all over in a most capricious way,
turning up now and then where least expected and where they
haven't been seen for years.

But the trails are far shorter than they used to be. At one time
these fascinating beasts, waving their trunks high above their heads,
moved through not only Africa and Asia, but Europe and North
America as well. In fact, one of the largest prehistoric remains of an
elephant ever found was discovered in Kent, England.

Its skeleton is fourteen feet high and adorns the British Museum,
or so Reggie told me, and I can assure you I have always found
him very precise. The next time I am in London I am certainly
going to see it. Having been through Africa's big-game country
twice without seeing a single wild animal, you can hardly blame
me. As I like animals dearly, the whole matter smacks a little of
conspiracy.

In New York I live directly opposite the zoo. I couldn't be
any closer without being an animal myself. My apartment is on
the eleventh floor, looking out on Fifth Avenue and directly down
on the Central Park menagerie. I see three elephants, two big and
one small, every day of my life. At breakfast I stare at playful
orangutans, pacing leopards, and yawning hippopotamuses the size
of a bus. I can all but see the whites of the eyes of a bona fide
rhinoceros, and I watch monkeys jump around in numbers nobody
would guess. I can nearly count the hairs in the whiskers of the
impatient gorillas and on the backs of the water buffaloes, wilde-
beests, and Thomson's gazelles.

At night the African birds and the bloodcurdling hyenas are
often restless in their cages. They make an awful noise. If you
live in my building there is nothing to do but lie awake and plan
to move. When I come downstairs in the morning to get into a taxi

I see zebras being fed, and the plumes on a quartet of African ostriches being fumigated. I pull away from the curb to the tune of a lion's roar.

The first thing I did when I got home from Africa was walk across the street and visit the zoo. I knew how the farmer felt who saw the giraffe.

Colonel Reggie Mayhew knew all about Kano. "The charge will be very small," he said, "I will tell you everything." Then he began to point. "Those are horsemen from Sokoto, Bornu, and Zaria," he said. "That is a caravan from the northern solitudes, men from the tin mines in the Bauchi Plateau. This man is a Kerrikerris, that man is a Kanuri. Kano is the magnet for the Nigerian country people.

"I've found around the world that it's city people who differ so much," he said. "Country people seem just about the same the world over."

A buffalo cart, half the size of a railroad caboose, lumbered through the crooked streets, brushing the mud walls and tying up traffic. Reggie and I lumbered behind it. For no reason that I could see, a man sat cross-legged under a tree, drumming on what Reggie called a *tambari*, and another man sat looking him straight in the eye, playing a mournful dirge on a bagpipe-like instrument. There was no limit to Reggie's cleverness. "That," he said, "is an *algaita*."

"The man or the horn?"

"The horn. They are playing for the amusement of the people in the jail."

The Kano jail is operated on an open-air basis, and the men and women behind the wall looked as pleased as Punch to be there in the shade of a tall palm tree that brought them all together in the center of the yard. Most of the Kano men were tall, lean, swathed in turbans. The women all wore calico robes of the same blue, which they dye themselves. They haven't found it monotonous for several centuries. And they all look alike.

Still, they have their distinctions. Wives and maidens who are so well off that they do not have to work and can, therefore, afford not to carry anything on their heads have a glamorous way of showing this to the less favored sisters who must toil. They amble around with small, fragile, and very empty glass bowls balanced on their heads.

An amazingly tall, distinguished-looking native walked proudly by us, carrying himself with great dignity. "He is rare in Kano," my friend said. "He is a Watusi."

Centuries ago there was a series of droughts in upper Egypt. Wretched families stayed as many seasons as they could, put up with one trouble after another, held on through hardship after hardship. More and more people had accumulated in the area during the good times and overpopulated the section, so that when great forces began to make it too barren to support them they were faced with want and destruction. The young men moved away. They migrated to peace and a better life. They were regal men, seldom less than seven feet tall, straight as pines, proud as peacocks. They were the Watusi, the tallest tribe in the world.

We followed the Watusi to the market place. The place was cheerful—I might say uproarious. A wild hoe dancer was spinning around on one foot and juggling a hoe in the air. Apparently this is a hard thing to do. Beads of sweat gathered on his chest, ran down his body in rivulets. A beaming, moon-eyed, thick-waisted man stood near him, never missing a twist. He was balancing on his head a bundle of rods tied together in homemade Roman fasces. He turned out to be the principal thief catcher of the Emir of Kano.

But the chief amusement of the natives is trading. The merchants chatter and giggle in front of bowls of maize, millet, nuts, potatoes, fruits. They unfold bundles of blue cloth. They wave trinkets at each other on long sticks. When they see a man with a spear they know they have a country boy on their hands. They laugh at his headdress, or the long feathers and claws in his belt, and cry with joy if he unshoulders his goatskin pack and starts to trade with them. A flock of spear carriers is likely to put a good part of the market in an uproar. The ones we saw certainly did. We found ourselves in the middle of one of these bull markets.

The visiting hillbillies had just laid out their packs. In front of the sellers' bowls they spread ivory, elephant meat, arrows, dry banana flour, pelts of strange shapes and sizes.

"Look at this fine corn meal, and tell me what you will give for it," shouted the leading merchant, or so we were told, for Reggie's interpreter was always about two sales behind each transaction.

"This arrow," answered the biggest of all the boys from the back woods, smiling as wide as the Kano gates.

"Whee, whee, did you hear that!" yell the merchants and on-lookers, in unbounded glee. It's the funniest offer you ever heard.

"*Sai wata rana* [Till another day]!" the spearman finally shouted.

"*Allay ya ba ka yawan rai* [May Allah give you a long life]!" all the merchants replied.

Soon new fires begin to light, and the spearmen and merchants are feasting on each other's merchandise and laughing into their banana brew. "Whee, wheee." They have a good time in Kano.

Now, it would be absurd to suggest a return to the state of the lowly Kanoite. But no one can pass lightly over the fact that he is very happy with "very little," while so many millions of us are very unhappy with "very much."

From morning until night this elementary fact impresses you as you travel the distant areas of the war-torn world. A British tank company rolled into Kano looking as out of place as a tidal wave in Indianapolis. The soldiers' faces were tense, their muscles taut. Their eyes were sharp. These men were well trained not to make mistakes. Something about them expressed what I imagine should be the motto of all machines: "To err is human."

They were clothed in the best that the Hudson Tube Age could supply. Only the finest steel, only the best leather, only the latest gasproof cloth. They ate food out of ingenious ration packages, not out of heavy kettles that swung over a crackling fire on hand-wrought cranes, and the food they ate had most of the properties of nature.

When they wanted to see a long distance they did not have to climb up on a platform in a tall tree. They sent up an airplane, stayed where they were, and got the reports through other eyes.

They had no end of devices like this. In fact, they had so many devices for talking to each other without being together that they lacked enough ears to listen. While their ears were busy under the headphones of an outside radio, these men in the tank used an intercommunicating phone which was clamped tight to their throats. No lowly Kanoite could possibly provide such a marvelous device as that.

The soldiers had all saved some money—not brass trinkets, or useless pieces of carved ivory, flowers, vegetables, cloth, or anything like that. They had saved some paper money. But they couldn't buy anything with it. Nobody would take it except one government place in the town, and that place was closed for the day. A few of them started a crap game and divided it around among themselves a little bit. But they were still hungry when they quit. Hungry and tired. And far from home. They thought of their king, but they took orders from a sergeant. They thought of God, but they went to church in a trailer.

To the Kanoites these Hudson Tube men must have seemed savages. Even the spearmen warriors looked at these "modern men" and laughed.

"What are you?" a lowly Kanoite might well have asked the tank commander, standing there in his bulging helmet, his head as big as that of a man from Mars, his throat phones around his neck, his gas mask high on his shoulder.

The commander could have given only one answer: "We are modern men."

I suppose that is all he could say.

But unwind this man, unwind his wires, detin him, strip off the coating of steel and leather, return him to himself—and what have you? You have an ordinary, good-humored, conscientious, gentle man, who, if at home, would be torn by every agony if a kerosene stove in his kitchen blew up and killed a puppy dog.

What are his wants, what are the wants of Leonard Paine, Corporal, wounded in the B.E.F., evacuated from the beach at Dunkirk, wounded three times in Libya? His wants are simple, and they have always been simple. He wants to be with his family, to work and to enjoy his community and his friends. He wants to be a part of that community, and to have his family a part of it. He wants to own property, not because he is greedy or vain, and not because he wants his property to do anyone any harm, but because he wants to feel some sense of security and to know that he himself is properly able to take care of those whom he loves and who are dependent on him.

He doesn't want some committee, or any person, to *give* him things. He doesn't look at himself or at life that way. It just does not sit right with him, any more than it would to stay home from the war.

Look at him closely at home in Hull, Yorkshire, as an unwired and detinned man. He is cleaner, more washed, than men have ever been in all history. He is healthier, and, on the average and except for war, he will live longer than men have ever lived before. He is better informed, went to school longer, hears more and reads more than has ever been the experience of any generation since the beginning of time. He is the most magnificent item for peace since the beginning of time.

He would not steal his neighbor's horse under any conceivable circumstances. Less than one per cent of his countrymen have ever stolen anything. As for shooting a man, killing anyone, he has never known a murderer in his life.

He works as a joiner in the building trades, and at thirty-five he is married and has one daughter. He loves his wife and that daughter beyond anything in the world, and they love him as much as life itself.

Ask him what a Communist is. "A Russian," he will tell you. A Fascist? "That's Hitler and his gang." Ask him how he likes the Americans. "They're a good crowd," he'll say, and let it go at that. He doesn't even dislike the Germans or the Italians enough to agree that he would like to keep on shooting Germans and Italians after this war is over, *and that ought to be a reasonable test of hate.*

None of the political leaders of any of the nations ever heard of Leonard Paine, or Richard Day of Massachusetts, Otto Lahr of Munich, Serge Popva of Stalingrad, Ricardo Pietri or François

Romier. Yet it is they who do the fighting. They do the dying.

Deep and dark their troubles flow. Who among them could have thought such darkness was concealed in their bright century, such horror compressed into only thirty years?

Is there no hope that human destiny can lay a lenient hand on all men? Is there no hope to soften sorrow's wound? Above the somber swell of war, even while men's hearts are torn out and dashed in their faces, there is the call of the soul for hope.

This is why kitchen-cabinet conspiracies, Washington plots by first-name functionaries, frivolous appointments, schemes that are already muddled before they are published in the newspapers, partisanship, nepotism, jobbery, and the creation of chaos have no place in this war or in the peace.

This is why cleverness and histrionics are so unappealing in our land, from which the best hope must come.

CHAPTER 13

General Valin Rides the Ammunition

Richard day of Massachusetts was killed while we were flying to Lake Chad.

I had gone to the field at four-thirty, an hour before the first streak of dawn. The pink single-seaters were being fueled and tuned up. The American pilots sat around a repair truck, looking more like a soccer team in their shorts than like a squadron of air fighters.

"Do you know how I can get a wire out of here?" one of the boys asked me. "They tell me there isn't a chance."

"Where's it going?" I asked him.

I could not believe my ears when he told me.

"You never heard of the place," he said, "but there's a telegraph office there. Coal City, Illinois."

His name was Lucian Ryan. He told me his uncle had run the general store in the days of Father's mines. If the words had dropped out of the air by magic he couldn't have looked more amazed when I started to ask him about Matt Keefer's farm and Harry Harkess, the son Billy Harkess named after my father.

"It doesn't seem possible we're 'way out here," Ryan said. "This is a long way off. I've never been across the ocean before. I certainly never thought I'd fly it."

We made a try at getting the message out.

"I want to say hello to the folks," Ryan said.

Next to transportation, communication with home is the most precious and difficult service in a war area. Every man misses it more than any other single thing. There is hardly a man in a remote war zone who wouldn't go without food for days in exchange for a letter or cable from home.

The sprawling war so complicates delivery that mailless months would have become an agonizing feature everywhere overseas if Major General George and Brigadier General C. R. Smith of the Army Air Transport Command had not stepped in and installed a mail service with American planes.

They carry army letters fast. Once a group of soldiers is settled, this army air organization swings into action and delivers the mail. General Smith is an old hand at this. Formerly president of our largest air transport line, he has managed plenty of mail in the air. Air Corps General H. H. Arnold and the Deputy Chief of the General Staff, Lieutenant General Joseph T. McNarney, who knows soldiering as well as any man in the world, co-operated with the Air Transport Command—and the mail flew everywhere to soldiers overseas.

But the airfield, of course, was not an established spot—men move through there too fast to get mail—and the field had no setup for personal wires. So the matter ended by my carrying Ryan's message with me, and sending a cable to Coal City from Cairo.

I had another cable to send for Richard Day of Massachusetts. It said, "Feeling fine. Don't worry."

I did not send it.

When we went up from the airfield in the early morning light all the fighter ships were behind us. The leader signaled that the formation was complete. Vernon Kerns of Ridgeway, Ohio, pilot of our munitions-loaded plane, set a course due east. He was pointing straight for Fort Lamy and Lake Chad, 300 miles away in the northern section of Free French Equatorial Africa.

We were flying over twisted, matlike jungle, as solid as the sea and as wild as jungle country can be. There was no vapor. It was clear on the ground. But we were flying through patches of thick, gray clouds. We broke out into the open only by fits and starts. As we came through the cloud banks, spotted all around us like hazy islands in a brooding sea, the wisps of dull white seemed to reach up and seize the pink ships marching behind us. They would disappear by one, two and three, depending on the angle of our view. Then they would emerge like bees out of a hive. We could never see the whole formation at one time. The scene from our plane was a giant game of peekaboo in the sky.

Three abreast, the fighters kept on our tail. At least we thought so until we got a signal from the squadron leader. Something was wrong. Something was very wrong. The leader came in over the earphones:

"We've lost a ship. Plane missing. We've lost a ship."

Apparently one of the pink ships had dropped a little behind and had been hidden for a few minutes during the in-and-out business with the clouds. Now even the rear planes were in the clear, and one plane was missing. The whole tragedy was as quiet and smooth as that. Into the cloud patches and out, into the clouds and out; all but one. Richard Day had not come out of the clouds with the rest of us.

We signaled that we would circle. We had hardly started when we saw a solid black spout of smoke, rising from the jungle like a narrow funnel and swaying like an immense, expanding cobra.

There was a short gash in the stubby trees, a brown tear in the solid green mass below us. Why this ship had fallen no one would ever know, but the shortness of the gash meant it had struck in a dive. This was no comet of glory. This was simple, awful death. But in this jungle country we could not even pay the respect of landing to claim one of our party in death. We could only notify our air base on the air waves, ask that a burial party be sent for this American boy, wheel back on our course, and go on.

I have seen many men die in this war. I have been close to men many times when they were killed—Scotchmen strafed on the airfields of the Trossachs, under a clouded moon and in the dismal haze of the brooding moors, Finnish scouts shot in the lovely pine forests of the Karelian isthmus, Frenchmen killed on the border of Italy, Poles drowned and dead in the North Sea. I have seen Russians die as their bodies were lifted from lifeboats on the shores of the Baltic. I have seen Englishmen die as I stood in the streets of London, and sailors brought ashore from the torpedoings near Gibraltar. I have seen countless planes shot out of the sky: a burst as though some giant paw had torn them apart, a plume of black, a sickening thud. Fire. But Richard Day is the first American boy I saw die in this war.

The quietness of it, the simplicity of this death. As always where trouble is on, it is the overwhelming fact of death and suffering that carries the meaning of war. Everything else seems so far away.

Death, twisted lives, the agony of blindness and of cruel wounds that tear men to pieces—these are the final realities of war, and only these. How much death there is that man can cause! How little he seems to cure! War is not a triumphant thing. It is cold and cunning death alone, or in a herd, that triumphs in war, takes men suddenly as their eyes grow cloudy and their chins drop, as their bodies strain against their harnesses and their arms quiver, alone in the sky; or takes men standing within inches of other men, who are saved, no one knows why, and who live to come home and be with their families and know once more the love of simple things. How difficult it is to see any pattern in life when you can see no selection in death, no choosing or weighing, no care or mercy in the choice, no blessing that we can understand! To any man who believes in God, his faith tells him that the death of each good man has its purpose and its blessing. But in war you find it hard to keep that thought. War confuses the depths of any man's soul.

But there are worse things than war. I have seen worse things than war in the Nazi-occupied countries of Europe. I do not think the slaves who built the Pyramids had less of life, less hope than men who die. None who are dead are further from life than Jews I have seen in Hitler's concentration camps. The early Egyptian slaves would have welcomed war, but it was too late for them. It is too late now for millions of French, Dutch, Belgians, Poles, Greeks. It is too late until the free men who are left stop this pagan force and throw back forever this evil enemy. Richard Day's death was to keep it from being too late for all the world.

For if free men do not, or cannot, make their stand now against the wave of paganism which is hurling itself with insane fury against us in the middle of the twentieth century, man as a creature of God returns literally and actually to the despotism which permitted tyrants of the Egyptian centuries to erect to themselves, in the blood and sweat and tears of their subject peoples, the colossal monuments of egotism towards which Richard Day was flying.

Yet the first desire of the human heart is to find something on which to lean. And this is the desire which is capitalized by Europe's totalitarian and America's national socialist leaders alike.

Thus, while one cuts a cruel and violent gash in the very web of civilization itself, the other performs a sad unraveling. For civilization rests upon individual conscience. Civilization is first and foremost a *moral* thing. Without the worship of truth, rooted in the action of its leaders, no government can exercise *national virtue*, and no war or peace can have a truly moral basis.

Neither rhetoric nor clever "conditioning of the public mind," nor brilliant formulas which disguise a group's plans while this is being done, not even the goodness of the cause which is disguised, can maintain the edifice. The ultimate ground on which the strength of the nation rests is the spiritual quality within the people and their confidence in the integrity of their government. Integrity is what upholds all, and the whole is menaced whenever bad government sets a bad example.

In our Government the separation of enlightenment and virtue, the separation of thought and conscience, was at the bottom of America's failure in any way to direct the world towards peace from the time Hitler came to power in 1933 to the outbreak of war in 1939. As our leaders pressed their views and expanded their words and promises at home, they fell further and further away from the ability to enforce any peace abroad.

For six years, while the world smoldered, ready to burn under the torch of the madman Hitler and the historic flame of Pan-Germanism, knowing and being warned by such men as Mr. Hull that war was coming, our national socialist leaders still tampered with the spiritual and intellectual honesty of our nation.

Our Government was run then, as it is now, by a small group thoroughly familiar with the power that such organization gives for the attainment and retention of influence and position. The tongue and pen were the cogs of the machine, just as they are today. A masterly camouflage of spoken morality was daubed over the grim reality of politics. Side by side with the misuse of speech, they entered into their vast pretense of "making democracy work."

They operated not for democracy, for their measures and orders, their appointments to the judiciary, their witch hunts and purges, were the antithesis of any confidence in democracy. They operated for the purpose of ruling the nation as they—in their wisdom—saw fit. They pursued the same program which led to such bitter trouble throughout the world: the elaborate suppression of facts and the doctoring of news to suit a secret policy.

The tragedy resulting from this is that our people will therefore never thoroughly understand our stake in this war or the full force and nature of our mortal enemies abroad. Our whole country—the men in our fighting forces, the loved ones of those who died, like Richard Day, the young and old on our farms, in the workshops, stores, locomotive cabs and pit cars, factories and offices—will never really see this war in its true perspective and grasp the underlying contrasts in our war against the Axis.

What could have been, and should have been, the most profoundly just and impelling crusade for righteousness and the way of God in all the history of man; what could have been, and should have been, the triumphant release of the American spirit in joyous dedication to the high duties of this glorious nation, degenerated into the maxim "We have been attacked."

What is still the common denominator which runs through our public mind at the hour that Richard Day is falling in the jungle? Doubt—doubt of oneself, of thought, of news, of men and measures. Doubt of life—doubt which dilutes the will at home and weakens all our powers—that restless and corrosive doubt which the sophisticated governmentalists call "the problem of home-front morale."

Regardless of our military victory, if liberty is to be saved it will be only by good example. It will be by religious conviction, by the faith of individuals who believe that God intends man to be free but also pure. It will be by those persons who feel communion with immortality and eternal life, and prefer the soul to the whole world. Liberty will be saved by those who set an example in this, and not by those who set the example of cleverness.

Richard Day fell in what was once German territory, the jungles of the Kaiser's Cameroons. In another few minutes he would have been in the clear, for we were coming out of the jungle area, onto the rolling plains of the big-game country. There he would have had the best of chances in a bad landing. Soon there would have been nothing under him more difficult than clumps of scattered trees and tufts of pale-yellow elephant grass. He was killed in the jungle. We landed at Fort Lamy.

At this Fighting French post I had arranged to meet General Martial Valin, Chief of the Fighting French Air Forces, on an inspection trip to his flying units in Equatorial Africa, Egypt, and Syria and to the Lamy mobilization of the French troops which I had understood I was to see.

The advance arrangements worked out as something of a miracle of modern transportation. The general left his headquarters in London when I left New York. His wire to me the day before said, "Starting Sunday." So did mine to him. We were to join each other at Fort Lamy. As I came down the coast of South America he flew down the coast of Europe to Gibraltar and on towards South Africa. As I flew across the Atlantic he flew to the mouth of the Congo. When I landed at the Liberian base he landed at Brazzaville. As I flew east from Accra he flew north from the French capital. Over oceans and from different directions, on two separate routes of 10,000 miles each, we kept our engagement within half an hour at Fort Lamy.

Walking across the field, trim in the light-blue shorts and open-collared tunic of the French desert uniform, smiling and looking at his watch, Valin came up to the door of the plane as I stepped down. "You're late," he said. "What happened to you? I thought we said we'd meet at noon. It's nearly twelve-thirty." I was glad to see him. He had been a good friend in London from the time of the fall of France.

Now Air Chief of all Fighting French, the general had had a brilliant career before the fall of France. Born at Limoges in 1898, he came from a great French military family. Valin served in the trenches in World War I with a special infantry unit made up of demounted cavalry forces and was decorated in the Champagne action of May 1918.

Immediately after the armistice he returned to Saint-Cyr and then went on to the military school at Saumur. Valin was one of the best horsemen of Europe, winning twelve steeplechases in one year in nearly every country abroad. He went to Morocco on active service in the Army and took a leading part in the Rif campaign of 1925. When he returned to France, later that year, he transferred to the French Air Corps, making up his mind that the whole effort of night flying had been badly neglected all over the world.

He used balloons in his first test of night operations, and by 1930 he was Europe's outstanding authority on night-flying matters. He began to study the problem of night flying in groups with landings in the dark, and as a staff officer of the 12th Air Brigade he developed this work on air tactics in the General Staff of the French Air Forces.

Hampered in every way by political obstruction, he pressed for the development of Potez 63s and went into action on the first day of World War II as Commander of the 33rd Air Squadron.

Valin's command was the only group in the French Air Forces to perform successful night reconnoitering, and he and his men were cited continuously in the military dispatches for their performances. By the time this stocky, alert officer had accumulated 1800 hours of flying, over 500 of which was night flying, he was serving as the Chief Intelligence Officer with the General Staff of the French Army in the northeast, which was the theater of operations against the German invaders.

With the signing of the armistice, his squadron flew to Africa. These men did not propose to stop their fight for France. Valin was condemned to death by Vichy.

The Fighting French were mobilizing an army at Fort Lamy to advance north from there for 1600 miles out of the jungle brush and across the Sahara, to establish an attack from the south on Rommel's base at Tripoli.

This was a great day in central Africa, and, as ranking officer, Valin was so generous as to invite me to review the troops with him as the contingents started for this new "southern front" in the Sahara Desert.

The troops did not know where they were going. They had no idea that they were heading 1600 miles north to battle with the Germans. The whole difficult undertaking was one of the best-kept African secrets of Washington and London. Half its advantage was its element of surprise.

These Frenchmen and French colonial troops had been marched into the jungle for long periods many times before. But they had always come back to Fort Lamy. Today they would not come back. They were going right through. The trucks had been checked over, the water drums filled, the detachments formed in convoys under native guides that would take them forward under a point-to-point arrangement.

Beyond Huri Turao, as they entered the southernmost depths of the Sahara, they would encounter one of the most difficult desert crossings in the world. Here winds shift the sands, changing the surface all day and night. There is no road, and none is possible. The sands would cover it even if it could be built. Trucks cannot even follow markers, for they too are lost in the constant shifting of dunes eighty to a hundred feet high. It does not seem possible that any equipment could operate. But American trucks had been tested for this, and American trucks would do it. As they sank, native crews with *ke-ke* logs would go to work under the wheels and dig the blistering sand away with their hands.

It would be slow. "It will be two weeks from here to Faya,"

Valin told me. "That will be a little short of halfway. Each truck should make about eight miles a day, but it cannot keep that up. General Leclerc planned five miles a day for the trip."

"How about oases?" I asked him.

"We're carrying the water all the way to Faya. There aren't any oases. There are one or two water holes called oases, but the water would give every man dysentery."

With the review over, and the last trucks rumbling to the north, Valin said good-by to his aide and climbed into Vernon Kerns's plane.

Although each of us had flown nearly a thousand miles since dawn, we still had a long way to go to reach Khartoum. And, all told, we had 2400 miles to go to reach Cairo.

We stretched out on top of the munitions crates, made ourselves as comfortable as we could, and Valin told me what had been going on in London since we had been together, and about his previous inspection trip to Syria with the Duke of Gloucester.

"Our Alsace Squadron, based near Alexandria, is fighting in a few of our own ships," Valin said, "but mostly in Hurricane Mark I's that fought in the Battle of Britain. The boys fight the ships magnificently." He was proud of their record. Flying and fighting in the air is in the blood of these heroic French pilots. The only limit on their achievements was their equipment, for, as an indication of how rapidly aviation advances in this war, the planes which were absolutely tops in the Battle of Britain are far too slow and awkward now. Valin was on his way to ask Air Chief Marshal Sir Arthur W. Tedder in Cairo to give the French boys faster machines. He always got along well with Tedder, and he knew the Fighting French needs would be met if Sir Arthur could possibly manage it.

We refueled at a desert outpost, desolate in the rolling sands of the Anglo-Egyptian Sudan. With the terrible tragedy of Richard Day in the morning and the difficulties ahead that afternoon, it was the worst flying day of my life.

We took off easily from the fueling station. But our radio aerial snapped shortly after our take-off. Our radio set was dead for both receiving and sending, and we went on the compass to find our way. We began bucking a strong head wind.

The scattered trees of the Lake Chad area, even the tufts of elephant grass, were far behind us. The country had thinned out from the African brush into the brown billows of the rolling desert. These are not the white sands of seaside dunes. The ground is dull tan, rippled with hard waves and pinnacles. Seifs, with long, continuous ridges; abrupt and menacing escarpments of fissured rock, twisted and molded into weird and angry-looking shapes by the wind and sand that stings and sears rocks and men alike; then areas strewn with boulders, like dark melons on a patch. These are the desert fringes.

Now there are long stretches of barkhans, the crescent dunes that shift ceaselessly before the wind, their tapering horns a mile apart and their center cones rising like dunce caps, shimmering in the glare of the sun. We were in the Sudanese desert, starting to fly nearly a thousand miles in the Anglo-Egyptian Sudan.

In this vast area every map is misleading. Names can be anything from a water hole or a patch of camel's-thorn to a cairn of stones erected over a burial place in the middle of nowhere. A whole group of names need not mean life, or even water. Thousands of square miles in these deserts have never been seen, unless by the *Bedawi*, the desert nomads.

Not a ground marker anywhere, nothing but desert and sky visible from the cockpit; nothing of any kind in any direction except one distant and strange object, the weirdest object I ever saw from the air. It was a solid mass of gray-brown structure, 7000 feet high, 30 miles square, rising straight up from the surface of the desert as Gibraltar rises from the sea. It was a haboob, the great desert sandstorm.

As it traveled it grew, pushing its strangely abrupt form wider and wider, like a constantly extending wall. The edges of this moving block of sand were amazingly regular. Its front came forward as a solid wall, licking up the sand in ripples at its base as it moved along the ground under a fifty-mile wind.

We turned. Kerns tried to go around the fantastically even edges and stay in the clear air, climbing at the same time to lift the heavy plane above this immense block of sand if our paths met. We could not make it. The wall grew steadily wider, the top grew higher, and the wind stronger as we came on. Now the air held a light mist of sand. Then it seemed as though you could reach out and touch the solid, towering mass.

With a sickening impact, a blast from our propellers, a shudder through every inch of our ship from nose to tail, we hit it. That storm of sand threw us like dice in a shaker. The munitions cases shifted. Valin and I, lying prone on top of them, shifted with them. With ropes, we tied each other to the largest case. Each time the ship dropped suddenly in a downdraft the cases would pause suspended and then crash to the floor, as though to batter their way through and make their break for freedom. How that plane stayed together I do not know, and neither does General Valin.

We were in trouble. With the night flight across the North Sea, it was the second time in a few months that I had been up against a proposition like this.

Now, in the rolling desert, this haboob was an older enemy than the Nazis. No age in the history of Egypt has missed its devastation. These storms destroyed the Zwayaan, and in earlier centuries a haboob buried the forty thousand men in the army of Cambyses who vanished in the desert on their way to attack Siwa. Death and the desert. The Arabs huddle in the sand, wrap themselves in their *furwa* of black sheepskin, hope that it will pass. But you have to keep moving in the air. You can't land in this moving block of sand, couldn't come down even if you could see the earth.

We kept all the altitude we could and held on. That was the trick, to keep altitude no matter what happened in the brown darkness of the storm's fury, and Kerns did it. But after half an hour of this, without our radio, we were lost.

Sand filtered through the cabin, filled it with a haze. High above, the sun was shining brilliantly. It looked like a solid red ball in the mass of sand. No rays. Just a red ball. That was all.

We had to try to find the Nile, and sooner or later we must fly very low to do so. The surface area over the murky water, wherever it was, would give us our strip of visibility and our only possible guide to Khartoum.

Wrapped in the folds of pelting sand, wondering every moment when it might knock out our motors, we dropped slowly until the altimeter showed 200 feet, risked a downblast that would throw us in the desert, circled in search of the river. Then we came up. Time and again for two hours we did this, boring down, circling at the fastest speed to steady the plane, hurtling up again.

Round after round. The lift as we climbed, the shudder in the wind as we leveled off, the drop and sickening tilt as we came down, turning always and struggling to head into the wind. Then again the long-drawn breath of the motors, pouring themselves out once more in a blast of power. The lift.

For two agonizing hours we cut great series of figure eights, end on end, across the dismal Sudanese desert. We saw nothing. We did not even know when we were low except for the black dial on the altimeter.

Suddenly we crossed the Nile. And in a flash we lost it. On the next drop and circle we were again over the strip of water, wild, ruffled, angry from the terrible wind but clearly visible a hundred feet below us. We thought we must be north of Khartoum. That was General Valin's best guess, and he was right. The current showed we were flying upstream. We stayed as high as we could. But we had to fly below a hundred feet, twisting and turning along the serpentine banks as we roared over the churning water.

There is a high steel bridge across the Nile outside Khartoum. It connects Khartoum with the native city of Omdurman, the famous Arab city where "Chinese" Gordon made his last stand and where Churchill fought as a young lieutenant in a hussar regiment, under Kitchener, in Churchill's early days of war.

General Valin looked at the map.

"If we are going to crash now," he said, "it will be against that bridge."

We piled some parachutes and some burlap against the front of the cabin. We blew up two "Mae West" life preserver jackets that were in the tail of the ship—good cushions to have on in a crash.

We folded our overcoats into big pads that covered our heads, and we tightened the ropes that held us flat on the high boxes. Then we hung on.

Once you are set in a spot like this, you get plenty of time to think. There is nothing else to do but think, and to wonder. There would be no warning of that bridge. Either we were going to hit it or we weren't.

Kerns or no other man could keep the plane level as we battered through the sand, but he fought that ship like a man possessed as it hurtled up and down in the hundred-foot range. I saw Valin fold the map and tuck it in his pocket. He lit a cigarette and started to smoke it. So did I. I don't know how long we flew like this. Time doesn't operate like time when you are in real trouble. It is simply lifted out of life.

Valin started to say something. I saw a flash of green. We both saw it. We shot over the steel beams of the bridge.

Kerns sighted flares shot up from Khartoum's Wadi Seidna airport. They had been sending them up steadily; uncontacted, we were three hours overdue.

A final blast seemed to strike us down, as though to be rid of us forever. Kerns hurled that plane onto the whirling field, cut the switches, killed the engines. We tore off our wheels, wrenched off our landing gear, gouged the hard sand in a crashing, thunderous rip of our belly on the earth, swung frantically, crazily, in a wild, headlong spasm, stopped suddenly in a breathless moment of agonizing silence.

Valin and I untied ourselves from the ammunition cases and got out.

CHAPTER 14

Diver Ellsberg on the Nile

There was news for me at Khartoum. Over military wires I received a message that Dr. Refik Saydam, the Prime Minister of Turkey, had died. Stricken suddenly in Istanbul, the funeral of the man I was flying to Turkey to see was being held as I read this message in a hangar a thousand miles up the Nile.

By midnight I had further word. Owing to the tenseness of the international situation, Refik Saydam's successor would be appointed at once. It would be His Excellency Sukru Saracoglu. Now Minister of Foreign Affairs, he would be Turkey's new Prime Minister. He had agreed to see me the day I reached Ankara.

But Valin and I could not get out of Khartoum. The Nazis were bombing Cairo's airports persistently. Planes had been stopped from Khartoum.

"We have been shut out for two days," the field commandant told us. "It looks as though you're in for a wait."

Rommel's progress was totally unknown. Indefinite orders had been issued. No one knew whether we could land anywhere in the delta area. If not, I would have to fly east from Khartoum, detour along the coast of Arabia, fly to Karachi, India, and then work my way up through Iran to reach Turkey. I felt a little as I had on the blacked-out moors of Scotland, waiting to fly across the North Sea to Finland. Difficulties were accumulating then, and they were accumulating now.

But our cargo couldn't wait, and neither could we. We decided to make the start. In the middle of the night we sent a message through to Air Chief Marshal Sir Arthur W. Tedder, Commander of the R.A.F. in the Middle East, in Cairo, via the British army signal corps relay from Luxor. We made a deal to get under way for Cairo at dawn. Air Chief Marshal Tedder's headquarters in Cairo telegraphed us that Sir Arthur was issuing instructions to the Heliopolis airfield, Cairo's military airport in the Heliopolis section of the city, and that he had worked out a plan. Sir Arthur told us to proceed from Khartoum as far as Luxor, 800 miles down the Nile and within 200 miles of Cairo. He would keep the R.A.F. commandant of the Luxor field posted, and he was instructing this officer to notify us of the situation in Cairo by putting down a signal.

As we would not be able to use our radio in that area, the Luxor commandant would signal with cloth. Large white strips laid out in a circle on the Luxor field would tell us that the Cairo airport was being bombed. This signal would ground us at Luxor, where the commandant would take care of us until we could get in to Cairo. A white cloth X on the Luxor field would tell us that the Cairo field was clear for the time being. This X would send us on in to Cairo. In either event we would have 800 miles behind us and be that much nearer our objective. Tedder's message ended: "Come on, and good luck."

Working all night by black-out flashlights and wrapped in their white robes, barefooted and scar-faced Sudanese transferred the cargo from our cracked-up ship to another C-53. "We finish before daylight," one of them said. They did.

I had a second message at the hangar. It was from Captain Edward Ellsberg, U.S.N., one of our country's quiet heroes, top man in the world in his line.

Captain Ellsberg had just arrived in Khartoum from the Red Sea port of Massaua. He was in Khartoum for a two-day visit, and I drove in to the city to have dinner with him.

This short, stocky, soft-spoken naval officer, holder of the Distinguished Service Medal, was the man who revolutionized salvage operations by his use of pontoons. He was the hero of the raising of the *S-51* off Block Island, consultant on the raising of the

Squalus and the *S-4* off Provincetown, inventor of the Ellsberg underwater torch, which emits its flame under water and cuts steel below the surface of the sea nearly as fast as you can cut it in the air, and author of five books on salvaging operations. He looked fresh as a daisy and pleased as Punch as he sat waiting on the broad veranda of the beautiful Sudan Club. He wore khaki navy shorts, his knees were bared and tanned, and his face was weather-beaten and wrinkled as a saddle.

"We're over the hump," Ellsberg told me, leading the way to the dining room. "We're in the clear on this. We've finished at Massaua."

Just to see the look on his face made you feel like proposing a toast. And well you might, for Ellsberg had just completed one of the grand jobs of the war.

Massaua is the Red Sea port of the inland city of Asmara in Italian Eritrea, near the northern border of Abyssinia. It had been Mussolini's most important naval base outside Italy. It was his gateway into the kingdom of Haile Selassie. After 1935 the Italians, good at construction work, developed Asmara in a big way. They erected elaborate buildings, transplanted shade trees to line new thoroughfares, lit them brilliantly at night by a unique system of indirect lighting. They built an air-conditioned hospital, large movie theaters, parks, and terraces. In Massaua they built levees, warehouses, a modern port. The Italians really did something in Eritrea. It was the only bright gem in tiny Victor Emmanuel's dull crown of emperorship.

When British columns attacked Abyssinia from the Anglo-Egyptian Sudan and returned Haile Selassie to his throne—the first re-establishment of an overrun state to be accomplished in World War II—they recaptured Eritrea through the back door.

They found Massaua's water-front shops and piers battered in from explosions. The fleeing Italians had blown up all Italian and German ships in the harbor and made it a graveyard of tankers, war vessels, freighters, supply ships, ex-liners. Two floating dry-docks, one large enough to handle 10,000-ton cruisers, lay wallowing on their sides, half submerged, fixed in the mud. The Italian scuttling methods had been thorough. They placed 200-pound bombs in all watertight compartments, blasted every bulkhead.

"Allied inspectors said it was impossible to refloat most of these ships or either of the drydocks," Ellsberg told me, "but Secretary Knox and Admiral King said they thought our Navy could do it. We filed away the inspectors' reports and went to work."

Ellsberg rounded up as many United States navy divers and salvage experts as he could find who had worked with him before. They were scattered among outposts of the fleet: in Honolulu, Dutch Harbor, Bermuda, Panama. He gathered thirteen. These Americans, and the native labor they had to train, did the whole immense job at Massaua.

The *Intent*, a 108-foot navy tug of only 310 tons, slipped out of New York under sealed orders and sailed 14,000 miles with this little band. It took the men two months to reach the Red Sea, but, once among the ships which choked Massaua's harbor, they began breaking new salvage records as Ellsberg had broken so many before.

The keen-eyed naval captain put on a diver's suit and went down into every wreck. For days this fifty-one-year-old officer roamed around in the black silt below, calculating the problems, figuring his plans, testing his guesses. He had no chart of this enemy harbor. He had no plans or diagrams of these enemy ships.

The thermometer ranged steadily between 115 and 120 degrees. He had thirteen experienced men where he needed a hundred.

Ellsberg had to find and rig up his own pumps, make most of his own salvage apparatus. There was no such equipment at Massaua, of course, and there had been practically nothing aboard the *Intent*. She was not a salvage vessel, like the *Falcon*. She was a plain, tough tug.

"We took Diesel engines from abandoned Italian tractors, ropes from halyards, even the pump from the Italian governor's swimming pool," Ellsberg explained to me. "But we really did the main job by 'cannibalism.' We went down into each of the sunken ships, extracted all the pumps the ships carried, got our tools, engines, and many motors out of the ships' engine rooms. We repaired this equipment in a shed, combined the pumps into batteries, and put them to work raising the hulls themselves. We dismantled six large gasoline-storage tanks on the shore and used them for pontoons. They weren't what we wanted, but they worked."

Few projects anywhere in this war, and none on this scale, reflect such genius for improvisation as Ellsberg showed in this task. And to the miracle of having done the job at all, after it had been officially reported impossible, Ellsberg added speed with a capital *S*.

Within nine months from the day the *Intent* arrived, Ellsberg, without plans of the enemy ships' interiors and not even knowing their weights, figured out and put into operation the project of raising each separate ship. Within that period every ship had been raised and was floating. He did not write off and abandon a single vessel. He raised them on their sides, tipped them upright. He raised them upside down, rolled them over. He did everything, and he did everything fast. He raised the 14,000-ton Nazi merchantman *Liebenfels* in record time. The official report had recommended that "the wreck of the *Liebenfels*, a menace to navigation, be detonated as a total loss." In exactly twenty-nine days, while he was doing all the other work, he patched this ship from stem to stern, pumped her out, lifted her on an even keel, and hoisted the American flag to her mast atop an ugly Nazi pennant.

Ellsberg raised the immense floating drydock, as big and sprawling as a railway shed. It was the worst mess, the most important and irreplaceable item, in the harbor equipment.

General Maxwell's men erected in this area one of the largest and most important overseas supply depots of the United States Army, the vital base of our African forces. In doing so they installed our service entrance to Egypt and the Middle East.

"Somebody had to clear the harbor for Maxwell," Ellsberg said, "and we needed the shipping back home. But I'm sorry I was away and couldn't have a crack at the *Normandie*." Then he showed me how the French ship would be righted and raised at her New York dock. "It's wrong to say that ship wasn't well built. She was well designed from bow to stern. The *Normandie* can be very useful. But, among other reoutfitting jobs, thousands of miles of wet wire, which would short-circuit, will have to be yanked from behind panels and from every part of the ship. That's an awful job. I'd rather raise her than rewire her."

Valin beamed when I told him Ellsberg's opinion of the *Normandie* on my return to Wadi Seidna airport, where he had remained while I went into town. "I like to think she was the most beautiful ship in the world," he said, "and that she will be again. I think there is something symbolic—maybe prophetic—about her. The day the *Normandie* is righted and floats will be a better day for France."

Valin and I turned in and slept near the hangar until just before dawn, when the Sudanese finished transferring the load. The new C-53 was ready on the runway.

But it had been raining hard all night, torrents as heavy and abrupt as the sand in the earlier storm. The field was too wet. We had to wait until well after noon for it to dry. Then the pilot lifted the ship. We swung north and headed down the Nile, over the mud villages and the tall pillars of the water wheels, over the bamboo-masted feluccas that spotted the water like swans.

Beyond the Nubian Desert we came out of the Anglo-Egyptian Sudan at Wadi Halfa, close to the four Borglum-like statues of Ramses II. We shut off our wireless, as we had to do in the war area, and started over the flat sands of Upper Egypt.

We flew low, following the course of the Nile. The great river wound through the desert like an even, unfrayed ribbon, sometimes dividing to come together again in the distance, sometimes wide, sometimes narrow as though it were squeezing through a pass between invisible mountains.

Red-brown-skinned fellahin worked their ancient wooden farm tools, ground their wheat and corn in circles as they walked behind water buffaloes, patiently raised the river water by their shadoofs as they had for centuries. Bucket by bucket, these well sweeps lifted the Nile and dumped its waters onto green fields. This was the season's flood tide. From the junction of the White and Blue

Niles at Khartoum the brown waters were carrying loam to the delta a thousand miles north. Life for Egypt.

The history of man is the story of a hungry creature in search of food. Wherever food is plentiful, sooner or later man has left barren, crowded areas and traveled there to make his home. Egypt made food, and food made Egypt.

But why the concentration of early civilization in the belt bordering the Mediterranean? Why was civilization concentrated not far from the Mediterranean coast on the European and African shores, and in Asia Minor, Persia, and China?

One peculiarity of the first belt of intellectual development is that it had generally low rainfall and generally high temperatures. This peculiarity made it necessary for people to conserve rainfall and irrigate the land. They had to think. *And when they did think they were rewarded.* This is the distinction of Egypt in the development of mankind and in the great drama of agriculture, which was, until the mechanistic network of a few moments ago, the great drama of man.

The complicated network of canals, well sweeps, and irrigation trenches which stretched below our plane, unchanged in five thousand years, gave new life to people who migrated to this land from the interior of Africa, the desert of Arabia, the western areas of Asia.

Over the First Cataract and the gleaming white dam at Aswan.

"That was the model for the great Mississippi River dam at Keokuk, Iowa," I told Valin, for no reason at all.

"Where?"

"Keokuk."

"Egyptian city? Further along the Nile?"

"No, Keokuk, Iowa, America."

"Oh," said Valin.

"The slogan of Keokuk is 'The Best City by a Dam Site.' "

"Oh. And you say that in French?"

"*La meilleure ville près de la digue.*"

"Is it?"

"So they say."

"So who say?"

"The Keokukians."

"I think," said Valin, "they sound like ducks."

Now we were over the ruins of Thebes, Greek name of the capital of the upper Nile. Homer knew Thebes, gave it the epithet of ἑκατόγπυλος, meaning "hundred-gated," but the German General Staff knew Thebes too.

Just as the Germans originated so little, but developed so much from the ideas of others, the first idea for their open strong-spot type of fortifications, as contrasted with the Maginot Line, came from Thebes. Meanwhile others used it before the Germans, of course, but the military conception of Hitler's West Wall and the open defenses in depth that Stalin installed to save Moscow were originated here. Thebes was unique in all the ancient world. It was never a walled city. Its "hundred gates" were not a hundred gates. They were open spaces between fortified temples. The defenders of Thebes let the enemy "into" Thebes and then annihilated them from these giant temple pillboxes by a close cross fire from any direction. And, furthermore, they connected these strong spots underground. Dr. Todt, who built Hitler's West Wall, came to Egypt in 1937 and studied Thebes. So did Rommel. General Weygand ran into them here then. "Our hobby is archaeology," Dr. Todt told Weygand. The irony of this is that Weygand's hobby really was archaeology.

When our pilot sighted Luxor he pointed for the R.A.F. airport on the left bank of the Nile, on the edge of the valley of the kings. Near the site of the excavations of Tutankhamen's tomb our signal was stretched out on the field, gleaming and clear on the reddish-brown sand. It was a giant white cloth X.

It was good news. In this way Air Chief Marshal Tedder was telling us that we could come in to Cairo. The pilot dipped the plane's wing. The R.A.F. commandant at the Luxor airfield would now notify Cairo's Heliopolis airport and identify us as on the way. The ship was set for the last two hundred miles across Africa.

When you fly alone in the desert war zone you keep very low, only a few hundred feet over the sand. This is the best protection, because enemy fighter squadrons will not break formation to come down and get you. All over the desert, dispatch planes or single ships on missions skim above the surface of the sand. This was our technique beyond Luxor.

The desert night, full darkness, follows quickly after a short twilight haze. It was twilight when we sighted the gleaming Mosque of Mohammed Ali on the high escarpments of jagged rock which make a backdrop for the city of Cairo. It was dark before we reached the succession of pyramids on the left bank of the Nile.

Suddenly, as we veered to the right and were making our landing at the Heliopolis airfield, shafts of light cut the sky, sheared and slashed the delicate beauty of the desert night. These were the lights of the twentieth century. Apparently our race with the Nazis, begun for me at La Guardia Field, and for Valin in London, was going to end in a photofinish.

Valin looked at me and laughed. "This," he said, "is what I call punctual."

Valin and I made for the door as the plane stopped. "Here they come," Valin said, "and here we go."

We each spotted a slit trench, and down we went. We didn't even have tin hats, which are a good thing to have any time, and especially if you happen to be lying in an open trench on the dive bombers' objective. We just had our fingers crossed.

Sixteen Stukas dove, one after the other, Indian file. I'll always remember that first one. And I'll always remember that slit trench.

In a few minutes it was all over. Valin and I lifted ourselves to our knees, first one knee and then the other. We put our hands on the hard, stony edge of the slit trench. Then we stood up. Your head doesn't clear right away after a thing like this. You feel very helpless. My nose was bleeding pretty badly, I don't know why, and it was a bad mess. We found ourselves holding each other up, and Valin was saying something, slowly, and I knew I was saying something too.

"We can have our chance at them while I am here," he said as we started to make our way across the field to the headquarters, his arm under mine as mine was under his. "I will get a plane, and I will take you with me."

I telephoned Air Chief Marshal Sir Arthur Tedder from the field house and told him I was on my way to Shepheard's Hotel.

Sir Arthur told me he would be waiting in his garden.

CHAPTER 15

The Evacuation of Cairo

CAIRO WAS EVACUATING civilians. Censorship was down tight on this and everything else, and it stayed down. Reputations were being made and broken fast now that the heat was on. The place was full of gossip. The Turf Club buzzed. Everybody's tongues were loose and going.

Martial law had been declared. There was a serious run on Barclays and all the banks in Egypt. Bearded Sikhs patrolled the streets. Every sort of vehicle carried civilian staffs east into Palestine or south to Luxor and beyond, billeting them along the Nile. The clerical staff of the American Legation was sent to Khartoum. The British Ministry of Information packed off to Jerusalem. Except for Paul West and his assistant in charge, our Office of War Information, after burning its files and photographs, had gone to Palestine.

Communications were cut. Thousands of people did not know where they were going, except that they were going out of Alexandria and Cairo. By truck, train, automobile, wagon, donkey, bicycle, or on foot, foreign residents with bundles moved like ants emerging from an anthill, spreading like minnows at the drop of a stone. When the hotels at Luxor and Aswan became full, refugees slept in the desert. When the food gave out they ate as best they could. When more came they shared what they had.

In Cairo itself Shepheard's Hotel was a labyrinth of luggage, trunks, kit bags, and boxes. Lieutenant Sumner Gerard, Jr., of our Navy, Major General Russell L. Maxwell's aide and one of the most helpful Americans in the Middle East, met me at the hotel, gave me my first picture of what was going on, and laid out a program for the following morning.

"You certainly timed this one," Jerry said. "It's been quiet here for months. Kirk says you are a sign of trouble anyway." Alexander Kirk was now our Minister to Egypt. The last time I saw him, in August 1939, he was evacuating American civilians from Berlin. Now he was doing the same thing from Cairo.

"You can choose your accommodations easily," Shepheard's Sudanese clerk told me when I registered. Looking wan, he tried to inject a little humor into our conversation by telling me the rumor was untrue that Rommel sent a flippant telegram reserving Shepheard's Hotel for his Nazi officers. "Propaganda," he said as he led Jerry and me to the elevator and turned my traveling case and heavy canvas shoulder bag over to a Sudanese bellboy. "Propaganda, I think."

These Sudanese giants are considered the Middle East's best servants. Tall, scar-faced, they still wear long white robes with a wide crimson belt and are never without their fezzes. At a distance in the long halls they look for all the world like orderlies wandering around in a hospital. They smile a good deal, and they know far more than they say.

The British were bringing up all the force they could scrape together. At some risk of Nazi air-borne invasion of Palestine and Syria, they were denuding these areas. The Holy Land was bare. Fresh troops of Sir Henry Wilson's Palestine-Syria forces were on their way through Cairo to the front, crowding forward in trim lines.

In the opposite direction, bashed-in trucks bearing the skeletons of torn tanks and airplane fuselages, ripped-up wings, jeeps and field kitchens, bashed-in trailers and scout cars, bashed-in lorries and motorcycles, clogged Adly Pasha Street. Every car was crusted with dust, so heavy and hard that it seemed like enamel on the windshields, and the dust on the men was as thick as the coal-dust coating that sometimes fills every pore of your face when you work in a mine.

Some of these men were very young, but most of them were not.

Every man looks old at a time like this. There were eyes that did not see, hands that did not feel. Some of these men had been fighting the desert war two years. They had been as far as Bengasi once under O'Connor, and nearly there again under Wavell. They had captured 25,000 Italians at Tobruk one year, lost 33,000 of their own troopmates the next. For thousands and thousands of hours they had been cut by the wind and dust, blistered by the sun, frozen by the cold at night. All this, the thousands and thousands of hours, the tired muscles, the large hopes and tries, had come and gone and been lost.

A Scotchman, swathed in bandages, his stubbled face drawn in terrible pain, leaned out of a lorry and asked me for a cigarette. These were battered men, weary men, their clothes torn, their hearts torn. There were others, in field ambulances, whose minds were torn.

One of the most astonishing things about war is how cities like Cairo and Dover can go about their business and function as they do at the very threshold of battle, death, and destruction.

I have seen Dover as normal as Asbury Park, New Jersey, when German fortifications, visible across the Channel, might open up at any moment, without the slightest warning, and shell the city: beer trucks unloading at the pubs, shoppers gazing into the store windows, traffic policemen busy in the business of the day, children playing on the sidewalk along the beach, near coils of rusty barbed wire. In Cairo there was music every afternoon in the lovely garden of Shepheard's. A good floor show operated each night in the roof cabaret of the Continental Hotel. The music was gay. The wine was good. The food was delicious, for there is no shortage of food in Egypt or, incidentally, any shortage of gasoline, sugar, coffee, or anything else. There was no rationing for the public.

The small, blue street lamps give Cairo the appearance of London, for Cairo, like London, is really two cities, one fantastic city by day and another by night. You see no more than little pins of blue light coming nearer or turning to one side in the crooked streets, traffic signals the size of a watch's dial, hear only voices in the dark speak the Babel of all languages. Air alerts sound, and suddenly the pin-point lights stop. The Germans fly their planes over Cairo, and on the outskirts they duplicate what I had just been through at Heliopolis as often as they can manage. Then ack-ack guns let go all through the city. But the Germans didn't drop bombs on Cairo. Cairo is not bombed. The reason: The Germans accepted Winston Churchill's warning that if they bombed Cairo, the R.A.F. would bomb Rome. The Germans knew that Winston Churchill meant what he said.

The horse racing was going great guns—the Junior Beginners Stakes, the Shahraban Stakes, the Tabarin Stakes, the Cozzika Cup. As for cricket, an immense crowd in the stadium roared while the Imperial Harlequins beat the Willcocks Sporting Club in a race against the clock.

Open-air movies showed Robert Montgomery, Madeleine Carroll, Rosalind Russell, Greta Garbo, Gloria Swanson. George Murphy and Ann Sothern played in a "Maisie" picture at Roxy Theatre. In Sweden I heard that Stockholm had the largest per-capita movie attendance in the world. Cairo must be next. The Egyptians are just plain movie mad.

Next to Lisbon, Cairo is regarded as the war center for proto-types of the lovely *agents provocateurs* who made E. Phillips Oppenheim a very rich man. Lisbon disappoints you in this particular, for the German girls are typically heavy-handed there and, I might add, none too beautiful. But Cairo shows the Italian influence in personnel, and I must say it is a great improvement. The beautiful ladies of the cocktail lounges and of Shepheard's veranda are very superior and very alert. These are women you read about every-where and see nowhere—except in Cairo. Many are Rumanians, or claim to be; some are Syrians, and a few are French. They dress smartly, dance lightly, laugh often, and produce well for the Italian Secret Police.

They have homes in the pleasant Garden City section of Cairo, or live at Shepheard's or the Continental or, until it was taken over by the United States Army Air Corps, at the Grand. I had seen one of the Cairo contingent time and again at the Ritz Hotel bar in Madrid. She was an Italian named Maria, well known in Spain.

Smothered in Russian furs, French perfume, Belgian lace, and
Dutch diamonds, she entered Spain from France with a German
"professor" who was traced to the Deutsche Akademische Auslandsstelle, the German propaganda and Gestapo training school
for foreign agents, located in Munich. In Madrid the German disappeared, and Maria blossomed forth with an American passport,
forged and completely false. She went around alone and passed
herself off as an American who had been married to the German.
"He has left me flat," she said, "And I need help." She was trying
to go to Brazil. Alert Ambassador Alexander W. Weddell put a
stop to that. So Maria produced an Italian passport. "My native
country, you know," she told me. Now Maria was sitting on a
stool, leaning across the bar in Cairo's New Star Café.

"How did you get here?" I asked her.

"I flew," she said, stamping on her cigarette and turning her
back on me. Then she spoke over her shoulder, "I work at the
Kars el Nil [Egyptian Ministry of Foreign Affairs], and, besides,
I am a language teacher." Her black eyes snapping, the tempestu-
ous Maria fairly stabbed me with a copy of Cairo's *Egyptian Mail*
and pointed a crimson-enameled finger tip at a classified ad:

> LANGUAGE COURSES QUICKLY. French, German, Italian,
> Spanish taught by a young lady teacher speaking fluent
> English. Write to "Lady," P.O.B. 365, Cairo.

I did not gather what Maria thought she was proving, but, whatever it was, she proved it. She handed me her check for an empty
champagne cocktail and stalked out the door.

Most of these espionage women maintain some sort of diplomatic status, some string to a neutral embassy, and all of them are,
in turn, known to the British Intelligence. It's a little like the
Chinese taking in each other's washing. But it adds its sparkle to
Cairo.

The sensation of the moment, however, the delight of all who
saw her, was an American. An optical combination of Veronica
Lake and Gypsy Rose Lee, this girl was a blues singer from a café
on Kansas City's Twelfth Street.

She was very pretty and very full of blues. Why she came to Egypt I don't know, but she sang "My Heart Belongs to Daddy" with the gusto of a Sophie Tucker and the volume of Aimee Semple McPherson's trombonist. She never faltered, and she never failed. She simply bowled over all officers: Americans, British, New Zealanders, Australians, Canadians, French, Poles, and Greeks alike. This American girl sang for the armies and spied for nobody. If there had been a cannon around the soldiers would have given her a twenty-one-gun salute.

The Restaurant Balalaika, on Opera Square, across the park, featured a collection of Egyptian muscle dancers—"Non-stop Comedy, Sensational Dancing, New Music." Six in number, they ranged from the short, fat Egyptian girl on the left to the towering gold-toothed Persian brunette in the center. As they danced they carried on a running conversation with each other, which was presumably the Non-stop Comedy, laughing back and forth in a most liberal way and chatting with a few of the more favored cash customers in the front row, emitting little yips at unexpected moments as though they had been pinched or in some manner surprised in the monotony of their terpsichorean miracles.

In the evening camel trains came in from the desert, the gawky animals tied nose to tail by their long, thin ropes and controlled by Arab riders on every second or third camel. The lead camel and two or three others wore bells. But the bells were only the size of a fifty-cent piece, and in the black-out you just heard a tinkle and the next thing you knew you were walking with or against, through or under, a series of desert hayburners who were swaggering along without a care in the world. Pat Timberlake and I got mixed up in the camels' ropes once. It's something like meeting an octopus. I never want to be entwined in a camel train in the dark again, with or without Pat. He is no better at ropes than he is with cameras.

Pat was busy as a bird dog gathering pilots and planes as they arrived from our country, working out our whole bomber setup as chief of the Air Forces Bomber Command in the Middle East. It was typical of him that, after planning the largest raid our air force ever staged, and one of the longest raids of any air force in the war, he led the attack himself.

General Timberlake was in a formation of four-engined Liberator 24s. From Cairo, he plastered Italy. He led his bombers in a sweep out over the Mediterranean, high over Crete and Greece, far above the waters of the Adriatic Sea. He led them over the length of Italy, from the heel of the country to the French border, wheeled there, and attacked a northern city in an all-out blast of American air power.

Pat had barely given the signal and turned the squadron back from the target when his planes drew ack-ack fire in a big way and were attacked by eighteen Messerschmitt 109-Fs. Seventy bullet and cannon-shell holes were counted in Pat's plane. Part of its rudder was destroyed, many of its controls were made useless. An engine went dead. Two of his crewmen were wounded. But Pat wasn't hurt.

We had dinner that night on the Continental roof. It didn't seem possible that Pat had been over northern Italy a few hours earlier and that this good friend had had such a close miss. Later, he recommended his boys for decorations. Then he turned one down himself. "Our bombers have lots of work to do," he told me, "and it's early."

All around the Middle East our soldiers and the R.A.F. are good. It's the hardest-hitting combination I ever saw. The American commander in Cairo who had to think of everything was Major General Russell L. Maxwell, commanding American operations in the Middle East. He knew the problems of supply backward and forward, which means that he knew the nut of the coconut in America's Middle East problem. This called for the closest, smoothest contact with our allies as well as our own people. An endless variety of problems and personalities headed into General Maxwell. He took them in stride.

He had an attractive, cool house on the outskirts of Cairo. It was a fine old colonial-type dwelling, looking much like Lieutenant General Hugh A. Drum's quarters on Governors Island, in New York Harbor. Jerry Gerard and the whole top military staff lived there, worked there at night. It was cool and comfortable. The general talked quietly of plans, policies, problems in the Middle East; of our construction of base depots and supply depots, the 14,000-mile life line to the United States.

"It could take a long time, and it will be very costly, but we can attract the Germans to the Mediterranean. We can attack Hitler here. . . ."

As is true of Ambassador John G. Winant in London, a narrower man in the confusing Middle East area, a man of smaller outlook and less patience, would be miffed badly by the many things which happen in any combined theater of the war. But General Maxwell was seldom miffed, because he understood the frailties of wartime organization.

As this American general talked about the problem of the war, you understood him. And what he said was "blood, sweat, and tears" and above all the terrible fact of this war—"We face heavy casualties."

On the diplomatic side, the United States Minister to Egypt, Alexander Kirk, had the backing of a long career in the State Department and came to Egypt after service in Rome, Moscow, and Berlin. In Egypt he did the same man-sized job I saw him do as America's top representative in Germany when the storm broke in 1939. I saw Kirk serve his country well in the most violent hour in Berlin, and by coincidence I was next to see him again in the most violent hour in Egypt.

There wasn't the slightest sign of nervousness at the American Legation. Kirk had been through a lot of this kind of thing before. He carried on as usual in his spacious house on the Rue Walda Pacha, quietly working around the clock there or at the Legation or on his small houseboat on the Nile, exactly as he had at Grunwald-Brahmstrasse 4 in the worst hours in Berlin.

Interestingly enough, Sir Nevile Henderson, Kirk's conferee as British Ambassador in Berlin, had been British Minister Plenipotentiary in Cairo in earlier years. How different the Nazi "wool over the eyes" would have been if Kirk's present conferee, realistic R. G. Casey, had been with him in Berlin instead!

For Britain's top political figure was not the Ambassador, but the Right Honorable Richard G. Casey, previously known so favorably to Americans as Australian Minister in Washington. Now, as British Minister of State with full cabinet rank, reporting directly to his associates in the British Cabinet in London, Casey shouldered the boiling and thankless political problem in the Middle East as well as the contact between the military forces and Whitehall. This is a terrific job, a real heartbreaker. He admits this. But there is a rugged determination in Casey's face, and well he needs it. I thought his eyes looked tired, but they lit up when he started to talk.

We talked of sheepherders from New Zealand who stood in the same whirling dust as the Pyramids, telephone linemen from Kansas City shut up in Japanese prison camps after defending our country in Bataan, store clerks from California villages sitting behind pom-pom guns in the icy blasts of the Iceland patrol, ex-salesmen from Yorkshire swinging gun turrets under the sun of Madagascar. We spoke of the troops you see here in Cairo, the men from South Africa, the bearded Sikhs from India, the tall Australians, the French and Greeks, the Welshmen, the English and Scots.

"This is still a war of men and personal decisions," he said, walking over to the tall windows. "We have been slow, but we are speeding up. The freedom that made us slow will make us strong." Casey motioned with his hand, as though he were indicating the desert.

"There's a lesson in history where we are standing," he said, "a lesson of contrasts in the Pyramids. The great structures of human progress can be built only by the free."

As for Egypt itself, there is nothing subtle about the national attitude you find there. It comes to you in government offices, in army barracks, in banking houses, and from the Egyptian in the street: "Egypt for the Egyptians."

There is a small, tight little clique in Egypt, an offshoot of the original clandestine societies in Syria, which is the spearhead of this Arab national movement. It expresses the only dominant political idea there is in Egypt, and it has persisted in this since World War I: "Egypt for the Egyptians."

However, the idea does not unite the country. Far from it. Egypt is as crowded and pushed with political differences and personal rivalries as 1939 France. To begin with, Egypt is a hodgepodge of division between doctrinaires, the King, the Palace, and some of the stray officers of the Egyptian armies. King Farouk is a difficult boy of twenty-two, sharp-eyed, suspicious, spoiled, who rules extravagantly, unwisely, and contemptuously. He is pro-Axis, pro-Italian. He has large interests in Italy, and Italy has large interests in him.

Farouk has done nothing to support the United Nations. He has plagued British interests, been an obstructionist in large matters and a nuisance in small ones. His attitude has embarrassed and harassed the British, and in this program he has centered his special attention on the British Ambassador, the Right Honorable Sir Miles W. Lampson.

At times of important negotiations Farouk refuses to see Sir Miles Lampson. He makes slurring remarks about the Ambassador and the Empire, uses dilatory tactics when matters of Egypt's relations with Britain press for immediate solution.

An affair, before Casey arrived, became so bad, and the King was so far off base, that Sir Miles Lampson had to enter the palace by force. This was hushed up, but naturally it was a public sensation in Egypt. The British Ambassador called on the British Army for a detachment of tanks.

The tanks clattered down the Sharia Ruston Pasha to the British Embassy. Miles Lampson climbed into an army car beside a brace of brigadiers and gave the word. The tanks started off for the palace, knocked the gates right off their hinges, and battered their way into the palace grounds. The whole cavalcade stormed up to the door of the King's residence. Miles Lampson alighted. The tanks trained their guns on the wide and handsome door. With his military escort, Miles Lampson demanded entrance to the palace and audience with the King.

There was much scurrying around inside. Lampson's chauffeur

blew his horn in impatience. The British Ambassador was admitted. Miles Lampson completed his affairs with the King of Egypt. He got into his car and signaled the tanks. "Keep off the grass if you can," he said.

The Ambassador and the tanks proceeded out of the grounds and returned to the British Embassy.

Britain had no choice but force at that moment in dealing with a surly young monarch. And, whatever blame Britain got in German propaganda for this incident, Britain was acting in behalf of the United Nations. But that's the way the wind blows.

As for the Egyptian people themselves, the seventeen million population, 90 per cent of whom remain illiterate, are totally apathetic towards the war. Even with the battle on the doorstep of the Nile they were more interested, like Ferdinand, in smelling the flowers.

German propaganda harps on every matter, blows it up into an abuse. German short-wave radio blasts tell the Egyptians that the Axis, and especially the Italians, will give them "a better living," "a new day for Egypt," "justice where the British do not know what justice is," and all kinds of typical Nazi tommyrot. But even this, and the natural tendency of a native to resent any country in control, has not made the Egyptian people pro-Axis, or even vigorously anti-British. It has simply made them pro-nothing.

Thirty-four thousand Egyptian troops stood idly by, twiddling their thumbs in their pleasant Cairo barracks, while the United Nations and the Axis battled for the Nile. Some Egyptian army officers told me they would like to fight, but they had no weapons, and this gave them an opportunity to blame England for not arming Egypt's army with modern equipment. The fact is, however, that England could hardly afford to arm the Egyptians under the circumstances of the King's attitude and the general political confusion in Egypt.

The Koran itself dominates, and must continue to dominate, all Egyptian and Middle East problems which have vexed the ablest men of Asia and Europe for centuries. For nothing can be done in the matter of individual freedom or peace which does not remain within the limits of the faith the Mohammedan Bible expresses.

The Koran inculcates dependence on Allah only, describes him as a fearful man: "From the crown of the head to the breast Allah is holy and from the breast downward he is solid. He has coal black hair, and roars like a lion at every watch of the night."

For life as it is lived in the Islamic world there is hardly a condition in which passages from the Koran, suitable for instruction, cannot be recalled.

To the Egyptian such devotional fragments represent his sustained theological, social, and political doctrines. It is the daily guide of Egypt's millions. A pitiless destiny awaits all people: "Unto every nation a fixed time is decreed."

Throughout the faith there is perpetual emphasis on the delusion of human destiny, and this is the basic political view of the Middle East.

Here, again, the British have a native problem. And here, again, they are criticized in their handling of it by both natives and outsiders, who offer no solution whatever except the liquidation of the safety of everyone in the area and the ultimate absorption of the area by the internal and external enemies of free men.

CHAPTER 16

Our Fundamental Strategy

Lᴉᴋᴇ ᴛʜᴇ ᴏꜰꜰɪᴄᴇ of the Chief of the Imperial General Staff in London, Sir Arthur Tedder's office in the Middle East headquarters is a simple, bare room. It is strictly business, quiet and quick. There is nothing to indicate that this is a nerve center for the Empire except the presence of one of the great leaders of England.

There has always been some tension the world over between air forces and the land and sea forces. No country has escaped this, although Germany is often pointed to, in error, as having done so. France came the closest to escaping it, by the simple expedient of smothering her air force entirely. In the United States, where our air force started out as a mechanical carrier pigeon attached to the Signal Corps, Air Corps General H. H. Arnold and Deputy Chief of Staff Lieutenant General Joseph T. McNarney, who became number-two man in our army through his brilliant work as an air officer and an organizer, may still face problems of co-ordination. But, public impression notwithstanding, America has gone further than any other nation towards dissolving them. In England the relation between the Army and the R.A.F. has been a far worse problem—a terrible problem, and especially in Egypt.

In the fall of 1941, in fact, Winston Churchill himself had to issue an order that the R.A.F. commander must give the commander of the Middle East ground forces "all aid, irrespective of other targets, *during battle*." A year later Churchill announced that "co-operation is now renewed." He was referring to the appointment of Sir Arthur Tedder, which he made on the recommendation of England's distinguished, sound-policy-minded field marshal, Sir John Dill, now in Washington as military representative of the Prime Minister in the combined chiefs of staff group and who was Tedder's loyal and energetic supporter in London as Chief of the Imperial General Staff.

At fifty-three, able Sir Arthur William Tedder, K.G.C.B., spare-framed and wiry, has been flying twenty-seven years. A graduate of Magdalene College, Cambridge, a rugby star, a Shakespearean scholar, a remarkable characterizer when he dallies with his pencil, a slave to his pipe and his Rodian Curly-Cut tobacco, this quiet-spoken Englishman served first as a colonial administrator at Fiji and as a soldier in the Dorsetshire regiment.

Then and there he fixed his mind on aviation. He did this with an intensity and resourcefulness which placed him in the most important commands the Empire could supply, brought him to the Middle East to succeed Sir Arthur M. Longmore after the battles of Greece and Crete, brought him a new air domain stretching from Gibraltar to the Persian Gulf and south to Madagascar, and brought him the spectacular rank of Air Chief Marshal of the R.A.F. and the ribbon of Knight Grand Cross of the Bath.

Tedder is frail-looking for a man of such action. But he is tough-muscled and tireless. His eyes smile, little wrinkles around them like the false strokes of a make-up artist who has tried to make him look older. His hair is close-cropped, his face is clean-shaven, and he is very trim; an able, determined, and cool-headed man.

In the course of advancement Sir Arthur filled many places. He served as instructor in the Royal Naval Staff College, the Imperial Defense College, the R.A.F. Staff College. He developed the Empire Flying Scheme and was director of air training. Then he became director-general of research and development for the Air Ministry.

Here he worked with, encouraged, and supported Watson Watt in the strange and expanding field of telecommunication. "Tedder meant everything in this," Watson Watt has told me. "I could have done nothing without him." I once traveled nine thousand miles with this modest, cherubic-looking friend—Fellow of the

Royal Society, scientific adviser to the Ministry of Aircraft Production—before we reached where we were going, for after this
distinguished British scientist had worked out the magnetic-ray
defense of England against Nazi bombers he traveled many areas of
the United Nations, installing his system at strategic points.

The system on which Tedder worked with Watt is known as
Radar.

Radar beams point skyward in a meshlike pattern, emitting magnetic rays from compact sending stations approximately the size
of a small sedan. A watcher sits before a dial at each of these sending units. The Radar dial reacts to any object which crosses its
path in the sky as far off as several hundred miles. "You might say
it operates on a principle similar to that of the electric eye," Watson
Watt once told me, "which creates an impulse and activates a
mechanism when any object breaks the ray. The Germans now
have their magnetic-ray system, but we like ours better. The Japs
had none at the time of General Doolittle's raid on Tokyo."

Even United Nations night-fighting interceptor planes themselves have miniature installations of Watt's Radar aboard. Watt's
beam shoots out in the darkness ahead of the ship, probes the air
like an invisible searchlight, and makes contact with the enemy
plane in this way. When you are flying at night it is practically impossible to see another unlighted airplane. But for Watt's genius
and Tedder's support in magnificent developments and the elaborate experiments which he had to conduct, our planes could not
locate and attack the Nazis at night. For Radar a grateful nation
recognized Watson Watt. He appeared on the King's Birthday List
in 1942. He is now Sir Watson Watt.

Today Sir Watson Watt is working on the task of expanding
his magnetic beams to all sorts of war operations, and the war is
being revolutionized by this quiet genius. The technical problems
involved in his work do not stump him at all. "Forget the impossible," he told me. "Few things are impossible." I believe Sir
Watson Watt's latest developments will surprise the world.

"Some day," Sir Arthur once told me, "if anyone erects a monument under the Dover skies to the saviors of Britain, I think it

should have three figures: one, a figure symbolizing the young R.A.F. pilots who beat the Nazi *Luftwaffe* when Göring had the Battle of Britain won and did not know it. The next figure ought to be of Dame Fanny Lucy Houston, who contributed the money and personally supported the design and construction of a new aircraft engine which won the Schneider Trophy races in a period when our government was not sponsoring air development, and by this act of stanch initiative made immediately available magnificent new engines for our Spitfires at the time when England would have fallen without them. The third figure should be of Watson Watt."

Sir Arthur did not say that it was he who persuaded Dame Fanny Lucy Houston to sponsor this development when the official purse strings for R.A.F. development refused to open, and that it was her confidence in him that caused this gallant woman to do it. Nor did he say that his eldest son, a young R.A.F. pilot, was killed while flying over Britain.

One thought dominated Sir Arthur's mind when we were in Cairo: the day when British and American planes would occupy airdromes the full length of north Africa, and when his R.A.F. and the American component could expand the fundamental strategy of our war.

Actually, our fundamental strategy does not feature places or positions as such. It does not primarily concern itself with any place in Europe or any positions the Germans hold. Our strategy is dedicated to the conception that Germany's defense of the fortified continent of Europe can turn out to be a Maginot Line.

Our strategy deals with a different matter than the so-called "soft underside of Europe" (which is not so soft) or "invasion prongs" or "invasion springboards" in the sense of straight forward assault. Military decisions are not being made on this basis, or from the geographic maps that we see. Most such conceptions, especially in the Mediterranean, look better and more promising on the map than they really are. And, in any case, they fall into the category of either prologues or epilogues. They are not the body, the main theme, of our strategy.

Our fundamental strategy is to lure the German air strength into the air and shoot it to pieces.

To create the lure itself is far more difficult than appears on the surface, for we cannot do it by seeking it out. We have to threaten Germany with masses of men and equipment, transported to and installed at such places that the Germans will attack such installations.

This purpose involves expeditions, long communications, sufficiently large operations on our part so that the Germans *must* molest us.

It is a vastly difficult problem to *attract* the *Luftwaffe*, keep it spread out and force it to come at us, so that by means of attrition of the German air strength we can make Germany's Maginot-like defense of the Continent impossible. We can afford to apply our air strength on a basis of attrition. Germany cannot.

Every expedition on which we embark, every move we make, is designed for the basic purpose of luring the German air strength into the air. The aim of *attracting* the German air strength, *spreading* it and *killing* it, is the prime motivating idea in our entire planning.

This is the aim of high-level planning in Washington and London, and in the Middle East. The maps which lead to the decisions are the maps of Germany and German war theaters which attempt to show the distribution of the German air strength. The problems, which are first weighed and studied by the Combined Chiefs of Staff, are the problems of how it can be so attracted *towards* us that we can get at it. The over-all, basic task of our military forces is to flush the German war birds, bring them in range of our guns.

This is the aim. And it was in relation to this program that Prime Minister Churchill flew to Cairo and took Sir Arthur Tedder with him to see Stalin in Moscow and, later, for his meeting at Casablanca with President Roosevelt, for more in this whole war depends on such men as Sir Arthur Tedder than one dares to imagine.

Working hand in glove with Air Marshal Tedder was Major General Lewis H. Brereton of our Air Corps, fresh from his experiences in India and now in command of all our military operations in the Middle East. Short, wiry, this flier's flier punches out his words. He gets right down to cases and swings hard. He is an operations man on the pattern of Major General James E. Chaney, practical to his finger tips, a clever strategist, a disciple of concentration, and a quick mover.

General Brereton's courage is legendary in our Air Corps and in the R.A.F. He was awarded the Distinguished Flying Cross for leading the attack on Andaman Island in the Bay of Bengal, shooting his way through a flock of Zero interceptors.

The terrain of the Middle East undoubtedly makes it the greatest natural theater for air operations, and General Brereton's eyes danced as he told me why.

"This is the ideal theater to attract German air strength. Germany must dissipate her air strength here," he said. "This whole operation is made to order for our purpose. It can provide more final effect than any place in the world. The feature of the Middle East is that we can lay out airfields anywhere. Here in the desert there is no limit to the size of any airfield, no limit to the number of planes or size of planes we can use. As far as ground facilities are concerned, we are foot-loose and fancy-free. The desert doesn't supply the *Luftwaffe* any cover. It is exposed every hour of the day and night, and we are finding our fliers are able to get at it. Pat Timberlake and his boys can always hit the enemy with everything they have—fighters, bombers, or anything. The enemy cannot get out of range, because when a land action starts we can follow close on the enemy's heels. We move our advance fields quickly as the action shifts and squash his planes wherever they fly.

"Hitler can lose a lot in the air in the Middle East as our stuff comes in to supplement Tedder's R.A.F. Which is my way of saying that Germany itself is vulnerable here. The Germans have to back up Rommel in the air or lose Africa eventually. If they keep their planes at home and lose Africa they lose their pivot for the defense of the European continent. If they send them here we will shoot down as many planes as the *Luftwaffe* puts in action. It could cost them most of their air force. And with a weak German air force unable to support and cover their powerful land army on the European continent, anything can happen on the Continent itself."

For a poser has accumulated in the whole German air picture. Subsequent to the Battle of Britain, the Germans have never demonstrated the air power expected of a country which had 35,000 planes before the war and is supposed to have produced 2700 new planes a month since then.

Göring shifted his planes out of Italy and Sicily to equip the attack on Russia. That didn't look necessary in the books. Hitler planned to go against Turkey while Mussolini attacked the Balkan flank in Albania. But when Mussolini needed air aid these German planes were shifted to his salient. Again, the *Luftwaffe* couldn't support Rommel in the air over Libya, November 1941, without withdrawing planes from the hard-pressed Russian front and had to sacrifice air power against Moscow to do so. And during each of these borrowing-from-Peter-to-pay-Paul moves, the Germans stopped bombing ships off the British Isles, because the British equipped small merchant ships with fighter planes that were catapulted from the air offshore and beat off the few German bombers with such success.

Leading airmen are very suspicious of this German air-force situation, however, and, in any case, they cannot be wrong by being suspicious. The worst mistake they could make would be to take the German weakness at its face value, take it for granted.

Russia did not show against Finland what it showed against Germany. Japan did not show against China what it showed against the United States. Germany may not be showing in the air on the Continent what it may show against England.

Consider the question from the German viewpoint, which we so seldom do. Germany's enemies fight from a single advance base. Both England and America depend on one tiny little island off the coast of France for harbors, port facilities, industrial production, and man power to maintain war against the German mass on the Continent. Our toe is in the door, and firmly there, but it is still only our toe. *On this single island depends Anglo-American par-*

ticipation in the war in Europe. Without this island, and its air and naval bases, Germany would control the entire Atlantic coast from the tip of Norway to Gibraltar. No aid to Russia could be transferred from England to Russia. Germany could not be heavily bombed, nor would any attack of Germany be possible. America could not maintain the Western Task Force in north Africa, and the only value in trying to do so would be to hold north Africa itself. "Unconditional surrender" by the Germans would be far, far off.

This is the great German prize of the war. The immensity of the reward is worth, meanwhile, any possible sacrifice in other places and justifies conserving the entire German air force if, by doing so, enough planes, men, and supplies can be accumulated to accomplish the fall of England. Furthermore, if this conservation gives the appearance of weakness and causes diversion of planes to north Africa, India, Russia, China, and the four corners of the world on the assumption that enough remain in Great Britain to meet the "weakness" of the *Luftwaffe,* the necessity for conservation turns out to be a blessing to the Germans.

The question is further stimulated through our knowledge of certain new types of German aircraft which they have not shown. They have developed an immense six-engine transport, carrying 130 troops and designed with a multiwheeled undercarriage for landing on rough ground. This plane is being made by Messerschmitt. It is the Messerschmitt 32.3. Junkers is experimenting with a new model, the Junkers 86, which is a high-altitude bomber that carries 2,000-pound bombs, and a modification of the 86, the JU-86PW, which is a long-range reconnaissance plane. The Germans also have an important new six-engine flying boat, the BV-222, with a wingspread of 150 feet and equipped with power-driven armament.

Against an attack, England has been divided into separate self-contained defense zones, each with its commander, each with its isolated telephone and military wire communication system, each with its single independent organization. As the Germans realize—for they have described it in their German newspapers—this is the fundamental of England's defense system. Should the Germans land two hundred thousand men in England by air, through saturating England's air defense these could be followed by a great many more. The question hinges on British air defense. If the Germans can overwhelm England in the air they can overwhelm England on the ground. The home defense falls of its own weight under such attack, because the congestion of the island makes England the worst possible battleground for the defenders. Fundamentally, you cannot have your arsenal and your supply depots on your battle-field.

The British Navy would have to leave the English Channel in the face of German air superiority. If the R.A.F. couldn't stop the Germans, nothing could. The evident ease with which it appears that the R.A.F. could, of course, stop the Germans is not the point. The stark fact remains that so much in this global war still depends on *one* factor in *one* place—the air over England.

It is this feature that no top military man in England or America ever forgets. And you can be sure the German High Command does not forget it either.

On the other hand, our strategy of attracting is based on what we believe to be the real answer to the riddle: "Where is the German air strength?" The United Nations commanders believe Hitler never had a large air force by 1943 standards. *They do not believe it ever existed.*

The only German air fleets ever identified have been five in number, each consisting of approximately five hundred planes of different co-ordinated types. In terms of their home stations and German designations these are German Air Fleets No. 1 (Berlin), No. 2 (Brunswick), No. 3 (Munich), No. 4 (Vienna), and No. 5 (East Prussia). That is the basic organizational setup of the *Luft-waffe*, and the field operating units which fly with the German armies are forwarded from this organizational setup AS A TASK FORCE and report back directly to the mother organization in the Rhine-land. For example, the force which operated with Rommel was forwarded from German Air Fleet No. 4 (Vienna) and reported into the central organization there. In principle, the headquarters of the ranking officer in the German Air Force in Egypt was in Vienna.

Considering Germany's original conception of fighting the war on the continent of Europe and looking at her design of a hard-hitting, closely knit, central air force, this would be a large air force. But the expansion of the war changed the proportions. As a result the real answer to the riddle is that Germany has not done poorly with an immense air force, but that she has made remarkably effective use of a relatively small air force which she is unable to expand further.

Therefore: Attract, spread, kill.

Therefore: Every military move, *anywhere*, is a prologue or epilogue to this, for this is the strategy of the war. The mass movements, the mass installations of the Army, are for the purpose of making this strategy possible.

CHAPTER 17

Rommel Won the Sand and Lost the Air

GERMAN SCHOLARS and military people always have been thoroughly excited about Africa's latent possibilities. It is they who have consistently advanced vast schemes for the control of waste and the development of Africa's wealth. The Germans intended to put Africa on a paying basis.

Viewing the Mediterranean as a lake within the land mass of Europe-Africa, no one ever exaggerated the German estimates of Africa's importance in peace or war.

The Germans established their north African military position to threaten the rear of any United Nations expeditionary force invading Europe from the Mediterranean. As a threat to such a force's rear and flank, the Germans were literally in love with this strategy of a point on the outside of their continental position and steadfastly committed themselves to support this vital position in north Africa at all costs. The German army and navy people made no bones about this at the German War Office.

"Nothing can happen to Germany on the Continent," Grossadmiral Erich Raeder told me in Berlin just before Pearl Harbor.

There are huge maps extending from the ceiling to the floor in the Admiralty room of the dapper Grossadmiral, and he got up from his chair often as he talked to illustrate the point on them. Raeder's jaw jutted fiercely as he drew his finger along the whole line of the Mediterranean shore—two thousand miles—and pointed to the equations between the three fundamental spots in north Africa: Algiers on one flank, Alexandria on the other, and Rommel's Tripoli base in the center.

"See," he said, "north Africa!" German eyes have a way of gleaming at moments like this. Raeder's eyes gleamed. "And Rommel is there."

Rommel is two years younger than Hitler. He was born November 15, 1891. At fifty-two, Rommel is average age for today's generals, very old for the ancients. Alexander was twenty-three at Issus, Napoleon thirty-five at Austerlitz and forty-five at Waterloo, Hannibal thirty-nine when he crossed the Alps, and Washington forty-five at Valley Forge.

When he was nineteen Rommel entered the German Army, serving with the 124th Infantry Regiment and going into the field with this unit as a lieutenant in 1914. After three years in World War I he was still a lieutenant. He was company commander of the Württemberg Highland Battalion. He had seen a lot of fighting on the ground, never had any contact with aviation.

After World War I, this discouraged soldier was an early and violent Nazi. He knew Hess. He took part in the Beer Hall *Putsch* of November 1923. Thereafter he wandered around in the Reichswehr, the hard little 100,000-man nucleus of the new German Army.

Rommel did not come into his own until Hitler took over. January 30, 1933, was Rommel's day. As a Nazi general he built the Afrika Korps, the army that was intended to maintain the vital pivot in north Africa and translate into reality the *sine qua non* of Nazi geopolitics.

The Combined Chiefs of Staff of the United Nations, in turn, have always known that Germany's north African position must be cleaned out before we could invade Europe's continent.

Yet all the democratic world rang with shouts for a second front in France. These were agonizing words to hear in Cairo. It was a heartbreaking hour. For a sudden and vast upset had occurred.

What was the situation?

President Roosevelt, Prime Minister Winston Churchill, the Combined Chiefs of Staff, every top man involved, knew that Germany could not be beaten by thrusts at any one point. They knew that a single second front would be a ghastly failure. The Germans had the interior lines of communication on the continent of Europe. Germany could protect herself in a central mass, for that was suitable to the design of the tight, concentrated organization of Germany's air strength, the most vulnerable element in Germany's war machine. Hitler could shift his reserve to meet any thrust across the Channel. No assault could be sufficiently concentrated to equal the size and depth of defense the Germans could bring to bear against it under the air umbrella of the compact *Luftwaffe*.

The main assault, the main second front, must be across the English Channel onto the coast of France. From the day after the fall of France, no leader I saw among the United Nations' command differed on this. The lost bridgehead in France, across the channel, must be retaken. I never encountered any change in this conception, in London, in Washington, or elsewhere among the men responsible for the military conduct of the war.

The decision was perfectly well known to the German General Staff, for no military secret was involved.

The German General Staff knew as well as anyone could that it would be futile for the United Nations to attack the continent of Europe without an air umbrella. No force could land without air support. That was elementary. The effective range of fighter craft, ours or the enemy's, is approximately 200 miles. That is to say, a fighter-type plane can carry enough fuel to fly approximately 200 miles from its base, fight at that distance a reasonable time, and return to its base. The United Nations had fields in only one place in Europe from which these fighter planes could fly. That place was England.

Therefore, if you took a string 200 miles long, pinned it down in England, and swung an arc over the coast of France you revealed the only feasible invasion area. This arc within which landings could be made would extend from approximately Saint-Nazaire, France, on the south to the lowlands of Holland. The whole bridgehead was within practical range from British fields, and the whole invasion area from Saint-Nazaire to Amsterdam could have an air umbrella.

The invasion bases themselves could be installed and maintained between Antwerp and Boulogne, might even include the Ghent and Courtrai areas, and possibly extend to Brussels and Lille.

The Germans began installing fortifications throughout the area covered by the air arc as early as October 1940, two months after the fall of France. By the spring of 1941 we knew how dreadfully formidable these defenses were. The German network extended fifteen to thirty miles in from the shore line, contained heavy guns and much material from the Maginot Line. The Germans drew heavily on their immense supply of captured French artillery and their own equipment from the West Wall.

The defenses duplicated those that I went through when I drove the length of the West Wall from Düsseldorf to the Swiss border in August 1939. It was evident what such open-type fortifications would mean in United Nations casualties. The Germans themselves found out in 1941. For it was Russian General Zhukov's system of fortified strong spots, to a record depth of ninety miles, which defeated Von Brauchitsch in the all-out assault on Moscow while I was in Finland and kept the Germans from entering the city by November 15 as planned.

The United Nations attack across the Channel would be far harder and more costly than the German assault on Moscow. It would involve landing troops in a thin line on the beaches, the men advancing through mile after mile of the pillbox strong-point system, exposed to withering fire, ambush, and separation. Troops which fought their way further and further into the morass would extend themselves a great distance, battered and weakened. Then they would be struck by at least fifty fresh German divisions which had not been under fire. This crushing and bloody moment would give the *coup de grâce* to our forces, push them back into the sea.

On the basis of logistics we could send any number of divisions across the Channel, and they would be slaughtered in this way. At the right time the Germans could concentrate against them on a ratio of three, four, or five men to one, and on an artillery ratio of *at least thirty guns to one.*

The single second front could not succeed.

The attack on the Continent must not be opened in one place

but in several places at one time. There must be at least two divided assaults, one to detract from the other in such a way that either or both could succeed.

But no attack would be feasible *anywhere* until the German air forces were made weak and helpless, nearly as weak and helpless as the French air force became when the Germans blitzed France in 1940.

The Combined Chiefs of Staff decided that the German air strength could be lured to north Africa and the area of Europe bordering on the north shore of the Mediterranean. For the German General Staff evaluated the area as a vital theater of *occupation*. Rommel in Africa was their answer.

As long as Rommel maintained Germany's African position, threatening the rear or flank of United Nations invasion forces, the United Nations could not invade from the Mediterranean. We could *only* invade from England. The Germans knew that north Africa was fundamental in the defense of Germany itself.

Therefore, the first step towards the invasion of Germany, basic in our entire war strategy, was to attract the German air strength to north Africa. Until we did this we could not fight our land war in Europe at all.

But luring the *Luftwaffe* and then throwing Rommel out of north Africa had an agonizing feature. He could always retreat. We could push him around, but we could not expel him. He could always give up sand.

That is what broke the heart and back of every general the British sent into the Western Desert. They knew that the operation from the Nile was futile before they started. Rommel could play shuttlecock in the thousand miles between Alexandria and his base at Tripoli. He might even go in for a little game of hide-and-seek if we outnumbered him heavily enough. No matter what the British did from Alexandria, they could not capture the Afrika Korps by attacking from one side.

"Sahara" means desert. The Sahara, the western area of north Africa, and the Libyan Desert are really one, along with the Arabian Desert east of the Nile and the Sudanese Desert to the south.

Known as the Western Desert, the Libyan Desert changes its name
to Sahara when you go west beyond the Tibesti, Erdi, and Ennedi
rock formations in Algeria.

Looking at the north African coast in terms of familiar American
distances, Algiers would be Denver, Tripoli would be St. Louis,
and the Nile would flow in the banks of Hudson. French-held
Algiers, in the western Mediterranean, is nearly 1,000 miles from
Tripoli, in the central Mediterranean, and Tripoli is over 1,000
miles from British-held Alexandria, in the eastern Mediterranean.

The only way to expel the Germans was to converge on Rommel from both sides. Under such conditions he would have to fill
the air with German planes or retire to Europe entirely. Here was
the place to attract, spread, and kill German air strength. But the
lure would require a tremendous operation. The United States
would have to take a position west of Rommel, all the way from
Casablanca to Algiers. Then we could attack eastward from Algiers
while the British attacked westward from Alexandria. In London
and Berlin at the time of our entrance into the war all this was
sufficiently clear to be described in *Time Runs Out*. The fundamental has never changed.

The British were ready to begin their part in this two-sided assault in May 1942. For that purpose the attack force of British
Middle East forces was based at Tobruk on May 1. American
troops would sail from England, Ireland, and the United States to
Algiers, landing also at Casablanca to protect the Algerian rear
and flank and to occupy Spanish Morocco if Hitler attempted to
close the Strait of Gibraltar by occupying the Spanish shore of the
Spanish Narrows.

This expedition, the Western Task Force, would embark as soon
as General Claude Auchinleck gave the word.

But General Auchinleck, in north Africa, never got started.
He was never able to give the word.

In one single day, in seven short hours, the highest and most
secret plan of the United Nations, the preliminary step to the battle for Germany, was liquidated. By evening that day, the coming
battle for Germany had to be postponed.

Until that sunset the fateful place was just a name that British Tommies had given a low pile of stones in the desert: Knightsbridge.

The smashing defeat was Knightsbridge. There Rommel ambushed the British, using strategy which Lieutenant General Hugh A. Drum of the American Army first demonstrated in a brilliant manner when he won the decision in the North Carolina–South Carolina maneuvers shortly before Pearl Harbor. Using tank-attacker units and fixed artillery in the manner that Drum had originated, Rommel destroyed in seven hours 230 of the 300 tanks that attacked him. This broke the backbone of the British armored force in the Middle East.

The final disaster was the fall of Tobruk.

The Tobruk garrison contained 63,000 men, vast stores, and all kinds of equipment. Tobruk was also the forward base for central repairs. And Tobruk had the harbor, the only safe port easily accessible to large vessels for over 1,000 miles between Sfax, in Tunisia, and Alexandria.

British Military Intelligence has established that Rommel expected to lose 20,000 men in the assault. But after Knightsbridge, when the armored brigades and the German-Italian infantry and motor transport swung into the assault on Tobruk, Rommel did not lose 20,000 men. He lost no men at all. Tobruk surrendered in twelve hours. And Rommel captured a third of the Allied Army. He took 33,100 prisoners. Tobruk contained companies of the Coldstream Guards, the Grenadiers, and other crack British regiments. There were a few Australians, many New Zealanders, a large body of Indian troops, and some R.A.F. men from Canada. But the largest contingent was South African. They were sent to work camps in Italy and Germany.

Tobruk's defenses consisted of high pillboxes and connecting trenches. It was a "Thebes" defense, too exposed. The arrangement had a tragic result. Rommel surprised Auchinleck the second time with the same guns with which he had ambushed him at Knightsbridge.

The surrender without a last-ditch fight was water on the German propaganda wheels, and they spun them over the radio everywhere. But the truth is clear. The commander surrendered to save outright slaughter.

This was on June 22, exactly a year and five months to the day from the morning the British first captured Tobruk from the Italians and took 25,000 Italian prisoners.

Rommel, wooing Italian support, didn't forget this. He sent the Italians in to negotiate and accept the surrender, tried to make it an Italian triumph.

The Italians came forward in an armored bus and met the British and colonial officers in a warehouse on the dock. The Italians beamed and took obvious pride in the fact that there wasn't a German in sight.

But while this was going on Rommel himself was very busy. He skirted Tobruk in a large, snub-nosed armored car, equipped like an office, bristling with three radio masts. He reorganized Von Stumme's and Von Thoma's brigades and diverted them from their positions at Tobruk. While the Italian officers were talking, Rommel sent out his armored forces to harass the rear of Auchinleck's army, retreating along the shore road towards Bardia.

Bardia, on the Libyan-Egyptian border, had been the limit of Rommel's projected offensive. To this point he would have advanced 800 miles from Tripoli. The first phase of his attack would be over. Rommel was not attacking the Nile when he left Tripoli. He was attacking only Tobruk. He had a sound, two-phase plan.

After Tobruk, Rommel planned to concentrate entirely on reorganizing that port, change his supply lines to feed him there instead of in Tripoli. This meant less transport through Italy, across to Sicily, and across the fiery gap of the Mediterranean to Africa under the protection of the *Luftwaffe* based on the Trapani airport and the fields at Comiso and Gela. Further, he would overcome the long and dangerous Libyan haul from Tripoli eastward. It meant co-ordinating the German railroads, the Yugoslav transport lines, and the Greek railways and terminals so that the German position could be served from Salonika and Crete.

When reorganized in this way, Rommel could stay in north

Africa indefinitely, conserve his air strength, and make Germany impregnable at home; or, always threatening the Nile, he could at some desirable time attack Alexandria and Cairo with great power.

But the British did not make a stand at Bardia. Nor did they stand further east, at Solum or Halfaya Pass. The British kept going. And so did Rommel.

In doing this Rommel changed his fundamental plan. Like so many Germans, he could not leave well enough alone. Then he clung to his decision, as though it were right, when he was wrong.

I met Erwin Rommel once with Kirk in Berlin. He is a vain man and very stubborn. Stubbornness has taken men far before and then cost them fortunes and thrones.

It cost Rommel victory in Egypt, and it cost Hitler the defense of Germany.

In the desert Rommel succumbed to the temptation to overextend himself, and he needed to use more and more air power. Rommel let Tedder flush more and more German war birds.

German victory looked easy, for there is nothing so impotent, nothing so tragic, so utterly forlorn, as a retreating army. The entire British Eighth Army, with General Ritchie dismissed and with General Auchinleck alone, was in full retreat along the coast road.

Forty thousand vehicles streamed out of Libya into Egypt. Battered tanks and fieldpieces, battered lorries and trucks, battered scout cars, staff cars, and trailers crawled and halted, stood still or edged a little further. Each carried its battered men, red-eyed, thirsty, dog-tired, and sick with the tragedy of retreat, retreat, retreat.

For three solid weeks—three weeks—under the news of victories in the air above them, this disorganized, discouraged, bewildered, but unbeaten mass moved back tortuously in the jam of that road.

Rommel's eyes were on the ground, and he was smiling. Tedder's eyes were in the sky, and he was smiling too.

The retreating army passed Sidi Barrani. Here the road is inland. The troops and vehicles filled the area between this and the sea. By now they were far inside Egypt, two thirds of the way from Tobruk to Mersa Matruh. The German 15th and 21st Armored

Brigades followed at a safe distance behind, tagging along, not pressing, not fighting.

The British faced another Dunkirk in the Nile delta. The Alexandria naval base had been closed. Most of the British units had gone out of the Mediterranean entirely, south through Suez to the Red Sea. Our naval attaché left to join them at Massaua. Cairo had evacuated civilians.

But, to the surprise of the Germans, when the British reached Mersa Matruh, the last British line of defense, they did not make their stand. They abandoned the line. It was an important, bold, and wise decision made by Churchill himself. The British simply did not have enough effectives now to man this position and hold it long enough for replacements to arrive from England and America. They had to keep going until the funnel shape of the area gave them a shorter line.

Behind the retreat the British were fortifying the one rear position which Churchill, if not many others, felt confident they could hold. And the British were doing a good job hour after hour in the air.

At El Alamein, within seventy miles of Alexandria, the line to the Qattara Depression need be only forty miles long. When you see the Depression, this freak canyon in the desert is a weird sight: a miniature Grand Canyon, a sheer drop from the hard, limestone surface of the desert. This drop varies from a cliff to a slight ledge, rough and saw-toothed. The Depression is below sea level, filled mostly with impassable, tide-like sand. Other parts hold clusters of volcanic rock, sprawling in the sand like giant brown crabs, the chain formations of half-buried crags stretching out in ugly feelers. The British began mining a line from the Depression to the seacoast village of El Alamein, fortifying the heights in the center. And they transferred General Wilson's Ninth Army from Palestine and Syria. Coming the distance it did, this new force could not have joined the retreating army further west than El Alamein.

Suddenly Rommel's advance guard, tagging along behind the retreat, encountered New Zealand units standing on heights south of El Alamein. They were under the command of Lieutenant General Sir Bernard Freyberg, holder of the Victoria Cross and by all odds the most able general the British had in the desert. Rommel made one thrust. He found resistance. General Freyberg's New Zealanders threw the German reconnaissance force back on its heels. This was the British stand.

Rommel retired at once. On their short line, the British were at last set to fight him. He knew it, and he made no fight. By now he had traveled over a thousand miles from Tripoli. He still had his task to do at Tobruk. He had never intended to fight this far into Egypt in the first place, and he wasn't in any way prepared to do so. The German air strength, as a whole, had suffered serious attrition in trying to support Rommel in his overextended position. The tight, compact *Luftwaffe* had been attracted. It had been spread, and much had been killed.

In Egypt, Rommel was a magnificent tank fighter and artillery-man. He was a field commander of the highest excellence using a compact and hard-hitting, specialized force trained under his maxim of *Sturm, Schwung, Wucht*—Attack, Impetus, Weight. But he lost his air power.

"Fantastic as it may seem," Sir Arthur Tedder told me, "at no time during the entire three weeks' retreat, when forty thousand British vehicles jammed the coast road—an ideal target—did Rommel make any attempt to bomb us."

This fact was the most important military revelation in the Middle East in the opinion of Tedder, Air Vice-Marshal Coning-ham, and our own Major General Brereton.

Rommel's failure to strafe the retreating army was not because he did not have planes. It was because Germany lacked a flexible air organization.

The misfortune is that the British did not counterattack the moment Rommel's light force contacted them at El Alamein. Auchin-leck's final failure, his failure to do this, at last cost him his command.

The British strengthened their El Alamein line and stood still. So did Rommel.

At El Alamein Rommel was too extended to concentrate on

establishing his new base at Tobruk. He kept his army busy going through it as a transit point instead of devoting every hour and every man to making it an unassailable base. For if Rommel controlled Tobruk impregnably, he could control Tripoli impregnably.

By the time the British stopped at El Alamein things were very busy around Salonika. Dockmen were getting ready to handle incoming rail shipments from Germany and transfer them to vessels for Tobruk. Axis ships were steaming into Salonika and other Greek ports in bunches. Soon heavy trains would be coming down from Germany to give Rommel what he needed to finish his job in Egypt.

But the trains had to come down through Yugoslavia.

CHAPTER 18

A *for Africa*, E *for Eisenhower*, F *for France*

As a prewar traveler I once rode the famous Simplon-Orient Express, providing Europe's de luxe service between Calais on the English Channel and Istanbul on the Bosporus.

This was the great route across Europe to Asia, through France, Switzerland, and Italy into the caldron of the Balkans—Yugoslavia, Bulgaria, Turkey. At Belgrade one section went by way of Nish to Istanbul and the other dropped south to Salonika.

Laboriously and fitfully, this southbound train wound a treacherous way over high trestles, into long tunnels, through fertile valleys, and along the deep gorges of Yugoslavia.

Now these were the mountains of Yugoslav General Draza Mihailovitch, valiant Serb, who fought against the Austrians when he was fifteen, against the Turks when he was seventeen, against the Bulgarians when he was eighteen, and against the Germans on innumerable occasions ever since. This was Mihailovitch's moment.

It was General Draza Mihailovitch, acting when he did and where he did, that gave the United Nations' reinforcements time to reach north Africa from England and America before Rommel's reinforcements could reach Tobruk.

In Yugoslavia were the only fighting armies of the United Nations on the entire continent of Europe west of Russia.

By guerrilla warfare General Draza Mihailovitch and his fiery band of Tchetnitsi had immobilized in Yugoslavia twelve Italian divisions, three German divisions, seven Bulgarian divisions,

181

and three divisions of Hungarians. His fighters, from every class of Serb, Croat, and Slav—reinforced by even a few German and Italian deserters—had blasted Hitler's occupation of Yugoslavia for months until it was effective in little more than the valleys, and there only at a bloody cost to the German forces.

General Mihailovitch had deprived the Germans of their Yugoslav prize by preventing them from exploiting the rich copper, chrome, and bauxite mines in any way. The Germans asked Mihailovitch for an armistice.

General von Dankelmann sent a message to Mihailovitch in his mountain headquarters. Two German officers and a representative of General Milan Neditch's Quisling government in Yugoslavia were blindfolded and led on the tortuous trip into the mountains.

Mihailovitch met them in an open camp, standing with his staff in a clearing. The humble German officers crossed the clearing, saluted, and stood to state their case. The trip to the mountain rendezvous took the Germans two days. They were in the presence of Mihailovitch less than two minutes.

An armistice? The fiery Serb replied that he proposed to fight until Germany capitulated. Then he sent General von Dankelmann's officers away.

Through a Gestapo agent who had worked for Von Papen when Von Papen was Ambassador to Austria and engineered Pan-Germanism there, the Gestapo located Mihailovitch's wife and both his children. They seized them in Belgrade. Gloating, the Germans announced this in the Belgrade newspapers. The Germans held his family and fifteen leading officers as hostages, gave Mihailovitch one more chance to surrender.

The tortured man replied from a radio transmitter, his firm voice coming from the mountains. Softly, clearly, breaking a hush that fell over his country, his answer came over the air. He spoke to his wife, and he spoke to his children by name. He told them to have courage, for life was not worth living without it. "I have the intention of continuing the battle," he said, "until the day of my death or until the day when the enemy has been driven forever from our homes and from our glorious land."

With the British standing at El Alamein, the Tchetnitsi again stormed out of their mountains. With a ferocity bred of seeing their women and children bayonetted in their streets, their villages ravaged, their homes sacked and burned, they cut all communications between Belgrade and Salonika in the entire Vardar Valley.

The first German military train for Rommel dove headlong into the gorge south of Zagreb. Four Italian and two German divisions backed up on each other and could not move through the blown-in tunnels or over the blazing trestles.

Hitler had sent Rommel the material to assault Egypt, break all bounds in the Middle East. But Mihailovitch, in one of the bloodiest forays of history, had cut the German supply lines in the mountains that had echoed his voice.

United Nations' reinforcements, our ships, guns, and men, shipped from England and the United States, reached north Africa first.

Such German convoys as did reach Tobruk put into port without the tankers that carried oil and gasoline. "Get the tankers," Tedder told the R.A.F. "Get them day and night."

"Don't pay attention to the other ships," Pat Timberlake told his American bomber pilots. "Forget them. We'll let them sail on through if we have to. We'll concentrate on the tankers and drop every bomb we have on a tanker deck until we see that ship explode."

And that is exactly what the British and American boys did. *Not a single tanker, coming to Rommel from any point, reached him at Tobruk.*

When General Eisenhower's Americans landed in the western Mediterranean at Algiers they caught Rommel literally off base. He was gradually evacuating the line at El Alamein, because the length of his haul from Tripoli was so burdensome and he could no longer maintain any air support at this distance. Rommel was preparing to fall back to Bardia, beyond which he had not intended to go until he changed his plan. General Montgomery's attack from El Alamein, beginning the Eighth Army's magnificent advance, speeded the momentum of Rommel's retirement into a devastating rout. *The* Luftwaffe *had disappeared from the air entirely.*

Tedder's R.A.F. and the American Air Corps obtained definite air superiority in the desert in all categories, fought the *Luftwaffe* literally to a standstill, beat the German fighters, beat their bombers. The United Nations won the air in Egypt, and with it they won the opportunity to engage the *Luftwaffe* again in Tunisia. Tunisia would attract German air strength to an important degree—so important, in fact, that the Germans could easily establish air superiority there. But it would face a second battle of attrition.

In conjunction with the arrival of our troops in the far-off western Mediterranean, the war went west. The race was on for Tunisia.

Our own General Dwight D. Eisenhower's Western Task Force, heavily equipped, and a contingent of British troops known as the British First Army, which, though of no considerable size, was nevertheless made up of veterans, started to land at Algiers at 1 A.M., November 8.

Originally twelve experts were picked to go to north Africa under Robert D. Murphy, men who spoke French not well, but perfectly; men who had lived in France, knew every flavor of French thought. All but four were drawn from our army and navy. Several had attended French military schools with French officers then commanding in north Africa. Two had been graduated from Saint-Cyr, another from the French School of Cavalry. These Americans began leaving for Algiers in September 1941, three months before Pearl Harbor.

I was in Vichy at the time they were establishing themselves in north Africa. It was now the middle of November, and we were on the last-minute edge of entering the war. General Huntziger, France's Minister of War, had been conferring with General Maxime Weygand in Algiers and was returning to Vichy to report to Marshal Pétain when his plane, caught in a fog, crashed in the Vichy hills. Under the leadership of the German Ambassador to Paris, Otto Abetz, the Germans moved in on Vichy for the funeral and used that occasion to put pressure on Marshal Pétain.

The Germans knew all about America's program in north Africa and did not like Murphy's setup there at all. Abetz insisted, in the name of Hitler, that Pétain put a stop to American activities in the Vichy colony. The marshal could not agree to this demand, for it put him in the position of shutting off aid to his own desperate people across the Mediterranean.

Pétain compromised. He agreed to Hitler's insistence that he fire General Weygand, whom the Germans blamed for the north African situation, but who actually neither instigated it nor especially facilitated it in its operation.

Marshal Pétain summoned General Weygand to Vichy. France thought he was being brought home to become the new Minister of War. I met the general at the airport. He was received like a returning Roman hero. The marshal's guard—white gauntlets, bulbous helmets, and all—was turned out in full force. Weygand bowed in an open car, drove slowly through the cheering streets to the marshal's headquarters in the Hôtel du Parc. I do not know whether Weygand knew he was being fired, as I did. I rather think not. But in any case, Abetz had cast the die. General Weygand would be removed as governor of north Africa. He would resign as a soldier of France. Abetz put the finger on Weygand. I had a world scoop, which I had to smuggle out in a cryptic cable from a police station in Lyon. And, as for Robert Murphy, he had a new problem in north Africa.

More and more Americans were rushed into Algiers, Oran, and Casablanca. Shipments were stepped up. Murphy worked like a trooper. Pearl Harbor hurt the shipments to him, but from then on he made a little go even a longer way in each of his French and native contacts.

Originally, Murphy did not "conspire" with French military leaders to overthrow the Vichy Government in north Africa, or to gain military support for a possible American landing. With the exception of invaluable Intelligence reports, Murphy tried to keep his whole project within the economic field and out of the military orbit.

The Germans had their own armistice commission of two hundred men in north Africa, plus a full contingent of Gestapo agents. For this and other reasons the French military leaders were not plotting military aid to the United Nations until they were prevailed on to do so by an energetic fellow countryman.

His name is Jacques Lemaigre Dubreuil, and he is the man with whom General Clark had the secret rendezvous when he went to north Africa on his famous trip in the submarine.

Lemaigre Dubreuil was the chief conspirator in the entire enterprise leading to the overthrow of the government and the co-operation of the French Army. He is a manufacturer of vegetable oils, with large extraction plants in Algiers, Oran, and Dakar. He was an intimate friend of General Charles Mast, General Staff Officer and Deputy Commander of Vichy's Algiers forces, and of General Émile Bethouart, of Mast's staff. He was also General Henri Honoré Giraud's closest friend in France.

Operating as a private individual, Lemaigre Dubreuil was privileged to go back and forth between north Africa and France in the conduct of his oil business. This unique status was very important. In Algiers he persuaded General Mast to lead a military revolt. In France he worked out General Giraud's participation, meeting with him openly and often in his villa near Lyon.

Lemaigre Dubreuil built up a guerrilla organization of four hundred young Frenchmen, outside the Army, in Algiers. These men did not know they were going to work for General Mast, and they knew nothing whatever about General Giraud. Lemaigre Dubreuil paid them, met them secretly in groups of twenty-five, employed many of them in his vegetable-oil plants. He called these young Frenchmen his "crew."

Then he went to Murphy. It was a wild-looking setup, but there it was. Mast would handle the attack on the Vichy north African government, using Lemaigre Dubreuil's crew for the first impact of the *Putsch*. Giraud would come from France. Vichy power in north Africa would be overthrown.

When the Combined Chiefs of Staff in Washington drew up the plan to attack Rommel on both sides by landing in Algiers, Murphy was notified of this and directed to supply further information regarding what could be expected from his contact with Lemaigre Dubreuil.

The energetic Frenchman told Robert Murphy that, if General Mast was convinced the American expedition could succeed, he could supply effective co-operation at Algiers and Oran. But, said General Mast, neither he nor General Giraud could do much in the Casablanca area. This was an honorable and exact statement of their limits. The whole Casablanca area was full of Germans, including the two hundred armistice-commission Germans, and the defenses were in the hands of French officers who had been appointed by Darlan and who were committed to Vichy.

General Mast and his officers, of course, would face Vichy firing squads if they co-operated and the American landing required a long fight or failed to succeed. They remembered the De Gaulle attempt to take Dakar. They were afraid the American expedition might be a propaganda affair or another case of "too little" or "too late." They asked Murphy to have some high American officer on Eisenhower's staff come to north Africa and reassure them regarding the size and effectiveness of the invasion plan.

In London, General Eisenhower picked Major General Mark W. Clark for the journey. General Clark took the famous gold with him on his own initiative. He didn't need it. He was there to give the military picture, demonstrate the invasion plan, and express the United States Army's guarantee of its success. And when he kept his rendezvous he found that gold was not part of his mission. General Clark took away all the gold he had brought with him, although it was lost overboard on the way out to the submarine with British Commando Captain R. T. Livingstone.

The two Frenchmen, and their associates, whom General Clark and his party met in the secluded house on the shore were Lemaigre Dubreuil and General Mast. This was October 26. The immense convoys had already left England and the United States and were on their way before they met. General Clark detailed the invasion plan. General Mast was impressed.

The submarine, under command of Lieutenant N. L. A. Jewell, of the Royal Navy, dropped Clark and his party off at Gibraltar so that the R.A.F. could fly them to London. Captain Wright, of our navy, stayed with the submarine, and under his orders Lieutenant Jewell put to sea again to get General Giraud. The submarine proceeded to a secluded French harbor in the vicinity of the Spanish border, came in submerged, then surfaced 1,000 yards offshore.

Sixty-five-year-old General Giraud nearly lost his life transferring from a skiff to the submarine's slippery gangway and was badly shaken by the accident. A British flying boat met Lieutenant Jewell's craft off Málaga and flew General Giraud and Captain Wright to Gibraltar so that the French general could wait there and time properly his arrival in Algiers.

Admiral Darlan was already in Algiers, visiting his paralyzed son. This visit was not connected with the invasion event in any way. Darlan had no knowledge whatever of the plan. Darlan did not know the Americans were going to land. He did not know he was going to be taken captive outside France. On that point there is no question whatever.

The first activity ashore came from Lemaigre Dubreuil's crew. In the middle of the night, operating in groups of twenty-five and dressed in their ordinary civilian clothes, for they were all civilians, wearing arm bands and carrying rifles, they took up their posts. At a signal from Lemaigre Dubreuil they seized the Algiers telegraph and telephone office and the radio station. In these and other spots they found employees wearing arm bands too. Anyone with an arm band was a friend. It was the mark of Lemaigre Dubreuil.

Admiral Darlan was staying at the governor's summer palace. At two o'clock in the morning Murphy hurried to tell him the Americans were landing and to ask his support. Murphy went to the admiral's bedroom. He was there when Lemaigre Dubreuil's crew arrived to arrest the Vichy leader. Lemaigre Dubreuil had kept Murphy and the whole American plan out of the picture with the men of his crew, and they did not know Murphy. The young Frenchmen were taking no chances. They arrested Murphy too. In fact, Murphy was under arrest as General Eisenhower's troops started to land, and until word could reach General Mast of this confusion.

When Darlan was released with Murphy, the admiral offered his services to General Eisenhower.

Lieutenant General Eisenhower's forces made three separate landings in the Algiers area. To the east of Algiers the American troops and the British contingent stormed the shore at Ain Taya, on the tip of Algiers Bay. The British Royal Navy blasted the batteries of Cape Matifou, and British troops then occupied that point.

The Americans controlled the three local airfields before 11:30 A.M., and the United States Army Air Corps moved in. Until that time the only air umbrella was supplied by aircraft carriers, from which, for the first time, the British were using a remarkable carrier-borne version of the Spitfire, known as the "Seafire."

General Giraud, in Gibraltar, had wished the Allies to postpone the disembarkation to allow time for additional French officers to get over from France, and he stayed in Gibraltar to superintend this. He did not arrive in Algiers until three days after the disembarkation, flying there with British Major General J. C. Haydon, Lord Louis Mountbatten's Commando leader and Britain's Vice-Chief of Combined Operations. General Eisenhower had concluded an Algiers armistice with Admiral Darlan.

General Émile Bethouart, General Mast's closest collaborator in the Army, had gone to Rabat, Morocco's Atlantic seaport between Casablanca and the Strait of Gibraltar. General Auguste Noguès, Governor General of Morocco, was there. General Bethouart's assignment was to gain Governor Noguès' co-operation and support or failing this, to arrest him and take over the Rabat garrison.

Governor Noguès received this able French officer at once. General Bethouart told Noguès the American troops were landing and asked him to co-operate or surrender. The Governor General didn't say yes, and he didn't say no. He told Bethouart that he wished to verify the landing through the commandant at Casablanca. Noguès telephoned Casablanca.

"No ships are landing here. This is no invasion. You are being duped," came the reply to Noguès. The landing which General

Bethouart had expected to start at 3 A.M. had been delayed until 7. Our ships were lying far offshore and were not visible. This was unfortunate for General Bethouart. The shoe was on the other foot.

Governor Noguès arrested General Bethouart as he stood in his office. He charged General Bethouart with treason and placed him in the Rabat garrison prison. Then he rounded up as many of Lemaigre Dubreuil's crew, who accompanied General Bethouart, as he could find.

As for Casablanca itself, the delayed American landing ran into full and effective resistance. Murphy's fears, Lemaigre Dubreuil's fears, the fears of General Mast and General Giraud, were being substantiated by blasts from shore batteries and French vessels at Casablanca. And none of the Vichy commanders in Casablanca paid attention to General Giraud's pleas to surrender.

The Germans thought they saw the whole convoy steam through the Strait of Gibraltar, and, furthermore, they thought it was going to Malta and Alexandria. German and Italian submarines were concentrated in the gap off Sicily to intercept it. The Germans did not know that many more vessels stood in the dark off Casablanca. Out of the total vessels in our Western Task Force, some made a feint as though they were going through the Strait and into the Mediterranean Sea, but turned south and took up their position off Casablanca and near-by Fedala. Our ships there ranged over an area of sixteen square miles.

Our men had to gamble on bad surf. Breakers are generally high on the Fedala beach, where the landing had to be made so that Casablanca could be taken from the rear. But the breakers were not high as dawn broke that morning.

Then, suddenly, lights began to appear all over Casablanca. The shore garrison's wireless started up in a big way. A broadcast had been picked up over the radio. The garrison in Casablanca was told it was going to be attacked.

Two Vichy French cruisers and four destroyers were ready to leave the harbor and responded to the alarm. They left. At sea they encountered an American cruiser, alone. The odds were bad, and the diversion of the American cruiser from her assigned job against the shore batteries was very unfortunate. But as for the sea battle itself, our warship singlehanded broke a record. She sank one Vichy cruiser, disabled and captured the other, and sank two of the destroyers.

The shore batteries opened fire on our men and vessels with the first streak of light. Our forces landed in Fedala's crescent-shaped harbor under the direct and converging fire of the 90-millimeter gun batteries on the horns of the crescent.

Another American cruiser intended to reduce the shore batteries on the crescent horns. Unfortunately, the shore batteries were not reduced. The men of the infantry and other units landed in the face of this cross fire, fought their way through the shore water and up the beach, stormed the gun emplacements themselves from the sides and rear, and overwhelmed the batteries in one of the most heroic actions of the war.

Word went out that things did not look favorable, that the objective could be taken with three to five days' more fighting, but that it would be very costly and that all ships offshore would soon be subject to submarine attack on the arrival of enemy craft.

This was November 11. The Casablanca action was in its fourth day. The second and most important phase of the Algiers operation —the advance eastward towards Tunisia to beat Rommel to his home base—had already been seriously delayed by the possible necessity of sending reinforcements to Rabat and Casablanca, back through the Strait of Gibraltar and down the Atlantic coast.

"Well?" said Robert Murphy to the strange man of Vichy.

Admiral Darlan produced a code book from his pocket, reached for a piece of paper.

One hour later every gun in Casablanca ceased firing.

The battle for Tunisia—and Europe—then started. The battle for Germany was on.

CHAPTER 19

With the R.A.F. in the Desert

I'LL HELP YOU find Coningham in the desert," Sir Arthur told me. "I'll send him a signal, and you can meet at his trailer." Coningham's secret headquarters moved all along the front.

Air Vice-Marshal Sir Arthur Coningham, C.B., D.S.O., M.C., D.F.C., A.F.C., "Mary" Coningham to all soldiers in the Middle East, and field commander of the R.A.F., is one of Britain's most gallant and effective officers. He is in direct command of the battle in the air. That suits pilots to a *T*. Born in New Zealand, educated in England, Coningham commanded early bomber groups which carried out raids over Germany from bases in England. He came to the desert with Tedder in August 1941 as Air Officer Commanding, Western Desert.

The next morning Sir Arthur sent his staff car and his aide, Squadron Leader Gerald Bray, to take me to the front. We set out in the early desert sunrise along the Mena Road by the Pyramids. A "redcap," as they are called—a soldier of the Corps Military Police—led the way.

"At night the Heinies send fake redcaps in our uniforms and on captured English motorcycles inside our lines," Bray told me. "They station themselves at remote crossroads and wait for a stream of our trucks, or mix in at some heavy traffic point when they can. They flag our trucks into making wrong turns, and the next thing the truck drivers know they are in a German ambush. Our own redcaps spend a lot of time riding around challenging each other to find out who's who."

Some of the Germans' own traffic police in the desert use a

motorcycle that is a battling tricycle. It has a motorcycle front wheel and seat, but two extra soldiers sit on divided boxes in the rear, riding backwards. Equipped with tommy guns, they use these for patrol all over the occupied countries of Europe. These, too, I first saw in Spain, sold to the Spanish Army.

Soldier helmets bobbed out of the turrets of lumbering General Grant and General Lee tanks like the heads of turtles from their shells. We passed rumbling convoys, searchlight batteries, and anti-aircraft units. There was larger stuff ahead: heavy artillery towed behind caterpillar trucks, anti-tank guns on treads and wheels, an assortment of fieldpieces; lorries and more lorries, their automatic wipers clearing a little *V* in the solid crust of dust on their windshields.

The road was jammed with motorized troops. For a while we were caught in a mass of tank-repair units and tank-carrying trucks. Signalmen worked at field telephones at the roadside. We drove around the machine gun company on the march, soldiers leading Arabian horses with knocked-down weapons strapped across their backs. Red flags, stuck in the sand on each side of the road, warned against unexploded bombs in a terse and convincing way.

Seventy per cent of the troops in Egypt were British. Men from Yorkshire, Coventry, London; men from the moors of Scotland and bleak huts near Lands End; store clerks from the Midlands, salesmen from Tunbridge Wells, bus drivers and postmen, miners, butlers and footmen, acrobats from the Strand, men who tended the fuzzy little ducks in Hyde Park Pond.

The British Army is a civilian army today. In 1936 the appallingly small army amounted to only 158,400 British regulars, plus 57,524 in India. According to the British Ministry of Information's published figures, British regimentals, including those in India, stood at 225,924 in 1937, 226,806 in 1938, and 234,624 in 1939.

Against this background the Germans have tried to stimulate the belief, especially in America and the British colonies, that Britain fights the war with colonial troops. The colonials have fought well in this war, and the whole United Kingdom is proud of the South Africans, New Zealanders, Australians, and Canadians, the troops from India and the far corners of the world. But the core of the Empire Army is British, and the heroism of the average British soldier is a magnificent thing. No men fight better than the British Tommies, and from the Coldstream Guards to the newest Limehouse brigade, English troops in this war are alike. They fight like hell.

We turned finally from the Alexandria Road to a trail, and then we left these tracks and drove for miles through the whirling sand of the open desert. No sign of habitation in the whole flat area, for there is none, only scattered mobile equipment, its low-pressure tires flattened in the shallow sand like the sprawling feet of elephants. Anti-aircraft batteries manned for instant action, flags to show emergency landing fields, stray planes sitting on the desert carefully dispersed, looking like tiny gopher heads sticking out of their holes on the plains of Montana.

We could hear our artillery: after the flash the hurricane sound of the shell, then at last the slow sound of the gun explosion. "Four-and-a-half-inch howitzers," Bray said. We could see our fighters and the Messerschmitts in the sky.

An immense tank encampment east and west of the trail huddled together for protection at night in a manner designed after the Boer War laager. An hour before daylight these vehicles had been dispersed over an area of four square miles, nearly a hundred yards of desert space separating each vehicle, making them nearly impossible targets from the air. Among them was the vehicle of a man who lived with the soldiers and carried his mark in purple paint across the hood and along the sides of a battered station wagon: CHAPLAIN.

We pulled up in a scattering of net-covered equipment dispersed in the sand like so many other groups we had passed before. The only thing that marked it was a number, painted on a sign and stuck in the sand: 230.

"Where is the trailer of the A.O.C. [Air Officer Commanding]?" Bray asked a soldier in a jeep.

The soldier jumped out of the jeep, saluted, and asked Bray for his identification, although our car carried the mark of the air chief marshal. British sentries know their business. The soldier pointed to a heavy-built vehicle, smothered in its camouflage web. If you can imagine a trapeze net falling down on the business wagon of a circus, that's what it looked like.

Coningham's trailer is small, a tan-camouflaged cubicle about fifteen feet long and seven feet wide, a bed across one end and a wardrobe and basin at the other, a telephone-cluttered field desk along the side. Pictures of Coningham's family in New Zealand stood on the desk, pictures that spoke quietly of life a long way off and telling at a glance much that free men are fighting for the world over.

The air vice-marshal was delayed in our engagement. Bray and I waited for him by his trailer. Near where we stood was the grave of a British tank officer. The hard sand blew in eddies around the gravel mound. The wind blows nearly all the time, puffs and wisps of wind, monotonous and tedious and always affecting you in everything you do. You have to keep your tent flaps closed, brace yourself against the wind no matter which way you turn. Wind is the surprise feature of the Western Desert. It is always blowing, always carrying hard sand into your food, your eyes, your ears, your mouth.

The wind is the chief complication in flying, too, for it is the wind that gets the sand into the air, and it is the sand which tears the hearts out of motors. An American airplane engine is good for only eighty hours in the desert; then it has to be shaken down into little pieces and put together again. Sand strainers have been improved marvelously, or our plane would never have gone through the haboob in the Sudan; but the grit is hard, and it gets through. Like termites.

The sun beats down mercilessly. The glare is blinding, cuts at you like the blade of a hungry sword, and the shimmering waves of heat wear your eyes and your brain. But, for all the action around you, it is strangely quiet. Like the walls of a mine, the dust-filled desert wind deadens every sound.

At night the cold can be fairly intense in the desert, putting a frozen crust on any water and frost on the fuzzy muzzles of camels, horses, and mules. You need blankets or a bedroll to sleep in. And you need very heavy shoes to walk in, for the desert is really a limestone plateau, as hard as Gibraltar, and the thin layer of sand is a mass of pebbles, shells, and stones. These clatter against truck fenders, jam themselves in all mechanized equipment, and roll under your feet when you walk. This is no beach. The battlefield is a rock quarry, flat as a pool table except for jagged escarpments, sharp as a crushed-stone road, barren as the sea.

The heat alone is not bad. It's about like Arizona, and anyone from Kansas City, St. Louis, or Washington, D. C., would never feel it. The thermometer goes to 130 degrees and higher, but not often. It's generally around 100 to 110, and that isn't a strain, except when you are inside metal. Then it is terrible. The heat inside a tank is simply indescribable.

Even with his body full of salt solution, asbestos gloves on his hands so that he can touch the metal without scorching his skin, even if he is in the best physical condition, an artillery gunner inside a closed tank in action in the desert has the toughest single job in this war. The official temperature readings show from 160 to 180 degrees Fahrenheit.

The dryness dehydrates you. At first you lose a good deal of weight and some strength. It takes conditioning to fight here, more because of the dryness than because of the heat, and it takes time. Rommel had all kinds of trick equipment for this, which he used in Germany to condition the Afrika Korps, and the British have much the same things, but the real training is the gradual accumulation of hours in the desert itself.

Yet, it's amazing the hold that the desert gets on ground troops and fliers who fight here. Father used to say that miners never complained about the one thing everybody feels sympathetic about: the fact that miners are underground. Men who are miners don't mind being underground. They like it. And they don't want to trade for a job shoveling coal on the surface.

It's something like that in north Africa. Troops and aviators who have fought from Narvik to Singapore would rather fight in the desert than anywhere else. I would rather be there myself than in any place I have been in the war. This is chiefly because of the difference in discipline and organization. Men fight in small teams and really feel they are accomplishing something. And they get very close to their machines.

In fact, men moving in machines, depending on machines, living in machines, and dying in machines blend with their machines.

The machine prides itself on having no nerve factor. But what does it do? At home, and in the desert, it amplifies and intensifies every nervous tendency the operator might ordinarily have. In fact, it introduces the nervous factor into the matter of civilization for the first time in the history of mankind. Neurasthenia, vast neurasthenia, coincides only with the development of the Hudson Tube Age, and in the desert you see the effect of this broad fact. You see it in the raw.

I was watching a mechanic working on a tank motor, bent over, when suddenly something snapped in this man, something in his brain, and he started to run blindly around until he dropped. These things happen very quickly in the desert. And very quietly.

Historically, even before 1914—so that the added effects of war can be excluded—there was a steady and mounting curve of neurasthenia in each country as it became more industrialized. The crowded countries of Europe led in this. From the beginning, around 1900, the matter centered in industrial cities and towns. As the mechanistic network grew, neurasthenia grew with it in absolute parallel. Germany was the most highly organized country. Germany was the highest in the neurasthenia curve.

Army signs on posts along the desert trails say: "Keep moving," "Step lively," "Keep going." So do signs back home. We can take the shock of this age in America. We have the relief of our land and of our high standard of living and the temperament of our free people. But on the peninsula of Europe, no. Unless something is done to disperse overcrowded Europe, as the laagers are dispersed in the desert, the meek do not inherit the earth. The fascist-communist tendency inherits the meek.

With our brave allies, we can beat in war the enemies of Europe and the world. But in peace we cannot break the rhythm of European self-destruction. The Europeans will have to do that for themselves, spread out, spread into their own lands, or there will always be tanks fighting in Africa. And Americans, who have no territory in Africa, and who need none, will always be dying in them.

When Air Vice-Marshal Coningham arrived he came in a captured German plane. It was a snub-nosed little three-place Fleisch-Storch, not good for battle, a sportsman's type of ship, convenient for hedgehopping between the different fields because you can pick it up and put it down on a postage stamp.

It is typical of the curiosities of this war, the strange bits of contradiction, the flavor of irony, that the R.A.F. Air Officer Commanding, Western Desert, would be tending to his fighting a battle, back and forth between his fighting fields, in a captured German plane.

Coningham stepped out of the plane wearing a pair of R.A.F. shorts and a bush jacket. He had no hat. His smoked glasses hung from his jacket pocket. Carrying a map under his left arm, smiling broadly, squinting in the sun, he waved to Bray and me. He strode across the sand and put out a cheerful hand. And I found out that Coningham has an arm like Thor when we shook hands in the desert.

"Hello," he said, "you look in the market for a tall drink of water. Come along over to the operations trailer; we can have one, and I'll show you where we are, what we plan doing, and how we are doing it."

Coningham, a tall, broad-shouldered, clean-shaven man, has a marvelous smile. He has a good, solid face, open and frank, a twinkle in his eye, a pleasant, rollicking voice. Coningham bounds when he walks, and anyone could guess he had been an athlete. He was a champion Rugby player of the Empire.

We went back into the trailer to pick up some things. Then down a ladder into the blowing sand again, trudging a hundred yards along half-buried telephone wires stretching to the operations trailer. This vehicle was a world of maps, telephones, desks, and slide rules, men and filtering sand all compressed into a space no larger than the basement of a small Long Island home.

"There go the Bostons to do their jobs," Coningham said as he pointed to a new-made crayon arrow on the glazed map, chalked in place by an officer who wore earphones. "They're off to bomb Tobruk. And there go the Alsace Squadron."

The British have been criticized for lack of dive bombers in the desert. When you see the action in the desert, the British theory is more clear. The fact is that in the desert the Nazis have not been able to hit tanks with their Stukas.

The target represented by several tanks is totally different from the target represented by a warship. It is one thing to dive and launch a torpedo against a man-of-war from a torpedoplane and quite another thing to dive and bomb a tank. On one occasion I saw eight Stukas fall off and dive on twelve of our tanks. The desert whirled in a cloud of sand. The sand settled. We still had twelve tanks. They had not hit one.

The oldest British and American fighter planes in the desert are faster than the Stukas and will drop them. The Heliopolis action was typical. The Germans lose Stukas as soon as they turn up to get away, for a Stuka has a top speed of less than 200 miles per hour.

The British preference is for types like the American-made Boston. "We use this plane as an attack bomber, torpedo bomber, night fighter, long-range fighter, pursuit, interceptor, or intruder!" Coningham told me. Its battery of machine guns is terrifically effective for strafing troops. One Boston carries as much volume of fire as an entire battalion of infantry. The new word in the desert for "strafe" is "Bostonize." Except on large objectives, like the Heliopolis airport, the effect of the Stukas simply cannot compare with it.

In a few minutes there was fast action in the center of the battle area we were in. Coningham put the pieces together for me as they came to him in flashes from all over the area: "About noon I sent out a wing of fighters to get some Stukas which were reported bombing our Indian boys. That's the flight there on the map. I figured to get the Stukas at their airdrome as they come home, but my boys report now that they are not Stukas. They are Rommel's best Messerschmitts, 109-Fs and 109-Gs which drop bombs and then fight. This is a fine bag of just the planes we want most to get.

The Stuka job was 'small fry.' Stukas are what Americans would call 'easy pickings' and what we call 'cold meat.' But as we stand here these Messerschmitts have been coming into their spot to refuel. We want those ships. We've got one, two, three, by George, we've got six! That's a good job, a whacking good job well done, Mr. Taylor, a whacking good job. Won't you listen?"

The air vice-marshal handed me the earphones. The words I heard were those of Air Commodore Thomas Elmhirst reporting. All was well. The boys were coming home. No son of England was lost.

CHAPTER 20

"This Is It"

GENERAL VALIN FLEW ME into the desert battle in a French two-seater fighter.

"Tomorrow's our day," he said. "We'll go to the Alsace Squadron headquarters at five o'clock in the morning," he told me in Cairo. "We'll fly to Alexandria." A little while before daybreak Valin came by my room, and we had breakfast. One of his aides drove us out to the Heliopolis airport. A fast, sleek, two-place fighter was waiting there, clean as a whistle, trim and hard as a bullet. The Lorraine cross sparkled smartly on the wings.

The British commandant of the airport escorted Valin across the field, and we stood waiting while R.A.F. mechanics tuned up the ship.

"I'll fly to the Alsace Squadron base," Valin told the commandant. "I'll work out with the squadron there. Expect us back here late tonight."

We fixed our parachutes. Valin and I climbed in. It's a tight squeeze in the seat of a fighter plane. You fly in space, but you have no space—not an extra inch. Valin tuned up the engines, listened as they roared evenly and clearly in the test, nodded to the commandant as he throttled them down.

R.A.F. helpers pulled the blocks, and we taxied across the field past the same slit trenches which had welcomed us both to Cairo.

We took off like a rocket. The ship just kicked up the dust and flew away.

The wind at our backs, the desert world opening flat and clear before us, the earth and sky burned by the brilliance of the sun, guns in the wings, there was no limit to our independence and our powers.

In a few hours where would we be?

The house-clustered hills of Cairo were bare, brown, broken-off scraps on our right. Now they were behind us as we flew low along Mena Road into the desert, the same road to Alexandria that I had covered with Gerald Bray. We were flying practically on the surface of the sand, as we had flown into Heliopolis from Khartoum.

The first landmarks in the blazing desert were the long asphalt bomber runways, giant black crosses, scarring the sand. These serve as miscellaneous landing fields at the rear of desert operations. Most of them have no huts or service equipment, just the flat stretches of asphalt, like half-finished and forgotten race-track straightaways in the middle of nowhere.

"It was hard to build these runways," Valin said, "and the British built them well."

From the air we could see anti-aircraft stations far back from the road, and tank-repair units scattered in the sand. Single planes —Baltimores, these were—stood in their pits, consisting of three-sided walls protected by sandbags. Other planes sat unprotected on the desert as though made for the spot, dropped and forgotten. Dugouts, looking like pockmarks in the earth. And here was an oily gash, the long, black scrape of a crash, the desert equivalent of the short, brown gash in the jungle near Kano.

A single Hurricane, Mark II, flying in the opposite direction and flying low like ourselves, passed us an instant after we sighted it. Planes coming towards each other at 300 miles an hour pass in a twinkling. An airman must be good to identify them at all. This problem of identification is one of the features of fighting in such fast ships. It's amazing how quick you have to be at it and how far off you have to make up your mind, lest it be too late. Two planes ten miles apart come together in one minute. Each is traveling the length of one and a half football fields every second. When they are three football fields apart they come together in one second.

Three fast-stepping Spitfires, headed west, crossed over us, their shadows racing across the sand and through a dispersed tank camp near the road.

In the distance we sighted Alexandria on the east and Edku at the mouth of the Nile. There was the Mediterranean, breaking into sight again as it had when Captain Ben Wyatt, U.S.N., and I came out of the Spanish mountains in a little United States navy plane and saw the lovely blue of this quiet sea, smooth and clear, and as gentle as though there must always be peace. Now there were the same beautiful effects of sea, beach, and distance, the dazzling tracks of the sun's gold on the blue, the bands of vapor in the middle sky.

In the Koran the earth is firmly balanced in its place by the weight of mountains, the sky arched over it like a dome. The first test of the wisdom and power of Allah is demonstrated in the challenge to man to find a crack in this sky if he can. The heavens are launched in seven stories, the highest being the habitation of Allah, whose throne is sustained by winged animals. Shooting stars are pieces of stone thrown by angels at impure spirits. The Koran poses as coming from Allah the question for Judgment Day: "Where are my companions in the sky about whom you disputed?"

We started over the stringy fingers of the Nile, the close-woven irrigation ditches in the delta crossing each other and breaking off like tracks in a railroad yard.

"Our squadron is based on the shore, east of Alexandria," Valin said. "It is hard to find. They will give me a signal."

The Fighting French field was on a patch of salt bed, a neck of land near Rosetta, where another French visit had been good for the world. For this was the site where an earlier French officer, Boussard, had found the key to the decipherment of the ancient monuments of Egypt when he found the celebrated Rosetta stone.

Valin banked the plane. The motors' rhythm broke, cushioned us as we came in to land on the salt bed, close by the camouflaged hangars.

The commander had the full squadron lined up to receive the chief of the Fighting French Air Force. These were the thinning lines of French veterans who, ever since the fall of France, still fought for their country, their homes, and their people from salt beds or any other land that permitted their wheels to roll.

They were a grand crowd, some of them very young and looking frail and fidgety in their khaki shorts, their heavy shoes, their large sun helmets. One of them was so small it looked as though his helmet might extinguish him as the snuffer does a candle. Others were much older, and many were gray. Much had happened to these men. Much was happening to them every day.

From the opening attack on France until the armistice, these pilots had been combat fliers whose courage and initiative stirred French hearts as they had not been stirred since Guynemer.

Pulling together the remnants of shot-up squadrons, fighting from every kind of field, landing they never knew where or bailing out when they had to, they struck at the Germans in the sky day and night. They fought the Germans around the clock. Man for man, they fought them to a standstill. With the fall of France and the signing of the armistice, they did not surrender. They kept on fighting, took their planes out of France, flew from Lyon to Algiers. They didn't even have maps; they didn't have anything but battered-up ships, the gas that remained in the tanks, and a French will to fight. One and all, they were condemned to death by Vichy.

They did what millions of other heroic Frenchmen would like to have done had there been any way to do it. But how could others do so? The country was totally blocked, completely disorganized. There were no ships to take Frenchmen across the Mediterranean to Africa.

The so-called Reynaud-Churchill proposal to "retreat to north Africa," made in the complete demoralization of the Government's hectic pause in Bordeaux, was never feasible for the French Army as a whole or any substantial part of it. There was no escape.

Even if there had been ships available at the Mediterranean

ports for men and equipment and had the demoralized retreat been stopped and reorganized in some way, the *Luftwaffe* dominated the air. Hundreds upon hundreds of German planes would have bombed the vessels and men to the bottom of the sea.

It is too easy to talk about what an army should do, three thousand miles away. It is cruel, reckless, and unworthy to speak of the French as though they rolled over and played dead. The French were badly led, indescribably badly equipped. They failed to provide themselves with good government and good arms. I suppose whoever wishes to hold the French responsible for this may do so.

But it is a corrupt and dangerous thing to say that the French didn't even want to fight for their country. It suggests that the French people thought they could get along with the Germans. The French never thought this. They have recognized the German menace for centuries; they never had any illusions about Hitler. There were ruinous divisions in French politics, and both the Third International and the Nazi fifth column were terribly effective, but there was no revolt by the people of France against war.

The French had practically no Allied support in defense of the French nation. As described to me by Field Marshal the Viscount Gort himself, the commander who led the British Army, the British Expeditionary Force was heroic but pitiably small. There were only twelve British divisions in France, three of which were there only for training and were not equipped for the field. Astounding as it may seem, thousands of British soldiers who advanced into Belgium to meet the Germans did not even have rifles. A common chant in the ranks was: "If we see them, what'll we do? Throw rocks?"

There were seventy-three fewer British divisions in France in 1940 than in 1918. And instead of forty-two American divisions there were none.

Meeting the full and terrible force of the German enemy, striking blindly with what they had, the French fought and died in the most terrible tragedy of the war. The nation of imagination and culture, the people who had never enjoyed machines, met the robots. An agricultural nation of forty millions lost an armament race with a manufacturing nation of eighty.

Even so, the United States, Russia, no country in the spring of 1940, could have withstood the attack of the German Army on its border.

That anyone should stand at a safe distance and speak badly of the defeated, crushed French, pass judgment on them with the casualness and sophistication of detachment and find them unworthy, is an outrage against common decency. Any man who does not think well of the French soldier does not know the French soldier. Any man who says, "They should have done better," is speaking of the blind who were trapped in a burning asylum and of the wretched who have lost all but their souls.

There is much of this soul in the Alsace Squadron.

Valin, the commandant, and I went into the little shanty, the officer-pilots' mess. There was a bar at one end, with a few bottles of whisky and a little wine and some lemon soda and a large keg of beer.

A strongbox stood in a corner. It had a padlock and looked as though it should hold Spanish gold.

The commandant drew a key from his pocket, unlocked the rusty lock, lifted the heavy lid, and brought out some maps. He handled them as knowingly as a magician goes through a pack. He gave one to Valin, and Valin handed it to me.

We had some hot tea, a plate of beans, and a chopped salad. The intelligence officers talked rapidly to Valin, and he nodded his head in the quick fashion of a Frenchman who follows each word.

Three of us at a time took off from the salt-bed runway—eighteen planes all told. This was a fighter sweep entirely. The French had no bombers. The objective was combat with a Nazi interceptor squadron which came aloft regularly from their base in the German lines somewhere in the neighborhood of Fuka.

In a desert battle formation the leader weaves his plane, dips his wings constantly. It's a strange sight when you're behind him. He looks so uncertain, so fretful and vacillating. He looks as though he were trying to make up his mind to leave you. But he is not. His job is to keep you from getting lost yourself—from an enemy bullet. By flying higher than the rest and weaving like this, he serves as the squadron's rear lookout. Every fighter-plane cockpit is so low that the pilot is blind in the rear. A fighter is terribly vulnerable to sneak attack from behind. As the leader, too, cannot see the rear he weaves and dips his wings so that he can look out the side of the plane and see behind. By flying in front, where all pilots' eyes are on him, the leader can signal instantly when he spots danger. If he is shot down, a second plane changes formation and takes the leader's place at once.

We curved out over the Mediterranean and came in towards the desert behind the German lines, flying very high. Here was the war from the air.

The Nazi tanks and armored equipment below looked like beetles. The units in each group wheeled and turned as though controlled by a single string, like trick ponies in a circus ring who whirl about at the crack of the master's whip. Cone-like clouds of dust trailed behind them, white plumes which grew up from the ground and shaped themselves in funnels.

The R.A.F. air work was starting before the tank patrol action was joined. The air boys had about finished, for in the mix-up of contact between tanks no bombers could distinguish our units from the enemy's machines.

Infantry concentrations in dispersed strong spots scarred the desert like pockmarks, with moles here and there showing artillery. It's hard to hide anything out here.

Dead ahead some British light tanks were shooting up German "M.T." (motor transport), and white puffs on an escarpment showed they were getting anti-tank gunfire in exchange. I could see a group of tanks unengaged and moving forward on the extreme left, their red German identification paint blazing on their tails.

"Nazi Mark IV's," said Valin. "They're open for Bostons."

The collection looked like the Caribbean convoy in miniature. The outside tanks were protecting their own fuel, ammunition, and tank-repair trucks. Except for very short periods, they were helpless without their supporting equipment, and their first job was to keep from getting separated. This was a brigade on the move, trucks and German cars huddling around an armored control vehicle.

"I hope for the Bostons," my friend said. But you move fast in a two-engine fighter, very fast. We didn't see what happened, or whether anything happened at all. For the next thing I knew somebody was shooting.

We got some shrapnel in our left wing.

It's a strange thing, being shot at. Somehow you figure it won't hit you. The plane ahead or the plane in the rear. Someone on your left or on your right. The other fellow, yes. He may get it. But not you. Everybody feels that way. I know I did.

With shrapnel the thing you see is the hole. It just appears. You get a bump, like an air pocket. We got a hard bump. Then you see that the wing has holes. And then your breath comes a little quicker—at least mine came quicker—because there may be other holes. You may be on fire.

Valin put the ship up. The whole squadron went up, then it broke. And I heard him say, "This is it."

Valin's machine guns started before I saw the German planes. We were in a mess of Messerschmitt 109s. These Valin could fight. The 109-F's, now carrying two cannons, no. The first Messerschmitt I saw went under us like a bat under a hat. It was hard to believe he was as close as he was, or how he had disappeared in an instant. There's nothing pretty about a Messerschmitt when you see it like this. As we turned, Valin let go at another. Short stabs of bullets, tapped out like the bursts of a staccato horn. If the Nazi hit us we didn't feel it. And apparently we did not hit him. We were fairly high. We had the oxygen on now. Two planes were coming in together on the right. They dove, and then we were alone. I don't know where the Messerschmitts went; I could not see them. But suddenly I saw one of our planes fall. It was as fast as that. The dreadful sight. It is such a terrible thing to see the first smoke of this flaming death. You want to shout, "Look out! Look out! You're falling. Do something! Do something! You're on fire, you're falling!" But you just sit there in your straps.

No, war is not a triumphant thing. Death, twisted lives, the agony of blindness and of cruel wounds, these are the final realities of war. All else is far away.

It is cold and cunning death that triumphs in war; death alone here in the desert or in the jungles of Lake Chad, or in a herd; taking a man suddenly as his eyes grow cloudy and his chin drops, as his body strains against its harness and his arms quiver, alone in the sky.

In this sad way, high in the sky, the world's Great Age begins. And a man is gone who loved and wept and died. One man. It was his whole life, as it might be yours and mine. One man. The hand of death came too near him, the implement to kill him worked in full. He is lost, to everyone who loved him, and to the world. He will never see morning again, feel the warmth and vigor of life, write a note or sing a song, come home or talk with a friend. He has no hope, and any hope of this world in him is gone forever. He, one man, whoever he may be, might have changed this world had he lived.

It is easy to write about the problems of war. It is hard to see death, and to know that every care and purpose of life has vanished like the wreck of a dissolving dream. No, not like a dream, but in agony. This is a hero's death. But it is a dreadful thing, and it is the essence of war.

He is dying. Falling. He is on fire, his hands and face consumed in flames in a death more hideous than any prison executioner could finally supply to the worst criminal known on earth. One man, in the struggle as vast as the sky, and complex beyond all measure. Men in their prime, dying one by one.

That the great democracies of this world, England, France, and the United States, did not in a single instance become so fantastically strong at home that there could have been no deaths abroad is a profound and terrible indictment of their leaders.

It is not enough to say that they spoke well or had good thoughts. It is not enough if only one man, no more, dies alone in this sky who might have been saved. It is not enough to look ahead, now that war and death and agony are here, and not look back.

This war is a series of agonies, a Calvary, which we can only climb on bruised and aching knees. If our leaders would win our pardon they must turn towards Almighty God and bow their heads in everlasting prayer that they be forgiven for their share.

CHAPTER 21

Palestine, Syria, and the Jews

I FLEW TO PALESTINE and Syria in a British plane with Air Vice-Marshal Robert George of the R.A.F., British Air Attaché to Turkey. "Bobby" George, long a mainstay in the R.A.F. and for three years in charge of British air development in Turkey under the terms of the formal British-Turkey Military Alliance, had reached Cairo on his way back from England.

Sir Arthur Tedder arranged this last leg of my flight. "I'll send you through to the Turkish border," he said. "We can put you down at a place called Adana. It is an ancient town tucked away at the tip end of the eastern Mediterranean."

The Turks agreed to pick me up there in a Turkish plane for the trip over the mountains and into the interior to Ankara.

"Bobby George will meet you at the airport. He's a grand fellow. You'll like him immensely."

In the middle of the night, before leaving for the airport, I made a broadcast to the United States for the Blue Network and another for WJZ, New York, and a recording for Egyptian State Broadcasting, Ltd. Gilbert Sedbon of Reuters fixed it up so that I could get a little sleep in Manager Ronald Ferguson's office in the blacked-out studio, while the circuit was coming through for America. It was routed by way of the British Broadcasting System in London, and this can be a tedious performance, waiting for the clearances and contacts through Switzerland and the British Isles. These are the times to catch up on sleep.

I drove directly from the studio to the airport after I had finished the broadcast, just before dawn. It was a drizzly Sunday morning, but before the plane was ready to take off the sun came up, the weather cleared, and the desert sparkled on the outskirts of Cairo.

"We'll go first to Palestine," Air Vice-Marshal George told me. "We'll put in at the new Jerusalem base at Lydda."

We headed east over the waste of the Arabian Desert, reaching the Suez Canal in about half an hour. Nothing could look straighter than this man-made ditch, and nothing could look more artificial than the sight of a large seagoing ship moving through the desert. You can practically see the smoke being puffed out of the funnels by a stagehand, all but hear the creak of the rollers as someone in the wings jerks this piece of scenery along. On the lake south of Port Said live ships and dead ships clustered the water, concentrated there at the entrance to the passage through the desert.

One of the military problems of the Middle East is that there have been no bridges across the Suez Canal. British engineers were now building bridges across the ditch, and they were having a tough time doing it. Repeatedly, day after day, German planes dropped mines in the Suez Canal. They put down magnetic mines, such as they spawn in the shallow water of the North Sea. The British improvised their way of picking them up. Seines were pulled by camels on the banks, who also hauled a cart which carried the motor and electrical equipment which neutralizes the effect of magnetic mines.

This mine sweeping is a fairly continuous process in the Canal, but the magnetic mine is growing obsolete. A mine which is set off by sound waves under the water is now being used. It is adjusted to the sound waves from engines and propellers, and it explodes with great effect when the ship is near.

Along with this, the Nazis strafe the bridge-construction crews and dive-bomb the ships as they pass through the desert. Suez has seen much action. Port Said, like Malta, is one of the hot spots of the war, the special target of the Nazi planes based on Crete.

The Sinai Desert beyond the Canal, one of the most arid areas in the world, is simply an ocean of sand. There isn't an oasis, there isn't anything. Just rolling sand, billowy and white. We crossed this to the border of Palestine and into the better country around Beersheba.

Bobby George pointed into the distance. He was pointing to Jerusalem. In a few minutes we circled the city and landed at the United States Air Corps base at Lydda and asked Colonel Singleton if he would let us have breakfast.

A camel caravan plodded out of the desert, the strange, bleating animals tugging at their light ropes, their blanket-bound cargoes divided across their backs like twin balloons. They are a noisy collection, bleating and neighing, crunching their teeth with a strange, sidelong motion of their jaws, shuffling their curious feet, banging their water tins against their flanks as they lurch along.

A big Tauric camel can carry his corn ration for a month, but he uses up all the water he can haul in something like two weeks. These gaunt, balloon-kneed, grotesque animals were dusty and tired. So were their Arab leaders. Caravans travel, generally, at night—from two hours before sunset until two hours after dawn. They figure on covering about twenty miles. After a month or so on the way, the whole outfit had probably missed its sleep to finish the trip to Jerusalem—a month to cover a desert which our plane covered in two hours.

"What's that mark on each camel's neck?" I asked Bobby George.

"It's the *wasm*, their brand," he told me, "put on by each owner, always on the right side. The left is unlucky, you know, in Islam. You will never see a left-handed Moslem."

"Is it true that there are ninety-nine names for Allah?"

"Undoubtedly," Bobby answered.

"And only the camel knows the hundredth?"

"Undoubtedly."

Bobby George and I went from one end of Palestine to the other, across the lush lands that tantalized the early world, and along the shore.

We flew to Haifa and then into Syria; to Tyre and Sidon, to Damascus and Beirut. Fertile valleys and hills, as gentle and alluring as any area in the world, rich in loam and valley orchards, beautiful as the fertile lands of California between the San Bernardino range and the sea.

But this lovely land throbs with discontent, friction between Christians and Moslems, feuds between the Christian sects. The Catholic groups, unlike the Syrian people as a whole, look to France. The Protestant liberals of Beirut look only to the United States. Yet these Protestant liberals hate Zionism, and they are directly identified and in league with the anti-Semitic Mufti of Jerusalem and all that the Arab anti-Semitic program stands for.

The Free French, under General Catroux, declared Syria an independent republic on July 2, 1941. The British pressed this on the Free French, and the British received due credit for it, for the British knew that the Syrians as a whole are more friendly to Britain than to France. An independent Republic of Lebanon was recognized two months later.

The question of Syria is far from settled, however, and as late as September 1942, Sheik Tajeddine el Hassani, President of the Syrian Republic, denounced the fact that the United States had still not recognized this first new nation born of World War II. The restraint has been caused by the agitation of the Syrians themselves for a Greater Syria—another indication of how difficult it is "to make men free"; for frequently, when you make one set of men free they want to make their neighbors unfree. Frequently the world gains one freed man and at the same time loses another. The politicians always speak in terms of pluses, and this tragic fact is persistently ignored.

The Syrian program for a Greater Syria presents the objective of incorporating Palestine, Lebanon, Trans-Jordan, and Iraq.

"These are really our countries," say the Syrians. "We can rule them better, and they belong to us anyway. You tell us that we are able to rule ourselves. If we can rule ourselves, we can certainly rule the Arabs, and we will rule the Jews. In short, the program for a Greater Syria is important to us. We think that Britain and the United States should arm us well, give us what we need, and then let us take care of ourselves."

The Axis knows well this appeal, mixes into the problem with great zeal. The Grand Mufti of Jerusalem was brought to Berlin, feted on the red carpet. Mussolini took the title of "Protector of the Islamic World." Hitler forgot his non-Aryanism long enough to make a remarkable self-appointment over the radio for Arab ears.

He stood at the microphone in Berlin and proclaimed himself "Descendant of the Prophet."

Britain has been embarrassed because she has tried to live up to commitments which she should not have made. Following this, she has tried to be honest in one of the countless areas of the world where political honesty is impossible.

For example, Husein ibn-Ali, England's first friend there in World War I, had been very useful, very effective in the war in the Middle East. He was entitled to great consideration there in the peace because of the fighting he did on the ground.

But in the peace Husein decided to be a dominant power in the Middle East. He was so persistent that finally Britain had to get rid of him entirely. Britain divided the country and put forward two of his sons as independent kings. These sons pledged themselves against their father and against the fulfillment of their father's ambitions.

But Britain had also made promises to Husein's rival in the interest of wartime co-operation during World War I. Ibn-Saud had not turned a hand in the war; he simply waited on the side lines throughout the war, gaining promises and not committing himself. In the peace, however, he called on Britain to make good her wartime promises.

Ibn-Saud finally took over Husein's pro-British movement in the postwar wrangle and used it to maintain the balance of power in his own land. He buttressed himself with the movement which had helped England win the war, and in which he had no part, and then used that movement to bargain with the British so that he could advance himself.

Britain went out on the end of a limb for Husein. Then the British gave a saw to ibn-Saud. Ibn-Saud sawed it off.

In the same flavor, there is a real problem for the British, and the world, in Palestine. And of this much I am sure: Even as a problem, to say nothing of a solution, it is widely misunderstood.

It is the problem of peace between the Arabs and the Jews, for, bitter as anti-Semitism is in Germany, it is even more bitter in Palestine. Zionism presses the question and stimulates one of the most poignant dilemmas in the world.

The fundamental of the Zionist movement is the establishment of a Jewish state open to all Jews on their renunciation of national allegiances and the revival of Jewish nationhood.

Starting as the ancient longing of pious Jews to die in the Holy Land, Zionism has been pushed forward by the tragic events of the Hudson Tube Age and the unspeakable persecutions by the Nazis in Europe.

There was a brief flurry of political Zionism in World War I, stimulated by the participation of Jabotinsky's Jewish Legion in Allenby's conquest of Palestine. This upsurge was stimulated further by the Balfour declaration and then by the Palestine mandate.

Ironically enough, the United States specifically endorsed the Jewish provisions in this mandate while Woodrow Wilson was still alive and contrary to our stand on the League of Nations.

We endorsed them in the American-British mandate convention of 1924. It was this mandate which dismembered the Promised Land into Trans-Jordan and Palestine.

And since that day there has never been any rest in the struggle between the Zionist leaders in Palestine and the Arabs. For Palestine is the Arabs' country. It is deep in Allah's world. It is the land of the Arabs, not the land of the Jewish people. Arabs have always been in the majority there, and one of the most ancient tragedies is that Arabs have always bitterly hated the Jews.

In late years, as England and America and the rest of the world have sought to direct Jewish populations towards Palestine, according to the wishes of Zionism, the Arabs' resistance to this has been violent and unrelenting. The Arab Government fights any attempt to have Jews enter Palestine, claiming that Palestine is the Promised Land of the Jews only to the extent that the Jews promised it to themselves and that the Jews must go elsewhere because they don't want them in their country.

This attitude on the part of the Arabs, this pressing of so-called "prior rights" by the Arabs, is the basis for British difficulties in dealing with the Jewish question. And it is the deterrent on putting into practice a program of sending Jewish refugees to Palestine, which looks so logical and natural in the eyes of so many Americans thousands of miles away.

This bitter and ageless racial and religious hatred is at the bottom of the problem of arming the Jews and creating a Jewish army in Palestine to fight with the United Nations. The Arabs cite Allenby's promises made during the last war, the Balfour declaration, and the Palestine mandate itself, pointing further to its acceptance by the United States.

The Arabs don't want the English to arm the local Jews. "If you arm the Jews," say the Arabs, "you must arm us."

The British know that whether they arm either the local Arabs or the Palestine Jews, or if they arm them both, there will be a massacre in Palestine. They are afraid of this.

Inadvertently, American newspaper advertisements by the American Committee for a Jewish Army of Stateless and Palestinian Jews, calling on the British to arm the Jews in Palestine, serve to intensify the Near East difficulties and are read over the radio by the Germans into Arab ears throughout the Arabic world.

As everywhere in the world, the shrewd German theme plays on "the injustices of the British Empire." Its thesis is that greedy and sprawling Britain has failed to give freedom. It claims that England has betrayed the Arabs, not because the Arab politicians themselves created an impossible condition but because the British are not freedom-minded. (As though the Germans are!)

Twisting the picture by oversimplification, the Germans point to Palestine, "stolen from its rightful owners and delivered to the Jews." They link the future of the Arabs as free men to the withdrawal of Britain from control of the Arab world. They fail to say that the Arabs would then be easy pickings for the Greater Germany.

Britain has no definite solution to this problem. She has accepted responsibility for it by commitments to both the Jews and the Arabs and by her agreement with the League of Nations. In effect, Britain has supported the side of the Arab nationalists. It is difficult to see how she could have done otherwise.

Taking Palestine and Syria and the Jewish problem alone, how could anyone find better evidence of the problems of making all men free? Or, in the history of this, better evidence of the care and caution with which the United States must proceed in its promises to the world during World War II?

Instead of attempting to impress all foreigners with omnipotence, our government leaders should warn all foreigners that ultimately the people rule here. Had Woodrow Wilson done that his road would have been easier and there might have been some chance of America's support. Our present leaders' policy abroad features their own omnipotence. This is a tragic blunder. It springs first from vanity, and then from a misgauged estimate of necessity. It is leading directly to bad promises and false hopes.

The success of any new body for international conciliation which may emerge after this war will once more depend on the peace settlements from which it springs and in which it is grounded.

The danger to the body is in the quality of the settlements, and the danger to the settlements is in the quality of wartime promises. Nations, especially small nations, do not forget promises made to them during war. They make memorandums. They have the memorandums in their pockets at the first sign of peace.

The tragic failure of the League of Nations did not center in the League as a conciliatory body. It centered in the peace settlements which the League was obligated to enforce. No body, sitting in relation to those settlements and bound to them, could have succeeded. And the settlements *originated in wartime promises.*

This will be true again.

The danger is already rampant, and an honest recognition of such danger and a mending of our ways are the most productive things that Americans could do at this time towards a better peace in the future.

Actually, there is no Europe as such, in an operational sense, any more than there is an India, or a China. There are 400,000,000 people in Europe, divided into twenty-six races. The best you can say is that, viewed in terms of comprehensions, there are four Europes: (1) the economic, (2) the social, (3) the political, and (4) the military. Each is shot full of crosscurrents and contradictions, expanding and contracting in the pulsations of a changing age. Any one of these Europes, to say nothing of the problem as a whole, is enough to baffle any European. Yet American words and American pens are distributing promises everywhere.

The problems abroad are astronomical. They are far more confusing than the conditions symbolized by Hitler, Stalin, or the British Empire. They are the sum total of these conditions, and much more. On one hand they are historic, deep-rooted in the tensions between landlocked peoples and seafaring nations. On the other hand they are fluid and dynamic in the distortions of the Hudson Tube Age.

Unless we recognize the priority of Europe's own demands, we cannot honestly estimate our effectiveness at all. And unless we adjust our actions and moderate our voice to fit the facts, and unless our leaders have modesty enough to admit they are not omnipotent and, further, to display to foreign friends that there are limits to both American resources and world wisdom, we shall only meddle. We shall not serve. For our policy of exaggerated internationalism is as dangerous, foolhardy, and destructive as narrow isolationism.

As for fitting the facts, a few of these facts have emerged already.

The Swedes and Norwegians are convinced that, on Russian Foreign Minister Molotoff's trip to London, Foreign Secretary Eden was forced to promise Russia a free hand in the Baltic area after the war. If asked, could Eden have refused? The answer is that Russia did ask and England did refuse. There is no secret understanding on this point, and the truth is that Russia withdrew its demand with excellent good grace, through the intervention of a great American who should one day be widely acclaimed for this. Yet the matter worries millions of Scandinavians, and it certainly worries Swedish Prime Minister Per Albin Hansson and Foreign Minister Christian Gunther. For you can be very sure that if Russia wants the Baltic after the war England and the United States cannot stop her. Nor could we keep Russia from controlling the Dardanelles, which is what worries the Turks, the British, and the whole Moslem world.

Great Britain has certain "prior rights" in the Orient. England sees her future there. Chiang Kai-shek does not. And Russia does not approve of Chiang Kai-shek.

England's aims in China could be composed with Chiang Kai-shek's, but they are not yet Chiang Kai-shek's aims. Nor are Russia's aims England's aims, or Chiang Kai-shek's.

Russia wants to control the China coast and the West Pacific. From the Russian viewpoint, *this control is fundamental.* It is rooted in Russian policy, both internally and externally. Internally Russia's industrial area of northeast Asia is in the Buryat Basin, north of Blagovyeshchensk, for which there are vast plans for expansion. Externally, control of the China coast is the prime bulwark of defense against Japan.

Russia wants independent Soviet republics of Manchuria, Korea, Sinkiang, Ningsia, and Shensi, in northwestern China, whether Chiang Kai-shek likes it or not and whether Great Britain likes it or not.

The Poles want compensation in the Vilna and Lwów districts, as well as all of East Prussia and Danzig, West Prussia to the Oder, and Silesia as far as Breslau. The Polish Government in Exile is very outspoken about this.

The Czechs have already insisted on their pre-Munich frontiers, and, of course, the Poles oppose this. The Serbs in Yugoslavia are on record for that part of Bulgaria which contains elements of the Greek Orthodox Church. They admit that this would expel the Roman Catholic Croats, but the Serb-Croat bitterness is very old, and this is one of the reasons the Serbs in Yugoslavia are fighting on the side of the United Nations.

With victory over Italy, the Albanians wish Macedonia, and the Albanian Government in Exile is quarreling now with the

Greek Government in Exile over the matter. The Greeks not only refuse to surrender Macedonia, but they have entered claims for the Dodecanese Islands and Cyprus.

The stand that the Belgian Government in Exile once took in support of the blockade against food for Belgium caused such bitterness that these *émigré* spokesmen will probably be unable to return to Belgium after the war. One thing is certain: they will have no control whatever over postwar Belgian affairs. This is more or less true of all the governments in exile. The simple fact that they are not sharing the sufferings and humiliations within their countries has completely eliminated the home support behind their representation. This, combined with many original weaknesses among the *émigrés* themselves, plus such controversies as the Belgian one at home over wartime steps they have taken abroad, even now places England and America, who honestly and unselfishly sponsored these groups, in a very unfortunate position.

"Making the world free," "peace," "the community of nations," "the better world"—these words mean essentially an interweaving of *local* situations, each one full of local quirks, local prejudices, charged with ardors which date far back, and hemmed in by determinations which give no consideration whatever to the world as a whole.

What country's government does not owe its political life more to the emotional satisfaction of its people and their near-term prosperity than to their intellectuality?

Once you leave our shores, the only voices you ever hear speak about a Better World Order are either German, Japanese, or American. The American governmentalists in Washington have taken a strange bedfellow in the fundamental of their position. The world wants no New World Order, and if they were less vain they could understand this from the "foreigners'" viewpoint better than they do. They would see that whereas the world resents the German idea of world influence, to the point where it is repugnant to all free men, their own idea of excessive internationalism is also for other reasons unacceptable.

A remaking of human attitudes is taking place in this war. The

global concept, stimulated by the war itself and by the new idea
of the world's size in the Age of Air, is one of the basic developments of the war. It is one of the great generating thoughts in the
history of man, just as the place of the common man was one of the
most generating thoughts in the earlier day of the French Revolution.

But how could anything be more evident than that this process
must be slow and that to visualize it—or to promise it—overnight is
a great disservice to the world? This world will not be made free
for hundreds of years.

The development of freedom is itself a lopsided development,
just as is the development of civilization as a whole, and the off-
center elements within it which have made it lopsided have been
the very people who talk the most about it, the politicians and the
speechmakers themselves. For America's own social attitude in our
allies' colonies, mandates, and dominions is, in fact, building up vast
problems in these places, in the name of freedom.

Tying themselves to America's war effort in the colonies of our
allies, America's national socialists are already creating vast confusion and disturbance abroad. Their folly is working against every
solution which our allies may find for their own problems in their
own lands.

In support of stubborn schemes for America's Better World
Order, the credit and substance of our citizens are being expended
now and pledged for the future in the same irresponsible way which
made such a scandal of America's WPA.

Having, year in and year out, abused the sound principle of
emergency public works at home, having paid for raking in leaves
when we should have been raking in rubber, having built the largest group of government buildings in the world when we should
have been building planes, having bought votes and political power
and stimulated political machines throughout the United States,
these same determined men have now put boondoggling on a
global basis.

The professional officeholders put a good face on this operation
by limiting their description of it to the elementary needs for help,

with which no one would disagree. Everyone knows the value of limited public works. Everyone saw the shame of the boondoggling that grew out of it. Now, again, just as they did in the United States, these bureaucrats do not restrain their International WPA. They want to win some kind of "peace of plenty" with their scheme and build up a program by which various areas of the world will become as infatuated with them as local mayors and state governors were infatuated with their WPA. This is the way they kept power at home. This is the way they intend to obtain it abroad.

In principle, this is exactly the same as the Baldwin-Chamberlain policy of sanctions, which failed so miserably against Italy, against Spain, and in every place it was tried, and of which Mr. Churchill was a wise and brave critic.

We set wage scales for labor abroad which make it impossible for anyone else to hire a native man or woman wherever the American Boondoggling Corps operates. Naturally, the governments and local authorities in these distant communities, who have the long-term responsibility for peace and safety, are outraged by this performance. It is one of the most deep-seated cleavages among the governments of the United Nations.

I saw young men of the American Boondoggling Corps pay a native seven dollars a day for the rent of a jalopy. This man stayed drunk from the day he delivered the keys to that car until he went to jail for throwing a brick at the head of an American military policeman.

Anything may happen when the representatives of our various and sundry government agencies show up. Take Bolivia. One fourth of the world's tin is produced there. Tin is vital now, sorely needed in the United States as a war material and for canned goods. The Bolivian contingent of the American Boondoggling Corps has a program in Bolivia which has so much politics and so little economics that it is doubtful whether Bolivia's tin will not stay in Bolivia *for the balance of this war.*

Coffee bulges all Latin-American warehouses. Each coffee-producing country has been given a quota for export to the United States. The reason we did not get more coffee was not because there were not enough ships to bring more coffee. It was because no one in the Board of Economic Warfare, in which thousands upon thousands of people are employed in Washington, had gumption enough to authorize lifting the quota whenever an empty ship was in any port where the quota had been filled.

Meat abounds in Australia. Mutton and beef are stored there in vast supply, and as much more is present on the hoof, for the shipping lane to England, which was formerly the market for Australia's meat, has been struck by the Pacific war. Because of this, American meat is sent to England. But is there any shortage of ships between Australia and the United States? There is not. A large and constant flow of American vessels transport and maintain men and equipment in the Australian theater.

Everyone in America knows that meat is scarce here. And the global boondogglers should know that our ships come back from Australia without meat. Month after month they return, for the most part, empty. The reason is simple. The global boondogglers, planning the world, have not found time to take care of this. "We are a big institution," they will tell you wherever you encounter them abroad. The real answer? Global fixers, incompetent in fifty directions when you see them overseas, are easily incompetent in fifty-one.

With the exception of E. R. Stettinius' Lend-Lease (the only really well-run organization of the bunch, along with the few groups which the RFC has abroad), nobody can make head or tail out of the swarm of United States government employees. There is the same hodgepodge duplication of federal offices as in our own country, and those who man these offices are a mystery to the natives and to each other.

The boys of the American Boondoggling Corps conduct negotiations independent of our resident government officials; ambassadors or ministers, generals or admirals mean little to them. They will, and do, pay American cash to local politicians who are in opposition to the present governments of countries which are friendly to the United States. They put such opposition "leaders" on their payroll, slip them American currency, and stage various political vaudeville acts which the Corps boys have thought out overnight. If their idea runs counter to American policy and embarrasses the President or Prime Minister of the nation, as well as our ambassador, that is just too bad.

"This is a smart man's war," I heard one of them say. "We've got to be smart, plenty smart, with these foreigners. The thing to do is play along with both factions. You know, play both against the middle. Give the fellows on the outs some dough. Show them we're on their side too. You know how it is, *money talks*. The good old American greenback, that's the thing."

"What do you think of Steinhardt?" another impudent employee of the United States government asked me one day. "Has he got anything on the ball, or *do you think we ought to get rid of him?*" This sophisticated young whippersnapper was referring to the distinguished American Ambassador to Turkey, Laurence A. Steinhardt, who for ten years has spoken for his country so ably in Lima, Moscow, and Ankara, and done so at the sacrifice of his fortune and his health.

"Do you know Mr. Steinhardt?" I asked.

"No," he said, "but he's making it hard on the representative of the Office of War Information in Turkey, and I think he's got a hell of a lot of nerve. I'm for canning Steinhardt."

Nothing restrains the Boondoggling Corps. They are everywhere. Up in Labrador the Canadians and the Newfoundlanders are scared to death of these men. Why? Well, Newfoundland is a crown colony of Great Britain. It is not a province of the Dominion of Canada. Labrador is a part of Newfoundland. The Eskimos in Labrador have always lived by hunting and fishing, trapping for furs and seining for fish. In this way an Eskimo family earns eight or ten dollars per week. The work is productive, and the community life has always been peaceful. In came the American Boondogglers. They paid such high wages and so much for furs that, overnight, the income of the Eskimo family became eighty dollars per week. An Eskimo is an Eskimo. When he got as much in a day or so as he used to make in a month, he quit work. He didn't go trapping, he didn't go fishing, and he worked but a few days out of thirty. The supply of furs decreased at once, there was a famine of fish, and the work slowed down to a stop. To overcome this the American Boondogglers had an inspiration, based on inexperience and immature social theory. They boosted their own fur and fish prices and their wage scales. They ran the Eskimos' income to $120 per week!

That stopped all trapping, fishing, and work for sure. So they put the price down. And when they did that the Eskimos couldn't understand it. Serious dissatisfaction spread in Labrador, and this, combined with whisky, created serious unrest. So the American Boondoggling Corps turned to the local Newfoundland authorities to put the Eskimos in their place.

"They're out of hand," they said. "Control them. We're spending a lot of money here."

If you were the Mayor of Okkak, Labrador, or of St. John's, Newfoundland, or if you were the Governor of Newfoundland, how would you feel about that?

Or if you were an American trying to build an airport, doing everything on earth you could to erect shelters so that the motors of American planes would not freeze and conk out when American boys flew these planes on one of the most hazardous flights in the world, and you could get no Eskimo to lift a hammer, how would you feel?

"What will happen when the Americans leave?" thousands of local administrators are asking themselves, all the way from Bermuda to Sydney. Who would say that this is the path to peace in the world?

When our Western Task Force landed in north Africa the urban natives immediately began to short-change the American soldiers. This is as natural as anything can be and has happened to every tourist who has ever been in the bazaars of north Africa.

Anyone with the slightest experience should know that a native will sell a piece of ivory or some homemade gadget to another native or to an experienced resident at a fair price for the locality. The native merchant will get as much as he can from any stranger who steps off a boat. That is, of course, elementary. But the boys of the American Boondoggling Corps did not know that. They were perplexed and dismayed because the natives "switched elephants" on them, collected free all the free American goods they could, stored them up, and then sold them to each other or to the American soldiers of the Western Task Force.

The national socialists' plan of suddenly, and from a distance, socializing the world holds back our war effort mightily. It is not only fostering trouble in the war zones and aiding the enemy, but it creates new and vast problems for the peace.

This is not the right companion operation to the war in which the best youth of our country are fighting and dying all over the world. This is not the purpose of America, of you or of me. Nor is this the time further to weaken our life at home and such stability as remains in friendly nations overseas. This is not the time for anything but victory.

This is not the time to pay an American workman from St. Louis $1,000 a month to fix electric wires on the airfield at Accra while privates in the United States Army are paid $50 a month to hold his pliers. This is not the time to build immense bases such as we are building in Eritrea with an understanding that only union labor be sent abroad. This is not the time to play into the hands of labor racketeers who require that any skilled American civilian electrician working overtime in Algeria be paid more per month than four-star General Dwight Eisenhower himself is paid. This is not the time to patronize *any group*, and hardly the group of labor profiteers who caused this "arsenal of democracy" to waste one and a half million man-*days*, not man-hours, in jurisdictional strikes during the first twelve months *after* Pearl Harbor.

What would you think if you were an American soldier in north Africa or Eritrea? Would you say this is a fight for a better world? Would this look to you like a fight for freedom? How would you feel about our Better World Order? Well, that's the way the soldiers feel about it in Eritrea and everywhere else overseas where men stand in the uniforms of the United States Army or Navy.

They believe, and they are right in believing, that a great injustice is being done by our government in permitting labor extortion in this war. They have no patience with the political ambitions of the men who make this possible. They are determined to correct this when they get home. And as they hear bleatings over the radio on the question of maintaining morale, they want to know what the definition of morale is.

These men will return to our country bitter and mad. There will be a reckoning for all this performance, called for by these men and shown in the attitude of the United Nations towards America in the peace. That reckoning is coming.

It is our own fault.

CHAPTER 22

Atatürk Is Turkey

AIR VICE-MARSHAL GEORGE and I flew along the coast of Cyprus and across the Gulf of Alexandretta to land at Adana. This is the Turkish frontier post near the Turkish-Syrian border, scene of Prime Minister Churchill's meeting with President Inönü and Prime Minister Saracoglu when he detoured three thousand miles to talk with the Turkish leaders after his conference with President Roosevelt at Casablanca.

The British consul in Adana is G. H. Clarke, and he is the only European resident. We stayed at the Legation, remodeled from an old church, and there we learned that a diplomatic mail pouch which Bobby George expected to take on to Ankara as a king's messenger would be delayed.

The pouch from Teheran was aboard the Taurus Express, which runs from Bagdad to Ankara and Istanbul. The Taurus was seven hours late.

After it left Adana the train would certainly lose another seven hours in the winding passes of the Taurus Mountains, for the railroads of Turkey wind like snakes and the country is as mountainous as Colorado.

The social and political nature of Turkey starts and stops in the fact of its topography.

Fourteen million rugged people live here, populating its plateaus, tilling its valleys. The hills are under deep snow in winter and early spring, and the icy winds of Russia blow across unimpeded. The summer is hot, especially on the high plateau in the center of the country. Ankara is situated there.

By our start at dawn, our Turkish pilot of the Devlet Hava Yollari had us high in the passes of the Taurus Mountains by early light. This was not the season for snow, but the winds had carried the desert dust and deposited it in the clefts of the mountains, so that the jagged peaks had patches of white on them like the concrete water-slabs on the sides of the Rock of Gibraltar.

As the plane broke out of the passes we came to the central plateau of lovely Anatolia, Greek for "Sunrises."

Struggling north and across the waters of the Bosporus, early men carried the civilization of a developed world into the wilderness of the European peninsula. These plains were the pathway of immortal figures.

Here Priam had been King of Troy when the face of Helen launched a thousand ships. And here, dating far earlier than the Greek invasion, scientists find not crude stone hammers and crude pottery, but beautiful statues, costly jewelry, and ornamented vases unknown to the Greeks. For this land had been inhabited by a mysterious race, in many ways superior to the wild Greek tribes, for fully ten centuries before the Trojan War. The ruins in Turkey are so old that in the days of ancient Greece the Greeks themselves marveled at such antiquity.

Here was cut the Gordian knot. This was the land of Saul of Tarsus, and these were his mountains. And in these plains herds of Angora goats and flocks of storks stood where Tamerlane the Terrible had overwhelmed the Sultan Bayazid. Over these plains passed the armies of Alexander and of Pompey.

This was the heart of the Ottoman Empire, whose soldiers' campfires had lit the skies from the Piave River to the Persian Gulf, whose armies had hurled themselves at the gates of Vienna and conquered all of north Africa for 3,000 miles west, to the shores of Tripoli.

Here, 14,000 miles from my starting place, I was at the outbound end of my journey. Angora, now called Ankara, was under our wing. There were its scattered mosques and minarets—and the surprise of seeing one of the most modern cities in the world, deep in the Anatolian hills.

This capital and a friendly sun, many mountains and few rivers, rich lands and barren plateaus, ancient roots and the lengthened shadow of the nation's founder—these are the fundamentals of modern Turkey. For the New Turkey is a combination of geographic compactness and Mustafa Kemal.

Of all the great war figures and important postwar persons, the man who was ultimately called Kemal Atatürk is least known. *Yet his actions gave the world the first indication of German defeat in World War I.* And his nationalism cut a pattern for less honest men abroad. Later, the peace of postwar Europe quivered often under the impact of his purposes, and the effect of his life is one of the most dominant qualities in the Asiatic-European world today.

Mustafa Kemal defined the power of the compact over the sprawling.

He took his lessons from the failures of the sultans' Ottoman Empire and applied them by repudiating two thirds of the Ottoman Empire itself. Then he applied them again in successive order against Germany, Russia, France, Italy, and England with a genius that mocked the plans of each of these Great Powers alone and all together.

If Mustafa Kemal were alive today he would be sixty-three. He was born in Salonika, at the top of the Greek peninsula, in 1880. His father, Ali Riza, an Albanian customs officer, and his mother, Zubida, the daughter of a Turkish peasant, named him Mustafa. This is a common Turkish cognomen. He grew to have a bewildering variety of additional names, but one of the first came from one of his school friends, who, with pleasant courtesy, called him Kemal. In Turkish "Kemal" means "perfection." This is interesting, for at the Salonika school Mustafa Kemal was a problem. He was strong and willful, and at the age of twelve he muscled himself out of the school when he took it into his head to thrash his German teacher.

"I want to be a soldier," he said. And soldier he became.

Kemal entered the military school at Monastir and then went off to the Senior Military Academy at Istanbul. He never came home again. In 1905 he founded the secret society called "Vatan," which plotted for the overthrow of dull Abdul Hamid, the Red Sultan. Everyone hated that man. Gladstone denounced him for his atrocities against Armenians and for a list of things a mile long. The free world heaped condemnation on Abdul Hamid.

What stirred Kemal, however, was the prospect of a free Turkey cut loose from sultans, from the past, and from all complications of the nation's sprawling Ottoman Empire.

In spite of his training as a soldier, Kemal was thirty-one before he went to war. He fought in the Army against Italy in 1911, when Italy seized from the Ottoman Empire her north African base in Tripoli. The Ottoman Empire did badly, but Kemal did well. He showed first-class leadership, fought in the front lines with conspicuous bravery.

Kemal's record earned him a place on the combined German-Turkish General Staff in 1914. Over long years Germany had acquired economic domination of the Ottoman Empire, and this area of the Middle East was, as always, the most important southeastern milepost in the march of Pan-Germanism. It was the key then, as today, to the *Drang nach Osten* (the push to the East). It was the bridge of The World Island, the German Heartland.

The German-owned Berlin-to-Bagdad railway crossed Turkey. Germans infested every department of the Sublime Porte, the Sultan's Foreign Office. The Turkish Army was German-trained. The teachers in the few Turkish schools were supplied by Berlin.

Kemal wanted Turkey for the Turks. "Beware these strange Germans," he said. Many listened, but the time was not right.

Kemal was a colonel when war came, and a rival named Enver tried to shelve him. General Liman von Sanders, however, gave Kemal the rank of brigadier general, and he found himself at Gallipoli. When the British withdrew from this tragic campaign in 1915, Turkey cheered Kemal as "Savior of the Dardanelles."

Then and there, aged thirty-five, he earned the title of Pasha. The son of Albanian Riza was now Mustafa Kemal Pasha.

The German Expeditionary Army was being organized to serve with the Turks in the Near East. The Turks called their task army *Yilderim*. Like the word *"Blitz"* in German, it meant lightning in

Turkish. And as in all directions the Germans copied so many other things and originated so little, they got the army name *Blitz* from *Yilderim*. The Turks originated it at the time of Napoleon's campaign in Egypt.

The so-called combined German-Turkish General Staff maintained contact between this Turkish Army and the Turkish nation by a single officer, who was not a Turk. He was a German, and he held the rather abrupt German title of *Bevollmächtigter General Stabsoffizier des Türkischen General Quartiermeister beim Stabe Yilderim*. This officer was Franz von Papen.

The bloody attacks ordered by Von der Goltz, in which the Turks charged and died while German support stood still, and the one-sidedness of Von Falkenhayn's sacrifices of Turkish troops, infuriated all Turkey.

In protest, Mustafa Kemal Pasha resigned as a member of the so-called Combined General Staff and took an ordinary field command. This action stirred the country, put Kemal in the orbit of national politics, and had an effect on his political career similar to that on Calvin Coolidge's career of his settlement of the Boston police strike. It was his springboard into the national political pool.

After the armistice Enver fled to Germany. He was assassinated there a year later. Kemal stayed in Turkey, saw British warships holding the Bosporus, British troops occupying Constantinople and the fortifications of the Dardanelles, French soldiers in Istanbul, Italian infantry in Pera, mixed European troops guarding Turkey's railways and roads. Foreign soldiers held Kemal's Turkey. They were *policing* it. And, true to history, "policing" was failing in each of its purposes.

Kemal dedicated himself to throwing out the "policemen."

When the British segment of the policing forces insisted that the remnants of the Turkish Army in Anatolia, deep in the center of the country, be demobilized, Kemal saw his chance. Over British protest he had himself named Inspector General of the Northern Area and Governor General of the Eastern Provinces. This was a long title for one who was expected to disarm the tattered remnants of the old Army, and Kemal used it to better advantage than that.

He settled himself in Angora. The village was squalid and dilapidated, as dirty as any Arab camp and as dull as any place would be in the middle of the plains. There were no paved streets and, of course, no lighting or sewerage. Instead of the magnificent Ankara Palas and Belvu hotels which stand there now, there was not even a so-called *han*, which for travelers in Turkey was a whitewashed edifice with an open courtyard where caravan drivers would leave their mules or camels at night and sleep above them on platforms.

Instead of the splendid Ankara Numune Hastanesi, a great modern hospital with air-conditioned operating rooms, elaborate research staffs, fine laboratories, there wasn't a doctor. Instead of the broad boulevards with their beautiful shade trees, their traffic policemen on revolving platforms, their Diesel sprinkling trucks and modern regulations, there wasn't a paved street or a sidewalk. There was nothing in Angora but goats, Kemal, and his comrades.

Quietly and in disguise, leaders from other parts of Turkey came to him: Rauf Bey, Ismet Pasha, Ali Fuad, Adnan Bey. And Adnan Bey's wife, Adnan Edib, came too, and spoke for the women of Turkey, for she was the most important woman in Turkey, the old Empire's outstanding author, president of the Green Crescent, Turkey's Red Cross.

Kemal became the Messiah of a New Turkey. But it was not easy. Everyone wanted peace. The country was weary, racked with pain and suffering. Kemal spoke of war. He pled, argued, led his listeners to the heights, spoke clear words with the fire of one whose life was centered in "Turkey for the Turks."

At the direction of Lloyd George, the hated Greeks occupied Smyrna late in 1919, and Kemal struck. Acting with almost incredible energy, Kemal galvanized his guerrilla band into an army, equipped it by seizing the international police force's supply depots along the coast. As he did this with one hand he wrote a National Pact with the other, modeled on the statements in the American Declaration of Independence.

On this basis Kemal formed a revolutionary government in Angora in the name of the Grand National Assembly, announced it as the legally constituted government of Turkey, and proceeded, literally and actually, to throw the Greek section of the international police army into the sea.

The British, French, and Italian allies had supplied modern equipment to the Greek section of the international police, based at Smyrna. Their postwar program was to eliminate the insurgent Kemal once and for all. The Greek force advanced onto the Anatolian plains, straight for Angora. Kemal and his army of ex-guerrillas met them near by on the banks of the Sakarya River.

Observers from the international headquarters, British, French, and Italian generals, looked on in amazement. The Greeks were slaughtered in the Battle of Sakarya.

Sakarya made Atatürk an international figure in the military world. Then and there France forgot the policing idea and made a private treaty with him. She delivered Kemal equipment for 40,000 more of his ragged men.

Italy and Russia supplied additional arms on Kemal's word that he would return the equipment "when he had established peace in Turkey," i.e., thrown the "joint police" soldiers out.

But, after Sakarya, Kemal did nothing for months. It looked like a "phony" war.

On the anniversary of Sakarya, however, Atatürk let go. On the 26th of August 1922 he attacked Dumlu Punar, the center of the Greek position, and before sundown the Greek Army was cut in two. First he routed the left side, then he routed the right. The soldiers of the historic enemy of Turkey were pressed into the sea at Smyrna, and all Turkey was delirious in the name of Mustafa Kemal Pasha.

In fact, the Turks were so happy about this that they changed Mustafa's title once more. They called him Ghazi.

In the 469 years since Mohammed the Victorious had stormed the Dardanelles at the beginning of the Moslem Era, only three Turks had been called Ghazi, "the Conqueror." The first was Topal Osman Pasha, Conqueror at Plevna. The second was Mukhtar Pasha, the original Conqueror of the Greeks. The third was the son of Ali Riza, who had said, "I want to be a soldier."

At Çanakkale the Ghazi met the British "police." When word of the coming encounter at Çanakkale reached Paris, London, and the other capitals, hard on the heels of the complete defeat of the Greeks, the statesmen of Europe were in a dither. They weren't getting along with each other, and they wanted no showdown in Turkey.

Quick wires went to General Charles Harrington at Çanakkale. The Ghazi marched his troops through the British lines with arms reversed. He had cleared Turkey of the Greek police army. After the non-resistance at Çanakkale he could now clear Turkey of British, French, and Italians.

He did this without firing a shot. He devoured the famous Lausanne Conference, emerged as the only winner at a diplomatic table set to carve him and his country. The bird ate the feast.

Ismet Inönü, then Foreign Minister and now President of Turkey, sat at the table in Lausanne and ate Turkey's feast for the Ghazi.

The treaty which emerged, the Treaty of Lausanne, wiped out Turkey's mandates over Syria, Palestine, and what is now Iraq. The Ghazi did not want these. He wanted a Turkey he could defend. He wanted Turkey for the Turks, and Ismet Inönü traded beautifully on that point. Eastern Thrace was restored to Turkey, giving her European status with the European powers, although nine tenths of Turkey lies in Asia. Constantinople was returned to the Turks. The international police army was withdrawn, a hopeless jumble of confusion and intrigue, and a terrible liability to the general relations of each country which supplied it. To the jeers of the population, every foreign soldier left Turkey.

The Ghazi threw out the Armenians himself.

Promptly he changed the name of Constantinople to Istanbul, and, because it was too vulnerable and too close to Russia and the Germanized Balkans, he did not make it the capital of the New Turkey. He remained in Angora, made that village the capital, and changed its name to Ankara. Starting from scratch, he built the amazing modern buildings of his new land.

Imbrie, the American consul, had to live in a freight car for a year. There were only two restaurants serving any European food.

Ankara's main street was unpaved, rambled aimlessly on the gray, sun-baked plateau. The Grand National Assembly, a tottering adobe structure splashed with stucco, stood at the head of the street. The Ghazi was elected President of Turkey there. He was forty-two years old.

A new nation, new thoughts, new hopes, new buildings, new names—including still another, and final, new name for Mustafa Kemal Pasha: Kemal Atatürk. Atatürk—"Father of Turks."

"We wish to lend the co-operative spirit to our neighbors, but, after all these years of blood and suffering, *the fruit of our labors is not the common property of our neighbors.*

"The curse of the world is tyrants on one hand, and, on the other, the meddlers and politicians who make good-intentioned promises that cannot be kept."

So spoke Atatürk, twenty years ago.

CHAPTER 23

Marshal Chakmak Calls the Russian Turn

THE UNITED STATES ARMY AIR CORPS'S four Consolidated B-24 bombers, interned, stood in an orderly row on Ankara's airfield. They were undamaged when they made an emergency landing there after flying from Palestine to bomb Rumania's oil fields.

Turkish soldiers, living in tents pitched behind each bomber, patrolled these planes day and night. Everything the crafts carried remained safe, including the Norden bomb sights. The Turkish authorities removed these secret devices and locked them in a government vault, which could not be opened except in the presence of our Ambassador, Laurence A. Steinhardt, whose career in Russia and Turkey ranks with Mr. Winant's in London as the most successful in American wartime diplomacy.

The Turks gave the twenty-eight American airmen a hearty welcome from the minute they touched ground. Along with three Russian aviators and a South African R.A.F. flying officer, our fliers were installed in a schoolhouse Atatürk had built in a model farm community outside Ankara. The attractive building was immediately converted into an American barracks, and a spacious commissary and a dining room were added.

The Turks built tennis courts and a baseball diamond for the aviators' amusement, gave them free use of a fine swimming pool. Interestingly enough, this pool was designed like an outline map of Turkey. Shaded by a cluster of trees, the pool was a big feature in the fliers' daily life.

Ambassador Steinhardt and Mrs. Steinhardt were favorites with the fliers; they went to see them constantly, took them canned

American food delicacies, cigarettes, magazines, and as much else as the Embassy could supply.

The Turks gave these men the full run of Ankara. They came into town, went to the restaurants and movies, moved everywhere among Turkish, American, and English friends.

The Turks treated five interned German Air Force pilots the same way. Taking advantage of the Turks' liberal treatment, three of the five Germans skipped the country. The Turkish press and public were outraged over this abuse of Turkey's honest adherence to international law. The incident merely amplified the general feeling in Turkey, for the Turks simply do not like or trust Germans.

The reasons are basic. The Turks, especially the present Government, know the Germans only too well. President Ismet Inönü, Prime Minister Shukru Saracoglu, and Marshal Fevzi Chakmak, Chief of the Turkish General Staff, disciples of Atatürk, all witnessed the disastrous treatment of Turkey by Germany in World War I. They are steeped in the Atatürk tradition of distrust and dislike for their treacherous neighbors of the north. "Beware these strange Germans," Atatürk warned. Everything that has happened in Europe since he died in 1938 has confirmed the view implicit in his warning.

British and American initiative has capitalized on this honestly and well.

An example of British alertness occurred in the matter of an airplane-parts deal in which the Turks were bitterly disappointed by the Germans. The Turkish Air Force needed important replacement items for some Messerschmitt 109s, Heinkel 111 bombers, and several Dorniers previously purchased from Germany. A military mission went to Berlin to buy these parts, but, by necessity or policy, the Germans said no. The Turks left Berlin empty-handed and exceedingly annoyed.

Air Vice-Marshal George and Wing Commander J. B. Mackie got wind of this immediately on the return of the Turkish officers to Ankara. The British offered to supply the German parts to the Turks.

The able British Ambassador, Sir Hughe Knatchbull-Hugessen,

approved the plan, and cables went out from the Embassy. Within thirty days the British made the important shipment by gathering together the needed parts from Messerschmitts, Heinkels, and Dorniers which the R.A.F. had shot down over England and over the Western Desert, and from German planes found hidden in Syria when Syria was seized from Vichy France.

To offset the good impression of this, the Germans asked the Turkish mission to return to Berlin. The *Luftwaffe* chiefs offered the Turks an immediate shipment of the latest German bombers and fighters. This sudden turn was without precedent in Europe, for the planes were not the regular Messerschmitt 109s or 110s. They were the famous 109-Fs, the very effective Junkers U-88s, and Focke-Wulf 190s.

The Germans proposed an initial delivery of twelve planes of each type. This offer was communicated to Marshal Chakmak and his war council in Ankara. The offer was not accepted by the experienced Turks, however, because it contained a proviso that the planes be accompanied by German technicians. Marshal Chakmak and Shukru Saracoglu knew that such an apparently sensible provision would be only the forerunner of a flood of German technicians entering Turkey.

It was in this atmosphere, and during the time of this decision, that I reached the headquarters of the Turkish General Staff—the Genel Kurmay Başkani.

The headquarters building, flying an immense Star and Crescent of the Republic, stands on a high hill. Floodlights illuminate the approach to this modern citadel. Long flights of stone steps rise in stages to a chain barrier, flanked by two bombproof sentry houses. Guards pace the barrier, heavily armed, stiff and menacing, the red spot of the Turkish crescent brightening the sides of their helmets. They are sullen-looking and menacing until they are satisfied with your pass, and then they smile in the sudden way that so many Turks have in showing their friendliness and their desire to help.

The entrance to the building itself is guarded by four sentries who stand between two Trafalgar-like bronze lions. Other guards stand at the wide doors, which lead to a granite corridor. More guards bar the way up a wide marble staircase to the second-floor office of the chief of the Turkish General Staff.

I first heard of Marshal Fevzi Chakmak from Sir John Dill, then chief of the Imperial General Staff in London and now military representative of Prime Minister Churchill in the United States.

"He is one of the best strategists in Europe," Sir John told me. I heard the same thing from Lord Gort in Gibraltar, and from Colonel Bernadotte in Sweden. I even heard it from the German military people in Berlin.

Marshal Chakmak is square-built, tough, a heavy man whose eyebrows and general physique give him somewhat the appearance of John L. Lewis. When I told him this he laughed, and I was interested to see that he knew not only about John L. Lewis in America but Joe Louis as well. "I understand they both fight," he said with a chuckle. Very little the world over escapes these Turks.

Gruff and able Marshal Chakmak was hard put to find a way to refuse the German plane offer. He and his government did not want the German technicians in Turkey, and, as the Germans were asking for an answer in a hurry, the matter finally resulted in a blunt "no."

To offset any threat from the Germans in the Caucasus, Marshal Chakmak was in the midst of the most important troop movement in modern Turkey's history when I reached the Genel Kurmay Başkani. He was transferring Turkey's main army from the Bulgarian frontier and the Dardanelles to Turkey's eastern border on the edge of the Caucasus. He was arranging his forces, day and night, seven hundred miles across the entire width of the country to a position opposite Batum and stretching south on the ridges of the mountains. This difficult and expensive operation was accomplished under the direction of Chakmak's right-hand man, General Kâzim Orbay, Commander of the Army of Anatolia, with headquarters at Erzerum.

Turkish Army Intelligence established that practically no German troops remained in Bulgaria, that they had left Turkey's northern border, the "front door to Turkey." Russian General Gregory Zhukov confirmed this. The few divisions on the Bulgarian-Turkish border had been sent to Russia and engaged in the battle for Stalingrad.

By deploying his troops away from eastern Thrace, the little patch of Turkey on the European side of the Dardanelles, about the size of Rhode Island, where hundreds of thousands of Turkish soldiers had stood for over a year, and by placing these troops on the opposite front, Marshal Chakmak was guarding free Turkey against German attack from the Caucasus.

But in any case, could Turkey fight? Yes, and better than we suppose. The Turks are tough. They have always been tough: Lowell Thomas once told me that Lawrence of Arabia called the Turks "the best natural fighters in the world."

They had 750,000 regulars fully mobilized and in the field. These were good troops, well trained, well led. They had 150,000 irregulars who were now prepared for, and would be very effective in, guerrilla warfare. These were formed in local companies, known as *Chetes*, which is the Turkish name for Commandos. They needed more British and American artillery, but what they had was good. They were weak on tanks, but their terrain helps them, for Turkey's mountains and lack of roads for motor transport disqualify mechanized equipment.

Turkey had 250 first-class operational aircraft, 400 more not good enough to fight the *Luftwaffe*. But Turkey is England's formal ally, and under this alliance the British have built magnificent airfields throughout Turkey. If Turkey is attacked the British have agreed to send onto these fields complete operational units of the R.A.F.—planes, personnel, organizations, and all. Tedder's R.A.F. is prepared to fight in co-operation with Marshal Chakmak's army the moment that Prime Minister Shukru Saracoglu calls for aid from Winston Churchill. That was settled, once and for all, at Winston Churchill's and Marshal Tedder's meeting with President Inönü, Prime Minister Saracoglu, and Marshal Chakmak at Adana after Churchill left President Roosevelt at Casablanca.

Regarding Russia's military position in relation to Germany, Marshal Chakmak and his staff, who have so frequently been better informed than England or the United States on immediate Russian matters, were not at all nervous over the apparent German successes in the Caucasus which thundered in the headlines of the world. This was reflected in a dispatch I sent from Ankara on July 29, as Hitler announced that Stalingrad would fall, and which appeared on July 30 in the New York *Times* and the other papers owning the North American Newspaper Alliance:

The highest military quarters in Turkey are not nervous over the apparent German successes on the Don River and Black Sea fronts.

They have received with special satisfaction word that Joseph Stalin has gone from Moscow to Stalingrad, Volga River industrial center, and has arrived there safely at this important hour.

They feel that Russia has held the most important point for her to hold, namely, Voronezh, at the junction of the Don and Voronezh rivers, a railhead of first importance.

The Turkish estimate is that Marshal Timoshenko has large Soviet armies concentrated northwest of Voronezh. These troops, say the Turks, have been there a long time and have not yet been engaged in battle. As Hitler's hordes batter their way eastward through the area south of Voronezh, over flat country but without highways or railroads, the German Army will find itself wearily stretched into Russia for a thousand miles.

These important Turkish quarters believe that then Hitler's army will be extremely vulnerable and that Timoshenko's Voronezh armies will drop straight down on them from the north. The Turks see great promise in this possibility if the Russians' withering descent on the German position is timed with and accompanied by the opening of a second front elsewhere in Europe.

"We believe that at the right moment this descent from the north could be decisive on the whole war," said my chief informant.

Gruff, able, tough-minded Marshal Fevzi Chakmak called the turn. He knew his business.

Realizing that Turkey's aim was to stay out of the war, however, in a final showdown would Turkey come to terms with the Germans as an alternative to bloodshed and possible defeat? Or would Turkey fight Germany?

This was a question for Prime Minister Shukru Saracoglu, and this was the question I flew from New York to Ankara to ask the

Turkish Government. The Prime Minister received me in his office
on the second floor of the Presidency, a modernistic, imposing
structure commanding a sweeping view of Ankara's handsome
buildings and the lovely Anatolian hills.

The Turk is fundamentally an Asiatic. It is difficult to get a
direct yes or no. But, like Atatürk himself, Saracoglu personifies
the New Turkey and a new kind of Turk. When His Excellency
Shukru Saracoglu moves about Ankara he is greeted by foreigners
and countrymen alike who know him as an excellent Turk and
respect him for his integrity and his appreciation of the common
man. This gives Saracoglu great strength in the tense hours of
Turkey's national life. His roots are in the people, and the people's
roots are in him.

Anyone would like this man. I was prepared to like him, and I
liked him the minute I saw him. Saracoglu is stocky, his frame is
heavy, and he fills his armchair with a solid bulk. He has broad
shoulders and powerful, stubby hands which give you the impression of physical strength. Yet he is rather pale, and he has an intellectual, sensitive face. Its heavy lines only give it balance and
character, instead of a look of age and care. Saracoglu has a sober
expression until suddenly he smiles and you see that he has humor
and a quick sense of life. He has thin-growing hair above a high
forehead, and, although he wears tortoise-shell glasses, his alert
brown eyes have seen much in Europe that others have missed.

Shukru Saracoglu was born fifty years ago in the remote village
of Ödemiş, near Smyrna. He was one of several children in an
ordinary peasant family. At the turn of this century for a poor
country boy in Turkey to show any interest in going to school was
amazing enough, but for him to wish to go to a university and then
to devote himself to obtaining a scholarship for a university in
Switzerland was nothing short of miraculous.

Under difficulties which we in America can hardly visualize,
young Saracoglu sought the European world, left Ödemiş for
Istanbul with his father in a horse cart, worked his way on foot
across the Balkans to Switzerland, and entered the University of
Geneva.

There he studied economics and political economy, world litera-ture, and the Romance languages, especially French. He was gradu-ated with honors, and with the burning desire to help his people towards the fuller life he had seen.

As Saracoglu prepared to come home in 1919, British, Italian, Greek, and Senegalese soldiers of the international forces policed his land. Two sounds greeted this robust intellectual on his return: the metallic thud of the dreaded foreign boots and the voice of Atatürk.

Then and there, under the impact of these bayonet flashes and the ineffectiveness of Sultan Mehmet Reshad, Saracoglu's formative nature crystallized.

Saracoglu joined Atatürk's budding movement at once. Known as the Milli Mücadele (The National Struggle), this movement was the forerunner of the Peoples' Republican National party, which Atatürk, Ismet Inönü, Refik Saydam, Saracoglu, and other early patriots did not form until 1928.

Saracoglu married, took his young and beautiful wife from her home in Istanbul to the wilds of Anatolia, and fathered two chil-dren. "This marriage and these children have been the blessing of my life," he told me.

Turkish policy was made at Atatürk's dinner table, and far into the night, in the little stone house. Atatürk relaxed with Saracoglu, and hearty, cheerful Saracoglu did not fawn on Turkey's Great Man, on Inönü or Saydam or anyone else. Naturalness was one of Atatürk's strengths, and it is Saracoglu's. There was a deep affection between these two men.

Inönü emerged from the critical Lausanne Conference an impor-tant figure in European politics, and, although Saracoglu had re-mained in Ankara, he shared in this diplomatic triumph.

When the great Atatürk died in 1938, Ismet Inönü followed him as President of Turkey. Saracoglu succeeded Inönü as Foreign Minister.

Turkish foreign affairs were very cloudy. Storms were rumbling on several sides, blowing hard on the water approaches to Turkey, threatening her vital interests and her life lines to the rest of the world. Mussolini was speaking again of the Mediterranean as *Mare Nostrum*, while Russia revived her historic claims to the Dardanelles.

Shukru Saracoglu overcame these complications with the Great Powers and emerged from these difficulties onto the world stage an important and respected statesman.

When France fell he and his government brightened the tarnished luster of European engagements by immediately notifying the British that this in no way diluted Turkey's responsibilities to England under the fifteen-year Franco-British-Turkish military alliance. Again, when Hitler asked for the passage of German troops through Turkey to the Caucasus, Turkey mobilized. Turkey was within an inch of going to war. But German soldiers stood still, did not cross the Bulgarian border into European Thrace. Hitler described this act, with typical irony, as "an assurance of good will."

At the time of the famous Clodius Trade Agreement, Saracoglu recommended that the Nazis obtain none of Turkey's priceless armament chrome, the thing they really wanted, earlier than January 1, 1943. Clodius stormed, Von Papen went back to Berlin. But he returned, smiling and suave, with a personal "letter of friendship" from his *Führer*. Clodius then signed the agreement without the chrome.

Now it was as Prime Minister of Turkey that Ödemiş's famous son, Geneva's brilliant scholar, Atatürk's fiery disciple in the National Struggle, and the United Nations' good friend in World War II served his country and guarded its place in the fiery world.

"You have come a long way," he said. "I understand you have come fourteen thousand miles by air." He motioned me over to a globe standing in a far corner of the room. "Show me how you came."

I traced the route for the Prime Minister, who interrupted to ask how it seemed to be flying the Atlantic, whether I had seen any big game from the air in central Africa, each detail of my voyage.

"That is an adventure I should like to have myself someday," he said, "and I envy, too, your trip to Finland."

We talked of Russia and Germany, for Turkey and her Dardanelles are caught between these two great powers. We talked of Palestine and Egypt. "No one will ever solve the problem in Palestine," he said. "There is no solving of some problems among men, and the problem of the Jew and the Arab is of that kind. So is the so-called problem in India. These are not so much problems as they are what you might call *conditions of life*. There is no single fault, although today many seem to feel that they can undo the conflicts of blood-bitterness and history by an arbitrary program of 'equality,' which is really not equality at all and which is so distasteful to other 'superior' millions that the result is only chaos and revolt."

We had moved over to a coffee table near his office balcony overlooking the hills, and, with typical Turkish courtesy, he had offered me the rich brew of his country.

"It is a mistake to view this war as anything but a catastrophe for Turkey, as was the last war. It is indescribably difficult for this country to maintain itself and survive, *and Turkey's policy is to remain neutral, if possible, and stay out of the war.*

"For those who live a great distance away it is difficult to realize the terrible problems confronting such a country as ours, enmeshed in a belligerent area. Our home industry, which we have tried so hard to develop since the founding of the New Turkey, has suffered grievously from our mobilization of so many workers consistently under arms and not producing. These represent nearly fifteen per cent of our entire male population. International commerce, on which so many of our Turkish people depend, has been disrupted in all cases and in some cases completely paralyzed.

"In spite of the commercial treaty and the specific trade pact concluded here for Germany by Dr. Karl Clodius, in the autumn of 1941, the German Reich has been unable or unwilling to keep up deliveries and has fallen down on its promises. The pact, creating considerable alarm in England, Russia, and the United States, provided for the exchange of goods valued at forty-five million Turkish pounds. Among other things, the Germans agreed to buy our tobacco, copper, grain, and tanning materials, while we were to receive badly needed spare parts for German equipment previously installed, electrical and farm machinery, and some war materials, including planes, tanks, and anti-tank guns.

"There has been little performance in the German promises, and we have not and will not export our materials to Germany until we receive German imports. The Germans offer explanations for this non-performance, but the result still stands. Before this war Germany controlled more than sixty per cent of Turkey's foreign trade. Today this figure is less than fifteen per cent." The Prime Minister looked out over the hills and began to smile.

"I'll tell you a story Stalin told me in Moscow," he said. "It's a little complicated, but it goes like this: A German soldier returned to Berlin from the Russian front with a slight wound and went to a hospital. Inside he found two doors, one marked OFFICERS, the other TROOPS. He went through the door marked TROOPS. Inside he found two more doors, one marked SERIOUSLY WOUNDED, the other SLIGHTLY WOUNDED.

"He went in the door labeled SLIGHTLY WOUNDED and found two more doors, one marked PARTY MEMBERS, the other NOT PARTY MEMBERS. He went through the NOT PARTY MEMBERS door—and found himself out on the street. When the soldier returned home his wife asked him what the hospital had done for him. 'Nothing,' he replied, 'but the organization was perfect.'"

I asked the Prime Minister whether he would give Turkey's official answer to the question of whether or not Turkey would take the leap and, if attacked, fight Germany. It was not a question on which the Prime Minister could be expected to make a public statement at such a moment, but he did so. The Prime Minister answered it for all whose eyes were on Turkey and the Middle East when he gave me the first interview he had granted in that capacity to any Axis or United Nations journalist. Later he approved the statement and authorized me to publish it.

Meanwhile, I had a little bad luck.

CHAPTER 24

The German Underground and Saracoglu

I FOUND that as my dispatches to the North American Newspaper Alliance appeared in the American papers a synopsis of each was wirelessed back to Von Papen from the United States by way of South America and Berlin. He had each text at once.

The German Embassy in Ankara questioned the Turkish Government as to why three of these dispatches were permitted. Each, of course, had been approved by the Turkish Government before it was released. That was the answer the Germans received, and nothing more.

The Germans do this kind of thing, go through such motions, all the time. Every American and British newspaperman in a neutral country abroad is used to it. At the same time, however, somebody in Berlin told the German Gestapo in Turkey to pick me up and start in again on the little pre-Pearl Harbor game of tag which they had been playing with me in various parts of Europe. The Germans had found I was trying to make arrangements to get into Nazi-occupied Yugoslavia. They can be entirely too good at finding out this sort of thing, as well I knew. I think I know where the leak occurred, but I am not sure.

I wanted to see General Draza Mihailovich in his mountains. I wanted to see him very badly. It was not far. People are put onto the Yugoslav mainland from a place outside by plane and by submarine. They are met there and passed on from hand to hand through the country. They are taken out again from a rendezvous.

The operation has to tick just right as to time and place and contact points for any safety behind the German lines. This all takes a good deal of arranging. Further, the setup inside the German lines is complicated.

The Germans have worked out some very clever decoy arrangements against your getting in, and especially against anyone's getting out. Also, the Germans keep changing their patrols and wire-barricade systems. When they are changed between the time you go in and the time you try to get out it is just too bad.

But it can be done, and I was in the process of arranging it when I found myself in the Ankara Numune Hastanesi, the Turkish National Hospital. I had malignant malaria.

This type of malaria has a long period of incubation before it strikes, and apparently I had been bitten by the right mosquito when I was in French Equatorial Africa. At Lake Chad General Valin had told me that there were several cases. Malignant malaria is out of the ordinary, and there is little malaria of any kind in Turkey.

I took seven injections before I started this trip. As I had been injected against tetanus recently, when I went to Finland, I did not need to duplicate that, but I was injected against yellow fever, typhoid, paratyphoid, typhus, cholera, and smallpox. There is no injection against malaria.

Quinine is on every barracks mess table in such places as the Lake Chad area, and you take five grains a day. But quinine is only a conditioner. It eases the attack, and its concentrated application is the chief cure, but it is not a preventative. You can swallow quinine until your heart's action makes your ears ring like bells, but if the carrier mosquito makes his stab you get malaria. And if the one-in-fifty carrier is carrying malignant malaria you get malignant malaria. That is not good luck.

I had a bad time with it, the only time in my life that I was ever dreadfully ill, for this is the type which needs a quick and able doctor right away.

Turkish Dr. Salahi Durusoy, with his special knowledge gained in Istanbul and Paris, was quick and able. Very quick, very able, and very kind. He told me the truth, which is not easy to get from a doctor when you are that sick. And he saved my life. Russian nurse Euginye Popva, whom Ambassador Steinhardt called from Dr. Shepherd's American Hospital in Istanbul, was marvelous. I was out of the delirium on the fourth day, then out of the coma that followed, and after seventeen days Dr. Durusoy told me I could leave the hospital.

The day before I moved out of the hospital the Germans moved in on me.

"Two gentlemen and a lady are here to see you," Miss Popva told me. "They are at the reception desk. It is difficult for the old man down there to get their message. But they say it is urgent that they see you."

There were no room phones in the hospital. I asked Miss Popva to bring up the visitors. Ray Brock, Ankara correspondent of the New York *Times*, had asked me to carry back to the United States a copy of the manuscript of the book on which he worked so long, *Nor Any Victory*, and Hart Preston was giving me a bundle of photographs for *Life* magazine. I expected Ray and Hart about that time.

The two men who walked through the door were not my friends. They were Germans. I couldn't have told whether the woman was German or not. She was rather attractive, well dressed, but I thought she was a little fidgety. I thought she blinked her eyes a good deal and seemed to fuss with her hair. Her nails were long and crimson red, and that is a little unusual now in Europe.

The men presented no cards, didn't speak their names clearly, simply smiled as pleasantly as you please and walked over to my bed. One was tall, clean-shaven, erect. He was thin-faced, angular, but his ears stuck out and were noticeable. I knew he was in the German Army from the way he carried his cane. The other man was of medium height, portly, and considerably older—about sixty— round-faced, heavy-necked, a well-fed burgher. He wore congress gaiters, such as my grandfather used to wear.

The elderly man spoke to me at once.

"You have been very unfortunate, Mr. Taylor. We hope you are well now."

"Thank you, I'm feeling much better."

"This is a pleasant room," the lady observed.

"Yes, I have been very comfortable here. The doctors are grand, and Miss Popva is a great help."

"We have come at the suggestion of mutual friends," the portly man said.

"Well, that's fine. Who?"

The woman glanced at the nurse. I asked Miss Popva to leave the room.

"Who did you say suggested you see me?" I asked.

The tall man stated the names of two prominent industrialists in Germany, non-Nazis. I hardly knew either of them, had only the slightest acquaintance with them, and I imagine they were not involved in the matter at all.

"We bring you their compliments."

"How did they know I was here?"

"There was mention in a DNB dispatch of your arrival and illness."

"Have you been in Berlin lately?" I asked.

"We have just left Berlin," the portly man said, as though he were saying that he had just descended from heaven. He kept nodding his head up and down and smiling, fingering a heavy gold chain.

"You plan returning to the United States?" he asked.

"I am on a round trip, to Turkey and back. This spell in the hospital makes me already overdue in the United States. Why?"

The tall man came close to the head of my bed, smiled warmly. "We are German patriots," he said.

"We believe you would like to get into Yugoslavia," the woman said, as easily as you would say "Reading, Pennsylvania."

So that was it. There had been a leak, all right.

"Yugoslavia? It isn't very healthy for an American to go to Yugoslavia. What made you think I wanted to go to Yugoslavia?"

"You would like to see General Mihailovich. You should not go with Colonel Radoyichitch. You must depend on the German underground."

I had not intended to go with the Yugoslav they mentioned.

Lieutenant Colonel Zhivoyin Radoyichitch, of the Yugoslav Army, had been flying supplies to General Mihailovich from the United Nations base in Egypt. I knew he had been spotted by the Germans. So did the colonel. He had stopped his trips.

"Are you in the German underground?" I asked.

"We are patriots," said the army man. "We are in the German underground."

"Well, that's fine. How are you going to put me in? I hadn't expected to meet you here, you know. What is the plan?"

The woman broke in: "We are your friends. We stand to help you. It is our way in the hope that on your return to America you will explain better the force of the German underground movement."

"I would like to do that, but whom do you deal with in America?"

"It is difficult to go into that now," said the portly man.

"I don't know why it should be private," I said. "If your German friends in America, like the rest of the Germans there, are against Germany in the war, they are certainly not under cover. Everybody wants to help the German underground."

"The situation is so complicated," she said, a distressed look on her face and a little pout on her lips, like Dieckhoff's pout when he sat at his desk in Ribbentrop's suite and spoke of America's coming into the war.

The tall man unbuttoned his suit coat, produced a square envelope from his pocket, gray and unprinted. He turned it over in his hand slowly and then drew out a piece of very light paper. He held it so I could see it. He looked at it as he spoke to me. So did the other two. So did I.

"This is your pass," he said. "It will take you in through Greece."

When I saw that paper, printed in German, some strange name inked in at the top but my photograph fixed in an upper corner, the whole thing plastered with the ugly black eagles of the German Reich, I thought it was all so childish that I nearly smiled. But you get a strange feeling. You get a little sensitive about things like this when you travel abroad.

"Where did you get this picture?" I asked.

The woman was always ready with an answer: "There were extra photographs attached to the entrance visa you filed at Ankara," she said.

They did not get that picture in Ankara. It came from the Gestapo in Berlin. It was taken in Washington, D. C., one of three dozen I carried on my previous trip. These were used as I went along. Going in and out of eight or nine European countries, you can use a lot of visa pictures these days. I used eight in and out of Germany.

When I started off again I had the photograph shop on Pennsylvania Avenue make additional prints from the negative. This lot came out of the developer lighter than the first. The picture on the paper in the German's hand, just my face showing, was one of the darker pictures. The Gestapo in Berlin had taken it from the visa I had to file there on my last visit. Berlin Gestapo headquarters had sent this "pass" to Ankara. These three people, of course, had no connection whatever with the German underground. Just the reverse. They were members of the German Gestapo in Turkey.

"We have arranged your transportation, but only for late tonight," I heard the tall man say. "You will go by car and boat if you are ready now." The same little difference came into his voice that comes into so many Germans' voices when they tell you what to do, that shade of something official that comes out when they direct anyone.

"All is prepared," he continued. "We are ready to escort you now as far as Izmir and turn you over to the captain of our little boat there. He will sail by dark tonight."

The woman broke in. "He is a good man, has made the trip often. He will put you ashore at Salonika tomorrow, and you will be on your way." She blinked her eyes merrily, smiled as sweetly as a cherub. "What an occasion! You will reach General Mihailovich at once."

"Our friends will meet you at the Salonika pierhead," the portly man said. "You will receive aid and directions there."

"But I'm leaving for the United States tomorrow," I said. "All arrangements have been made. Everyone has been very kind. I have to travel to America flat on my back. I'm going in a Turkish plane as far as the border. I'm going on to Cairo in a British plane, and then I'll start across Africa the next morning. I have to fly each day, something like ten days at fourteen hundred miles a day, and this means a lot of connections on both sides of the Atlantic. It's going to be a complicated trip on a cot."

The woman broke in again. She never sat back in her chair, always perched forward on the edge and ready to say something. "Relying on you not to discuss this, we have come as we have," she said, "in the hope that such an opportunity to you as a journalist would cause you to change your plans."

It did not seem possible that they intended to keep up this foolishness. But the Germans are strange people. And although I didn't feel very well I felt well enough to be pretty sore. After the really complicated monkey business I had been through with the Gestapo at one time and another in Germany, Sweden, Spain, and Vichy, I was getting more annoyed by the minute that they should have tried to set such a clumsy trap.

I could practically hear a square-headed German sentry on the Salonika dock say, *"Ausweis, bitte?"* and see him take that fluttering piece of paper at the dark pierhead. It would be the last piece of paper I would ever have in my hand.

This was a stupid Gestapo play, a very stupid one. I told them so.

Now that, as you can conceive, roused a powerful commotion in the room; quiet, but powerful. The first thing the tall man did was to step closer to my bed, reach down and smash my head with his fist, and give me a bat with his stocky cane. I couldn't touch him. If I had had a gun under my pillow I would have shot that man.

The portly one grabbed a few papers off the small table beside my bed. My brief case was in the old-fashioned wardrobe on the side wall of the room. The woman pulled at the handle, tore the wardrobe open, and there it was.

The portly German and the woman went out the door as Miss Popva came in. Miss Popva wrenched my brief case from the woman's hand and let out a yell that gave me a souvenir. The tall man dropped his fancy cane.

But they didn't even hurry across the courtyard in front of the hospital. They just walked away while everybody on the floor was trying to find out what the commotion was all about.

Wonderful Miss Popva dressed me and got a taxicab. Then she took me downstairs, put me in it, and rode over with me to keep my engagement that afternoon at the Presidency. I was going there to say good-by to His Excellency Shukru Saracoglu, and to receive the generous courtesy of the statement he had promised me before I left for the United States in the morning.

At the gateway to the Middle East, standing between Germany and the vast prizes of the *Drang nach Osten*, with German troops on his doorstep, with German might on all sides, he spoke for Turkey:

"There are nations who would thwart our hard-won Turkish independence, who protest against our constructive nationalism and say it is merely a cover to hide a desire to conquer our neighbors in the Balkans, and who maintain that we are not capable of economic administration. They are mistaken. The first and foremost idea of the New Turkey is not political but economic. We want to be part of the world of production as well as consumption.

"Pan-Islam represented a federation based on religion. Pan-Turanianism represented a federation based on race. Both were wrong. In Atatürk's view, and I quote him, 'Pan-Islam really died centuries ago at the gates of Vienna at the most northern point of Turkey's advance in Europe. Pan-Turanianism perished on the plains of the East.'

"We want no force, no conquest. We want to be let alone and permitted to work out our own destiny. Upon this is erected the whole structure of the New Turkey.

"For centuries the Turkish Empire was a conglomerate human mass in which Turks formed the minority. One reason the Ottoman Empire fell into decay was that she was exhausted by the bureaucracy of rulership itself. The Ottoman Empire, stretching from Tripoli along the Mediterranean to Egypt, Palestine, and Syria, through Turkey and the Bosporus, into the caldron of the Balkans, laid itself open to trouble at every turn.

"Turkey's compact frontiers have been defined. The troublesome minorities have been dispersed. For a century the Armenians, Greeks, and Jews conducted 90 per cent of Turkey's commerce. These minorities in the Ottoman Empire comprised the commercial majorities. Turkey's best tobacco, which glows in cigarettes all over the world, grown around Samsun, was practically all raised by Greeks. Thousands of Armenians and Greeks, who had not been born in Turkey, intended to return home as soon as they could accumulate from our lands the wealth to do so.

"On the other hand, the Turkish farmer had limited himself to primitive methods, used the crude plow pulled by oxen or water buffalo, maintained a primitive self-sufficiency.

"This meant we had to build an entirely new nation, operated by and for our own people. We had to uproot the impositions of foreign businessmen, uproot the capitulations which permitted an alien to be tried in foreign consular courts, to have his own post office, and to be immune from personal taxation by Turkey. We called on all alike to live under Turkish law.

"We have built our nation.

"Now we are faced by great armies and great uncertainties. But behind our compact frontiers we propose to make our stand and work out our own salvation for our own fourteen million people without interference and without undue aid from even our most welcome friends.

"If we are attacked, we are ready. We will fight. In this melee we pledge ourselves to freedom, and to this we dedicate our lives as free Turks. Any appraisal of Turkey's future action which ignores this ignores the fundamental of Turkish devotion and Turkish honor. We will be free."

I asked the Prime Minister how he thought Germany would appraise Turkey's future action.

"The story of Von Papen is the story of Germany, past, present, and future," the Prime Minister told me. "There is more consistency in the story of Von Papen than there is in *Mein Kampf*."

CHAPTER 25

Von Papen Is Germany

Franz von papen is doing nothing for Nazi Hitler that he did not do for the German Kaiser and as a traditionalist German under President von Hindenburg. He typifies the *consistency* of official minds in Germany, the *consistency* of German purposes, and the *consistency* of the German idea that the end justifies the means.

Von Papen arrived in Istanbul as German Ambassador to Turkey five months after Atatürk died. He arrived April 27, 1939.

The ex-chancellor of Germany ensconced himself, Frau von Papen, his daughter "Steffi," and his eight dachshunds in one of the most elaborate embassies in the world, sleek and imposing in a graceful curve of the Ayas Pasha Caddesi.

Below him, in downtown Istanbul, the glittering form of Byzance shouldered itself high in the mass of Turkish houses and dominated the ancient, narrow streets and the old bazaars.

In uptown Istanbul, Pera, life moved about Von Papen in the tempo of the cosmopolitan world, with the elegance of the Champs Élysées, the smartness of Fifth Avenue, the beauty and form of the Avenida Beira-Mar in Rio. This life coursed along in imported automobiles—American, German, and French cars, polished and suave—and purred in rhythm with the click of cocktail glasses in the embassies and cafés.

In the evening it beat its rhythm to the good music of the Pera Palace, the Tokatlian, or the Maksim Bar, for Pera can be a very gay place at night, bright in the glow of neon lights, the shimmer of Schiaparelli gowns, and the sparkle of jewels from Cartier,

Mappin & Webb, and the Kremlin. Franz von Papen was very much at home with the foreign elements in Turkey.

Born October 29, 1879, and named after St. Francis of Assisi, young Von Papen grew up on the rich land of his father's Westphalian estate. He entered the Bemberg military school, was then graduated from the Lichterfeld military academy in 1898, and was a second lieutenant in the important 5th Westphalian Uhlans. Step by step Von Papen paraded through the grades of the German Army on a prancing horse: the Military School in 1902, the War Academy in 1907, the German General Staff in 1911, becoming captain and military attaché in 1913. Spy in America thereafter.

He did the Germans' uptown work at the Plaza Hotel and Delmonico's, operated a downtown spy nest at 123 West Fifteenth Street, Manhattan. He tended to the burning of no less than forty ships at piers in eastern harbors, directed U-boats against American liners everywhere, served as the connecting link between Irish Rebellion organizations and Germans in the United States, and paid off the whole German espionage ring here—until exposed by the Providence *Journal*. Our State Department threw him out of our country on December 4, 1915, while he was serving as German Military Attaché to both Washington and Mexico City.

After World War I, Papen tied himself close to Marshal Hindenburg. When narrow-eyed, imposing, mask-faced Hindenburg, born the same decade as Marshal Pétain, was elected a stopgap German president and moved into 71 Wilhelmstrasse, he brought with him Franz von Papen, his glittering protégé. Papen became Chancellor of Germany.

"The Kaiser made Hindenburg his Commander in Chief, and he double-crossed the Kaiser," was Admiral von Schröder's reaction. "Ludendorff won Hindenburg's battle for him, and he betrayed Ludendorff. President Ebert put Hindenburg in a place of honor, and he betrayed Ebert. The right-wing conservatives made Hindenburg president, and he double-crossed the right-wingers. The left-wing radicals are supporting Hindenburg, and he is double-crossing the left-wingers. Now Papen will double-cross Hindenburg." (P.S. Papen did.)

When Hitler came in, he served Germany through Hitler. He went to Austria as Ambassador.

In a typical Papenesque setting, Papen started the skit of his fateful sabotage of Austrian Chancellor Kurt von Schuschnigg in the Concert House on Lothringerstrasse during an intermission. He ended it February 12, 1938, when he lured Schuschnigg to the nightmare meeting with Hitler at Berchtesgaden. Papen capped the skit off by entering Vienna with Hitler himself, "reporting to History about the return of Austria to the Third Reich."

Fresh from his Austrian coup, Papen was now in Turkey to talk about the Dardanelles. Germany had installed him for the purpose of obtaining special rights in The Straits which would give Germany control of Turkey itself.

Papen's task was to combat the legacy of Atatürk, to overcome Atatürk's deathbed declaration to Ismet Inönü, who succeeded Atatürk as President of Turkey, that Turkey must always stay on the side of England.

Fourteen days before Papen arrived, England and France guaranteed the independence of Greece and Rumania and offered similar terms to Turkey. Underneath the rhythm of the imported cars and the click of cocktail glasses diplomats and military people were busy over long-distance wires, and every messenger who came to Turkey from London, Paris, or Berlin came to the center of the most grim and important intrigue in Europe.

Things developed badly for the Germans.

On May 12, fifteen days after Von Papen arrived, Foreign Minister Shukru Saracoglu concluded a mutual-assistance pact with England and France, announced "effective collaboration between Turkey and Great Britain, and mutual aid in the Mediterranean." France gave Turkey the sanjak of Alexandretta, a province and harbor tucked in the eastern corner of the Mediterranean on the border of Syria and Turkey. Known as the Republic of Hatay, Atatürk had claimed this strategic spot ever since founding New Turkey.

Foreign Minister Shukru Saracoglu obtained a loan of fifty million dollars from Britain to be spent on English armaments and prepared to welcome a military mission. Further, he offered Turkey's aid in arranging a mutual-assistance pact between Russia, England, and France, a move which able Maxim Litvinoff, later Soviet Ambassador to the United States, had long urged but which the leaders of England and France had been dismally slow to consider.

Shukru Saracoglu was convinced Russia would be the decisive influence in the coming crisis. Just as Secretary Henry Stimson saw the Japanese vista at the time of Japan's invasion of Manchukuo, Turkey's great statesman saw clearly that the lack of a military alliance between Moscow and western Europe had been one of the outstanding accomplishments of Nazi diplomacy in the years from 1933 through 1939.

The British and French failed to accept Shukru Saracoglu's sound offer. Before long it was too late.

German and Russian signatures had intertwined on the Non-Aggression Pact in Moscow. Papen had accomplished the greatest diplomatic triumph of the war.

Interestingly enough, this German-Russian deal which made World War II feasible for Hitler started with the Japanese.

For years the Japanese have been better informed about Russia, have known more about Russian military affairs, than anyone except the Russians themselves. This is equally true today. The Japs have the Russian picture on an hour-to-hour basis. Japanese private contacts and Japanese army and navy espionage have been and are extremely successful all over Russia.

Originally Hitler and the German General Staff, except Field Marshal Wilhelm Keitel, had a low opinion of Russian efficiency and therefore of Russian strength. German industrialists and bankers, particularly Walther Funk, president of the Reichsbank, supported these estimates. As for the German people, the historic fear of the Teuton for the Slav was assuaged for the moment. There was a common story in Germany; it shook the rafters in the beer halls, for when the Germans are wrong, they are more thoroughly wrong than any people on earth:

"What animal is most like a man?"

"A Russian!"

The Japanese could not make all this tally with what they saw. On the surface their facts looked silly, and there was later a confounding hour when the Russians showed up so poorly in the Finnish-Russian winter war of 1939-40, but the Japanese had the facts. And Japan had hopes.

Russia is the great threat to Japan. Russia's coast line envelops the Japanese islands. Russian airfields, such as the immense installation at Vladivostok, can smother Japan with bombing planes; Japanese coastal waters are easily mined from Russian ports. Dark as a sullen cloud, the shadow of the paw of the Russian Bear falls square on Nippon.

Japan's prime objective in diplomatic and military policy rested in the hope that Germany would fight Russia. Her task was so to impress Hitler by the figures of Russian strength that Germany would fight Russia early instead of risking attack from Russia later at some bad moment after Russia grew too strong. The sooner the better, because, of course, Japan was being hurt already by Russia in China. Russian military aid was China's principal foreign support, and it was growing.

The Japanese Ambassador to Moscow went to Berlin. He and the Japanese Ambassador to Germany arranged through Von Ribbentrop to see Hitler at Berchtesgaden. This was in early May 1939. The Japs had the picture from A to Z. The Russian military information, such as Russia's possession of 28,000 tanks, the Russian industrial production and railway-construction figures which the two Japs gave Hitler, even such details as the two-tier land-mine system, looked fantastic. But their facts were true.

They showed Hitler the production of the steelworks at Magnitogorsk (which cost the Russians $417,000,000 to build and is the world's largest steelworks) and denied that this plant was a failure. They stated that Russia was getting 850,000 horsepower out of the Dnieper Dam, and that Russian hydroelectric developments were producing 20 per cent as much current as all Europe. The figure was 42,500,000,000 kilowatt-hours. The German engineers had estimated 18,000,000,000.

Keitel emerged from these discussions the military man closest to Hitler, Hitler's personal Chief of Staff, and liaison man between Hitler and all armed forces. For the Japs' figures, tables, and maps, the Japs' names of places and people, the Japs' estimates all along the line confirmed in detail what Keitel had contended in principle.

But the Japs oversold the idea of Russia's strength. Hitler himself had not been unduly worried about Russia at his rear; he thought he could go against Poland without fighting England and France, but he was not sure. The Japs advised Hitler to attack Poland, as he had been preparing to do, and then keep on going—against Russia—after the attack he was preparing against Poland—"before it was too late." Fine, if England and France did not declare war and thereby commit Hitler to battle on two fronts. But suppose France and England fought him on the west?

Hitler and Keitel took the Japanese data on Russia "for study." Then they sidetracked the Japs' plan. Hitler got busy in Ankara.

Franz von Papen was the man to handle Hitler's next move, not Joachim von Ribbentrop. Nazis dealing with Communists was touchy business. But wasn't Franz von Papen, the Westphalian prince, descendant of Charlemagne, already urging on Hitler a pact with Russia, and wasn't he clubby with Soviet Ambassador Alexei Terentieff in Ankara? Wasn't Papen an aristocrat who had never spoken out against Stalin?

Papen, like Schacht, Dieckhoff, and other traditionalist Germans whom Hitler sent abroad, always served the Nazi purpose with every breath without appearing to be a Nazi bigwig.

One of the few men in America, for example, who really had Dr. Schacht's number was United States Secretary of the Treasury Ogden Mills. And what is more, he made this painfully plain to Schacht in his own house on Long Island. He did it in the presence of such men as Sir Montagu Norman, of the Bank of England, but it was to no avail. The Schachts, Papens, and Dieckhoffs lay their plans too far ahead, and lay them too well. For British leaders seem to insist on taking Germans at their word and then, like drunkards, promise never to do it again. "Many European leaders," Sir Robert Vansittart once said, "think of the French as though the French were Germans, and think of the Germans as though the Germans were British." But it has always been like that.

Papen received the hurry-up summons from Hitler. His large, blue, ambassadorial eyes blinked with delight at the Berchtesgaden call. A German military transport picked him up at the Ankara airfield and whisked him off to the *Führer*. This was May 13.

When he returned to Turkey by plane fifteen days later he went straight to Istanbul. He carried with him a phonograph record of British Prime Minister Neville Chamberlain's voice. Genuine, it had been taken by concealed microphones and revealed selected parts of Chamberlain's confidential and private Munich era talks with Hitler.

The gist of the Prime Minister's words was: "If you [Hitler] plan to extend Germany's economic influence in the east of Europe, His Majesty's Government will assume an understanding attitude."

This committed the British Government. If Germany attacked Russia, went east for oil and wheat and victory, England would not interfere and would not go to war to help Russia.

Soviet Ambassador Alexei Terentieff had a magnificent summer home on the Bosporus at the mouth of the Sea of Marmara, a few miles from Istanbul. Like almost everyone in Ankara and Istanbul, he spent the hot season of June, July, and August on these shores. His villa was at Beuyuk Dere.

Papen sent a message to Terentieff. They arranged to meet in one of the innumerable fishing coves, for each fished often, and the unsuspicious seclusion was ideal.

Papen told the Soviet Ambassador that Poland would be "redeemed along with Danzig." Germany would not quarrel with Russia about a division of Poland. The question was whether or not England and France would stand pat on their alliance with Poland and fight. Papen did not think so. *He quoted Hitler directly as convinced that England would not fight if he attacked Poland, and that, if she did, France would not join with England on this issue.*

In any case, Papen stated, Germany could and would defeat

France in not longer than *one year*. Then where did that leave England? England must fall. Aid from America was too far away for fast work like this. Therefore, argued Papen, the proposals of the British mission then in Moscow under William Strang, who lacked cabinet rank and was in Russian eyes tarred with the brush of his association with Lord Runciman, were dangerous for Russia. For if Russia fought Germany when Germany attacked Poland, Stalin would only be pulling a British chestnut out of the fire. Russia, not England, would have to do all the fighting against Germany in Poland. Look at the map, said Papen. Look at the map and stay out of this. The Russian Bear is Britain's goat if Russia comes in. Everything to win, if Russia stays out, for Russia will get what she wants in Poland from Germany and avoid all war. Stalin has nothing to lose by standing aside.

Terentieff carried the story to Stalin. And he played the Chamberlain phonograph record in the Kremlin.

A week after Terentieff returned to Istanbul, Stalin telegraphed him to obtain a concrete proposal from the Germans. From Stalin's point of view and the viewpoint of the Third International the pact was fundamentally desirable. *It would permit Russia to win the war in Europe by staying out.*

Terentieff went to the cove in his fishing launch once more. He passed Stalin's word to Papen, and Papen passed it to Hitler. Papen went to Berlin. Hitler left Berchtesgaden and met him at the Chancellery.

A non-aggression pact would be signed. The important trade treaty, which I saw being negotiated at the Berlin banks between the Russians and Germans, would be signed at the same time. The Trade Pact would be for seven years. The Non-Aggression Pact would be for ten.

In the Non-Aggression Pact Russia was given a free hand in the Baltic, the traditional center of her strategic interest in northern Europe. She was given a 600-mile strip in western Poland. Hitler, through Papen, would force Turkey to abandon her military alliance with England and France, signed with General Maxime Weygand. This would leave Turkey open for attack by Russia any time Russia wished to take over the Dardanelles. By these steps the pact would give Russia her two basic military and strategic objectives without firing a shot: the Baltic on the north and possession of the Dardanelles, the pathway between Russia's Black Sea and the open Mediterranean on the south. And Russia would have the buffer area she wanted in the form of an enslaved Poland.

Papen delivered the German terms to Terentieff in the fishing cove. This world would never be the same from that moment.

Immediately after the German-Russian Non-Aggression Pact mysterious fires broke out in the harbors of Istanbul, Mersin, Antalya, and Alexandretta, Turkey's ports to the seas of the world. The object of the German intimidation was the creation of an atmosphere of confusion, the prime technique of Nazis and the Third International alike. It hoped to accomplish Turkey's abandonment of President Inönü and Foreign Minister Shukru Saracoglu and in this way break Turkey's close friendship with England and France. Papen was out to break the Turkish-British-French alliance.

Papen's striped-trousers and frock-coat *Blitz* fell a cropper in an early stage, however, for now Russia herself was demanding from Shukru Saracoglu the control of the Dardanelles that Germany had originally sent Papen to Turkey to obtain and which Germany still hoped to obtain behind Russia's back.

Foreign Minister Molotoff called Shukru Saracoglu to the Kremlin. He and his wife made the journey alone.

"You will be anxious and worried in Moscow," Madame Saracoglu said. "I would like to go with you."

The Communist Third International had stimulated demoralization in Turkey, hand in hand with the Nazis, but for Russia's special purpose as well. *Pravda* bellowed on its front pages: "The Anglo-French Alliance means Turkey will pull British and French chestnuts out of the fire. For the Allies want to extend the war into the Balkans. The consequence of this understanding between the Turkish ruling classes and the Anglo-French imperialists is that Turkey virtually enters the war."

Turkey's Foreign Minister was kept waiting two weeks in Moscow before he was received by Foreign Minister Molotoff. This was, of course, not just carelessness. The Turks were furious. Their newspapers screeched for Saracoglu to come home. Saracoglu said nothing, publicly or to his government. He just stayed in Moscow, smiled, waited.

When Molotoff finally received Saracoglu a less patient man would have been alarmed and useless. Molotoff hinted at certain demands. Saracoglu skillfully kept them from being demands, kept them on an informal basis, never let them jell into an official matter, never let them require an answer from his government. It was a statesmanlike operation. Then Saracoglu saw Stalin. He was to see him many times later, and their contact is close today, but in this first meeting Stalin himself set the course.

"I want to disabuse you," Stalin said, in substance, "of any fears of Russian demands."

"We have received no demands," said Saracoglu, "and we have no fears." This disciple of Atatürk, the Ghazi, knew his business.

By the same token Von Papen failed. Apparently no one, German or Russian, was going to intimidate Shukru Saracoglu and the Turks.

Goebbels tried his hand in Germany. His *Völkische Beobachter* announced that Turkey was unneutral, declared that Shukru Saracoglu would "bitterly regret" his association with England and that the Turkish Government was not representative of the Turkish people.

"Turkey is in the orbit of the war," shouted Goebbels in the Berlin Sportspalast. "Turkey may share the destiny of Poland."

The Germans implemented all this with action. On April 4, 1941, when Rommel started his new attack in Libya, heavily engaged the British from the west, and recaptured much land, Papen staged a revolution to the east of the Nile. Its purpose was to spread out the British, weaken them through the favorite German formula of the *use of space*, and thereby win in both places and in the whole. Drawing heavily on the experience of his *Yilderim* days, Papen chose his old Arabian stamping ground of Iraq.

He used nearly 1200 German agents for this operation, directed

them from a brick house two blocks from the glittering German
Embassy on the Ayas Pasha Caddesi.

The men most helpful to him were Georg Werner von Hentig,
a cultured diplomat of the best German traditions, chief of the Near
East Bureau of the German Foreign Office, Dr. Fritz Grobba,
Germany's "Lawrence of Arabia," traditionalist German and non-
Nazi whom I have seen many times in Berlin, Paul Schmitz, prewar
foreign correspondent of the *Völkische Beobachter* in Cairo, and
Dagobert von Mikusch-Buchberg, known to thousands of Americans in university circles as a conservative German scholar and as
the translator into German of Lawrence's *Seven Pillars of Wisdom*.

In Papen's *Putsch*, Rashid Ali-el-Gailani, an opportunistic Iraq
politician, staged a palace revolt against pro-Ally Premier General
Taha-el-Hashimi. Papen, traditionalist German, pride of the
Junkers, planned this as a forerunner of a general Arab revolt
against Britain.

The British had only 2,000 men at the Iraq port of Basra. Every
British soldier was badly needed against Rommel, seven hundred
miles west of the Nile. But the British transferred more troops to
Basra. The British Navy moved in, sent ships and an aircraft
carrier into the Persian Gulf. Major John Bagot Glubb's Desert
Patrol cranked up its mechanized units. All together, the British
blasted Von Papen's Arab stooges out of the air, out of the sand,
and out of the premiership, and fought Rommel in Libya at the
same time.

Papen chartered a plane. He flew to intercept Naci Sevket,
whom he had made Iraq's Defense Minister and who was trying to
reach him in a hurry.

This was Papen the German traditionalist at his best. The jig
was up; Germany had lost. So he did his German somersault.

"Germany is unfailing in her interest in you and all Arabs," he
said. "We withdraw our support reluctantly, and only temporarily.
The way to Arab freedom is through the destruction of British
power. If we divert more aid to you and your friends we reduce
our strength for that accomplishment. Ask peace from the English. Gain peace. Give in temporarily, and wait."

Traditionalist Germany, defender of Islam, fountain of anti-Semitism, champion of Pan-Arab sentiment against Great Britain, simply washed her hands of the whole affair. Germany's immediate program had failed. Therefore, on with the next thing. Traditionalist Germany left her Arab front men to be shot, just as the Germans will one day leave any ally they have.

Overnight, when the United States entered the war, Von Papen became the purring and cooing friend of Turkey.

German blasts against Shukru Saracoglu came out of the newspapers. Plug-ugly Gestapo agents buried themselves, and the most pleasant Germans entered Turkey. The new German group is attractive and gentle.

Papen features Von Ribbentrop's sister, Frau Jenke, married to the German Commercial Attaché. She leads the parade at the German Embassies in both Ankara and Istanbul, for the Istanbul Embassy is used only in summer. Debonair Frau Jenke wears the best furs, conducts the most important musicales, introduces German artists, actors, playwrights, and singers, the best names of the amusement world in Germany.

Under the direction of Von Papen the German Embassy became the most congenial place in Ankara. His purpose is the concentration of a German appeasement group in Ankara which, under his leadership, is preparing to save Germany as Germany loses the war.

This Von Papen, pride of the Junkers, gentleman-jockey, ex-Chancellor, is a colorful, even glamorous, figure in Ankara. Now sixty-three, he is a little like a spry but aging movie star. He is straight as a ramrod, precise as a pin. Immaculately dressed, he is always suave and always smiling. His cold blue eyes have a quiet and open stare. His mouth is thin. A short-cropped, gray-sprinkled mustache high-lights the features of a canny man.

Ruthless, clever, and unreservedly ambitious, Von Papen moves about Ankara with the full equipage of a German nabob—shining black Maybach-Zeppelin limousines, swastika flags fluttering on the fenders, military and naval aides done up in quantities of gold braid, saluting and clicking their patent-leather boots wherever he goes. He plays tennis daily at the smart Ankara Tennis Club, often with his attractive daughter Steffi, goes to Axis cocktail parties, attends the concerts, beams at public celebrations. But the Turks see Von Papen as the plush and polished advance agent of an army which may someday attack. It is not a role to make anyone the toast of the town.

The traditionalist element in Germany, however, supports Franz von Papen with great confidence. It is now Von Papen's mission in life, in behalf of traditionalist Germany, to see that Germany is saved for her "destiny."

The German traditionalists, all over the world, intend to keep us so busy thinking about the Nazis that we shall make the dreadful mistake of believing we have eliminated the German problem when we have eliminated the Nazis. This would be a fateful error.

When we get rid of the Nazis we shall not have got rid of the German problem, any more than we did when we got rid of the Kaiser.

If our task were only to get rid of Hitler we should have one set of fairly well-defined military, economic, and social problems. Because this alone is formidable, and because we have such an avalanche of conflicting government opinions on how to do it, we have a tendency to mistake a problem for a solution. We have our labels mixed. Even our own propaganda within our own country has stimulated this fateful confusion.

I am sorry to say that this conception, in many instances unwitting, permeates the minds of many Germans who fled Nazism and sought refuge in our marvelous country and in England. The determination to preserve German unity remains strong among stray members of post-World War I Germany wherever they are. Many of these refugees have, unconsciously, served the long-term German cause in this way.

We have been smothered by literature written by refugees and others in England and America, dedicated to persuading our publics that this war is an ideological matter. We have all heard: "Hitler will be a prisoner of the Army." "The happiest day in the lives of millions of ordinary Germans will be when they get rid of Hitler." "Only the young people are behind Hitler." (Hitler was thirty-three when he struck for power. All Germans younger than fifty-four are younger than he is.) The implication is that there is no German problem as such. This is a dangerous over-simplification. The idea is that Germany can exercise her former place in Europe and can do so without danger to all free men after the Nazi hoodlums are eliminated. That is not true.

Ever since the days of Frederick William, German expansionism has been a persistent feature in European history.

It received many rebuffs, such as World War I, but it has greed and vitality and is the force always at work in all German-speaking communities in Europe.

Hitler's National Socialism in Germany speeded up this process. But Pan-Germanism is deep in the ordinary German as in the younger generation. It has grown and thrived on alibis. The traditional Germans were preparing their new alibi in such talks as I had in Berlin, elsewhere in the German-speaking area, and in *every neutral country in Europe*—namely, Sweden, Switzerland, Spain, Portugal, and Turkey.

The identical needs necessary for the *Herrenvolk* domination of Europe, the Middle East, Africa, and the German geopolitical Heartland are expressed by the Nazis and the ordinary Germans in Germany. The Germans as a whole are clearly in love with the thought of a German world, and I single from the German people the more important men there only because they are, naturally, the ones who are in a position to put up the coming smoke screen and fool the free people of the world, including, first of all, us Americans.

The only basic cleavage between the Nazis and the up-and-coming German industrialist, diplomat, general, or what not in Germany is the question of speed.

The Nazis wanted to achieve everything Germanic in their own time. The more conservative Germans were slow in acknowledging the Nazi popularity and the Nazi influence over the German people. They dreaded the Nazis' effect on them, and they disliked the cruelty in the Nazis' treatment of Jews, but they never differed with the Nazis' attitude towards a Greater Germany. Every move that the German traditionalists have made, every step they have taken in the broad area of policy in this century, has always contained the basic conception of Germany as the dominant world power. They had, at all times, the really Germanic feeling—namely, that the end justified the means. Actually, for the Nazis, it was just a question of: "We stoop to conquer."

CHAPTER 26

The Great European Dilemma

Naturally, when you see the Nazis in Germany you notice that they believe Germany must follow Hitler to victory or die and that the future of Germany and Europe must be settled in this war. The Nazis have a vested interest in World War II and in no other.

But the traditional Germans in Germany believe this war is already lost.

The traditionalists in the German Army and Navy, in industry, in the universities, and especially such men as Von Papen in the diplomatic service, are convinced that if World War II goes to its end Germany will suffer an irretrievable disaster.

They have only one solution for Germany that I could find among them: "If Germany is to be saved for her destiny the war must not be fought to the bitter end."

The traditionalists believe that Germany can cut her losses, *disarm, but retain blood and industry*. The ordinary German hasn't thought it through beyond this. The leading industrialists, the powerful Junkers of East Germany, and men like Von Papen, Schacht, and Dieckhoff have completed their thinking. It is they who supply the final words in the sentence: Germany should cut her losses, retain enough blood and industry to resume the struggle later, and *accomplish Germany's destiny in World War III under new alliances.*

If this sounds premature, it would be well to remember that this is exactly what Germany did after World War I. It was only twenty-one years before the new German alliances permitted Germany to make the next try.

The traditional German elements I saw in Germany and Turkey make capital of the blood-bath which would follow the dropping of the German guard, and claim advantages to the world by saving the butchering of Germans by a "cooling off" period.

The Poles had no "cooling off" period when the Germans crashed into Warsaw. Neither did the Dutch at Rotterdam, or the heroic British in the terrible blitzes, or the French, the Belgians, the Norwegians, the Yugoslavs, or the Greeks. Nobody had a "cooling off" period. Now there is to be one to avoid the slaughter of Germans. It is perfectly amazing how the Germans get away with the same thing each time they lose.

Important factors can influence free men into once more forgiving the Germans at a time when the so-called conservative element in Germany will look like lilies and sound more free-minded than any free group in the world. There is no penitent so vocal as the caught thief.

This appeal will be effective on the American and British mind, when it comes, because the Germans are cold-blooded when they have a chance to slaughter people to their own profit and we are not. On such a basis—and the outlook favors that basis—defeated Germany will come out of this war at least as well as Russia, incalculably better than the France which she overran, and far better than heroic England.

Actually the Germans have good reason to believe that England and America will shrink from permitting a blood-bath of Germans on the Continent and that the German people will not have to face from the British and Americans what they have faced from the Russians. *The most important traditionalist elements in Germany, such as Von Papen, do not believe Germany will have to fight to the end on the Russian front, and they are convinced they can avoid the ultimate debauch of Germany.*

The essence of this is that Germany would fight World War III in due time. Make no mistake about that.

For this reason we must go the whole distance with Germany this time, once and for all. Germany must be "beat to the ground," to use Mr. Churchill's words, in Germany. Germany must accept

the consequences of complete defeat, not by "unconditional surrender" or any other such painless method which permits Germans
to decide for themselves when it is wise to stop the war, but by
military punishment for their own military assault on the free men
of the world.

Germany must pass through not only grave internal convulsions
but also a psychological revolution which will permit her to be so
purged of Pan-Germanism that no German will ever forget what
it cost to exercise this greedy notion, and so that this idea in German *minds* is as defeated as in German arms.

Then there is only one hope. It is the fundamental for any prospect of peace in Europe. It is the point from which any realistic
consideration of European affairs must start. It is inherent in any
map. Any and all talk about "tomorrow's Europe" is utterly meaningless without it, which is one of the reasons why the talk about
Europe has been meaningless so far.

The one and only hope for Europe is THE REVIVAL OF A STRONG
FRANCE.

The revival of a strong France is the main obstacle Germans see
standing between themselves and expansion, just as they have always seen France as their obstacle in the west and Russia in the
east. Whatever European system may be devised after the war,
Germans the world over, home Germans and refugees alike, do
not want a strong France. If you do not believe this, ask them. If
they hem and haw about it be on your guard. I am afraid that if you
remind them that France was the first large democracy and that
France was the *only* important democracy on the entire continent
of Europe, you will find that they do not display much interest in
the democratic principle.

The intention in the German-speaking community inside Europe
and outside is that the personal relationships between England and
Russia will not prevail after the war, and that America will be distant. Accordingly, if England and France are deeply separated the
absolutely certain division in Europe would be favorable to the
resumption of German supremacy on the Continent. In this way

Germany would finally emerge as top dog in Europe, come what may.

"France is finished." "What could you expect of people who rule themselves as the French did?" "France is living in her past glories." These are dangerous and diabolic words. They are water on the German wheel.

France is a freedom-loving country. American and British relations with France are basic for world peace. There is no better protection against a long-range German political scheme.

This is one of the chief reasons why Germany did not occupy all of France in the beginning. The Germans knew and hoped that by occupying half of France the French people would fight among themselves. This had two purposes. First, it would remove the threat of a French minority boiling as a unit under the Nazi yoke and threatening to erupt, to Germany's military disadvantage. Secondly, French quarrels would discourage Frenchmen, and the world, regarding any real future for France as a nation.

Yet to lose sight of the position of France in the long-range political outlook is to let down our guard on the future peace of the world.

France must have the honest patience, the constant hand of aid, the vigorous and tolerant support of all free men. By driving a wedge between England and France, the United States and France, free men and France, Germans make their most important contribution to the preservation of German power and the continuity of a Pan-Germanic purpose.

France and England have not been, are not now, firm friends. This cleavage between the two great democracies of Europe is a calamity for Europe and the world. But it is not as bad as it appears to be, and *the first step towards peace and safety in Europe depends on the establishment of British-French unity*. For England is France's only possible supporter in Europe, and France is England's only possible bulwark on the Continent. The prime policy of the United States, to which all European matters are secondary, must be to facilitate British-French unity *and to join it in a formal tripartite agreement between England, France, and the United*

States. The joint arrangement of these three great democracies in Europe is feasible. *If it is impossible, what is possible?* Nothing less than this holds any hope in the post-war world. Anything more than this at this time endangers this fundamental arrangement itself.

The solidarity of France and England should not be regarded as impossible. The world has too much at stake. Not only is it the *sine qua non* of any protection against Pan-Germanism but it is the only really workable program in Europe. Inflate it into a community of all nations in Europe, and it fails. Make it compact and strong, and it can succeed. This is fundamentally a problem which the French must solve through the joint support of England and the United States. Basically, France must see her future with England and America together, not just England or America, or she has no future at all. Nor have any other free people in Europe a future unless this attitude on the part of France grows and flourishes.

If Great Britain in the past had pursued a courageous policy and had been militarily strong instead of pitiably weak, the influence and policy of France and the Slav states in the east would have been totally different from what it was in the last ten years, and there would be no war in Europe today. However, there is a new factor now which is immensely encouraging and justifies a view that the combination which once failed will not fail again. This factor is the terrible experience to which our British friends have been put. We do not have to believe that England will revert to the vest-pocket army and air force ideas of the nineteen twenties and thirties.

As for the place of the United States in this, our devious plans for a Better World Order—whatever that may mean besides the impoverishment of the United States itself—our dull and fatuous assumption that we can set all well with words and dollars and a "police force," are as meaningless and misleading as Chamberlain's Munich statement of "Peace in our time" and work directly against this prime Anglo-French objective.

For in our attempt to be everything to Europe and the world we would fail to be everything to England and France. Americans must assume that the solution of only this first problem will require masterful handling, concentrated and unencumbered. It can be done, but it can only be done as *the* program, not as one ring in a thirty-ring circus.

Wise men favor workable plans, always and in anything. Plans are not less lofty simply because they are limited. In fact, the simple label of "lofty" is small compensation for the failure of vast schemes that collapse of their own weight and die in a spasm of confusion and despair. Like Atatürk's plan for Turkey, in contrast to the old Ottoman Empire, there are many advantages in the compact versus the sprawling.

Wise men know that you cannot stand shoulder to shoulder with everybody. Those who should be friends may stand together. You need not make enemies of the others, but you cannot make friends of the others simply by calling them friends. The test of statesmanship is to choose your allies wisely and well, and then stick to them. This is hard enough, but it holds the prospect of success. And surely, if the roots of the tree are not strong enough to support a trunk they cannot support branches and leaves, birdhouses and watchtowers, candles and ornaments, in the lightning, the rain, and the hail.

The British Commonwealth is both our physical and metaphysical bridge to the world. The French nation is the trunk of democracy in Europe. France is the continental counterpart of the American Republic, and this nation has no older ties than it has with France. If these ties are too frail for unity of purpose, what ties elsewhere are stronger?

As for France's ability to survive on the Continent, the fundamental economic problems of the peninsula are not there. It surprises many to realize that *France has the best-balanced economy in Europe*. Her agricultural areas balance her industrial production, she grows her own food for her population and imports practically nothing. Her exports go to the world markets. England is her best customer, and 20 per cent of her exports go there. England is also her principal supplier.

France has space. Only as many people live in France as in Italy —forty-two million in each country. France is not crowded and pushed. France is no more densely populated than the state of Ohio.

France has raw materials. She possesses great natural resources in her soil, subsoil, climate, watercourses, and maritime location. She has timber and iron ore, bauxite, potash, salt, pyrites, antimony, and coal in full abundance. She mines certain quantities of zinc, lead, manganese, and gold. Her watercourses give her a canal network which affords cheap transportation and good irrigation, and water power for the hydroelectric energy of our new day. France is basically self-sustaining.

She could be largely rehabilitated by the repatriation of her own gold, for France has a gold reserve second only to the United States, and it is safely guarded in the Western Hemisphere. The rehabilitation of France would be no drain on the American partner in the Tripartite Alliance. Instead of no stabilization of anything, it could be possible to stabilize *the dollar, the franc, and the pound sterling,* and even to issue an international unit, but only if these three currencies *alone* were involved.

As for the French people themselves, the defects in the people of France, the things which some at a great distance call weaknesses of character, and the shades of temperament that contribute to the problem of France today are not peculiar to the French; they are human and will occur in any alliance, and all of us in our different ways are liable to them.

Yes, France is bitterly angry within herself, more divided than at any time in all French history. In this both England and America must show great patience, but the aim is worth the patience and represents a worthy test of England's and America's statesmanship.

Those who love France and wish for peace someday in Europe must reach out and embrace, cling to and hold, work for and cherish above all else a will and prayer: the will and prayer for the unity of Frenchmen, a strong and vital France, and, with this, the return of close and indivisible relations with England.

I believe that in due time the French can and will do it. The French are a proud, brave people, God-fearing and true. There are men in France and outside France who have integrity, patriotism, and unflinching courage, thousands upon thousands of them.

There are men in France and outside France who have wisdom, talent, and the deepest love for freedom and justice, thousands upon thousands of them. I cannot but believe that as time and events run their terrible course leaders will arise and determined Frenchmen and Frenchwomen will be found to follow them.

Then it remains for their course to be towards both England and America and our course to be towards them.

Anglo-American conquests of Italian colonies in north Africa resulting in their delivery to France could do much to lay the groundwork for the unity of the three great democracies. The joint declaration to the French people that this is the purpose of our fight in the central Mediterranean would point to the fundamentals of our joint attitude towards France, and in such an atmosphere as that France could and would do more for herself, within herself, than seems possible today. For the defeat of Italy, in *behalf* of France, is the first way to establish the integrity and value of Anglo-American deliveries to the French.

That their ancient enemies, the Italians, bellowed their way into World War II under Mussolini or anybody else and took a bumptious hop-skip-and-jump against France at what they concluded was the painless last moment, beat their chests, and turned loose their phony legions when France was prostrate, is something no Frenchman can even speak about. He just explodes. Whatever nations deliver Italian north African colonies to France, in retribution for Italy's attack, will endear themselves to every Frenchman. And every Frenchwoman.

Only a strong France, within the democratic alignment of the British Commonwealth and the United States, can supply anything to which the smaller nations of Europe can tie. For, superimposed on the peninsula's impoverishment, is the implacable force of long-term fear throughout all Europe.

This can be overcome only by having the balance of power rest in an Anglo-American-French bloc.

With all the delinquencies in England's balance-of-power policy on the Continent, the policy supplied, nevertheless, immense benefits from the White Sea to the Mediterranean in removing from the minds of millions the threat of engulfment by any single, dominant, continental nation.

It is true that in practice Britain's balance-of-power principle was full of twists and somersaults, but the principle itself holds more promise than any other policy. The other great policy in Europe was the continental policy of collective security, which secured nothing, expired in the shambles of the League, and was buried at Munich.

If, therefore, Americans could see the reduction of fear in Europe they could see a future. Only the injection of the Anglo-American-French balance of power holds the slightest promise of any such reduction of fear, because the great irony of this war is that the defeat of Germany will not dissolve fear in Europe. It may even accentuate it.

The sole alternative to an Anglo-American-French bloc is that the United States withhold making any alliance with anyone and in this way retain some balance of power itself by staying out of Europe entirely.

For the fundamental of Europe is the emergence in the Hudson Tube Age of two immense land powers settled and established on the Continent itself, each powerful, each virile, each ambitious. Russia and Germany stand face to face. As Germany is weakened and becomes prostrate in World War II, all Europe will fear Russia and Communism, just as all Europe feared the powerful Germany before World War II. Come what may, World War II leaves the people of Europe stricken by fear from the White Sea to Gibraltar, from the Orkneys to the Golden Horn.

Norway, Sweden, Finland, the Baltic states, and the Low Countries feared Germany. They will fear Russia no less. Belgium, France, Switzerland, the Mediterranean nations, the Balkans, and Turkey feared Germany. They will fear Russia no less. England feared Germany. She will fear Russia no less.

Russia is fighting Russia's war. No fair-minded man can criticize Stalin or take exception to Russia for that. A realistic and single-minded Russia is the best kind of helper we can have. If Russia never did another thing in this war she would have done, already, more for the United Nations than could even have been hoped or expected. Much of her strength comes from her single-mindedness, her refusal to be an adjunct of any nation, her repeated triumphs in having other nations (all of them, at one time or another) come to her. Russia will be equally single-minded in the peace. Much like Atatürk, whom he so closely resembles, and Shukru Saracoglu, Atatürk's disciple, Stalin has made the rest of the world statesmen depend on his strength *because they failed in being strong themselves*.

Russia is Russia's ally. Again, from the Russian point of view, that is sound and proper. And one fundamental fact will emerge: Russia will make every effort to avoid entanglements of any kind which do not advance the aims of the U.S.S.R.

That this has, and will, involve shifts in Russia's alliances with other nations, and that it contains the absolute certainty of diplomatic surprises, should surprise no one. For the U.S.S.R. predicates its international policy on two convictions: one, that proletarian Russia is the potential, if not eventual, object of attack by the "capitalistic states"; two, that the governments of "capitalism" regard themselves as the potential, if not eventual, objects of attack by Russia, "the homeland of world revolution."

The U.S.S.R. has never had confidence in the friendliness of certain powers or in the animosity of others. The Russians view with contempt the machinations of "bourgeois diplomacy," and one can hardly blame them for that.

Say the Russian leaders: "Do not the records of the democracies of Europe—England, France, and the others—in their actions regarding Manchukuo, Ethiopia, Spain, Czechoslovakia, etc., prove that in effect they helped the Fascists?"

Say the Russian leaders: "Out of all these circumstances, who do you ask us to believe is fighting *for* Russia?"

From Russia's viewpoint, Russia's ideal position is to *return to neutrality*, whenever that is possible, in what the Russians described as "a conflict between imperialistic rivals for the redivision of the world and the spheres of influence."

Whether or not Russia marches, if she can, to Berlin or even to the Rhine is hardly the important factor. The Russians took Berlin once in 1760, they marched to Paris after the collapse of Napoleon, and if circumstances permit they may wish to march to distant Berlin again. The Russians themselves will decide that, no one else.

It is beside the point to say that Russia may restrain herself and be agreeable on the Continent. Even if the Russians were angels the result would be the same. That is the agony of the situation. For no matter how Russia behaves the fact that there is an all-powerful, dominating, single force of such immensity on the Continent will of itself create deep tensions and profound reactions against it.

We have never known what it means to have a powerful rival, any powerful rival, on our borders. Europeans do. Generation after generation of Europeans have been threatened first by one strong power and then another. It is an old, old story. We have no idea how this fact can permeate every thought, every emotion, every plan of a nation or how treatment of this is the basis for the success or failure of government leaders in the eyes of their people. We do not appreciate the power of this fear of the strong one, any strong one. It surpasses every other influence in Europe. It *is* the instinct of survival, and the Europeans have reacted to it in accordance with the European habit through all centuries.

Normally, with the Nazis eliminated and Russia standing strong, millions and millions of Europeans will support a rebirth of Germany as a bulwark against the "Russian menace." And they will do this, ironically enough, whether or not Russia is, in fact, a menace. The existence of any single dominating power on the Continent, no matter what its intentions, will alarm and paralyze all Europe profoundly and set in motion every kind of counterplan against it.

A permanently well-armed America must stand ready to absorb and soften these fears, and guide them in a good, constructive direction so that better than otherwise relations can be maintained with the Soviet through the depreciation of fear and the enhancement of democratic prestige.

Therefore, the Great European Dilemma, which is Russia, should

be regarded constructively and realistically, and not with mis-
givings on one hand or false hopes on the other. That Russia is the
Great Dilemma is clear and uncontrollable and will emerge at the
first sitting of any conference, no matter where it is held, who
attends it, or what the circumstances. Words from outside Russia's
borders will not determine Russia's policies. And those who skirt
around this in overextending America's place in the Europe of the
future skirt around the fundamental of the whole problem of peace.
They are simply talking plans they cannot control.

Hundreds of men in the United States and England, especially
on the governments' pay rolls, are speaking and writing glowingly
about postwar matters about which we shall have little, if anything,
to say.

The British and the Americans will not make the peace. The
Russians will do that. By its location, by its relatively overwhelming force at the point of action on the Continent, Russia will possess
absolute veto power over any suggestions made. If they like what
we suggest, they will do it. If they don't, they will do as they
please. Make no mistake about that.

Russia was not involved in the last "peace" at Versailles. Russia
wasn't in the picture. Now the tables will be turned. This side of
our own willingness to fight soon again, the only word that will
really count in Europe will come from the Kremlin.

Today, in war, millions look upon Russia's prodigious and un-
foreseen strength as a blessing and treat the probable dominance of
Europe by Russia as Russia's due. But the recollection of even such
heroic contributions as Russia's can be short, and her unexpected
strength will not finally operate in Russia's favor. For the memory
of this force will not react in the same way after the war. Tomorrow, in peace, millions will look upon this same Russian power in
terms of its use by the Third International. Instead of pointing to
Russia's performance in the war as one of the most glorious examples of fortitude in all history, which it is, they will see in that
performance full justification for the latent dread of Communism,
which extends everywhere, to England, to South America, to the
United States, and knows no boundaries. If, in contrast to this, we

really want world freedom we must set the example of freedom. That is our first duty to ourselves, to our principles, to any democratic coalition, and to the world. To do this we need a new start, not in Europe but at home.

CHAPTER 27

Our Boundless Future

Throughout all times, men have tried to be free. For this the bravest and best men on earth have fought and died. The heroes of freedom have always and everywhere been the greatest idols in the world. And the poets and writers have been their soul-builders and preachers. Only passing opportunists are insensible to the magic of the rays which stream from the idea of freedom. For self-preservation is only part of the desire for development.

However, when the need for self-preservation comes into conflict with the desire for self-development, opportunists have their chance. Under such a condition powerful men can step forward, as they have in the United States. Soon, only the powerful men are free.

The Roman republic rose against the despotic world as America rose against the religious and economic limitations of Europe. The banner of freedom passed from tired Athens to Rome, for the early Roman Empire was a republic, *res publica*, a public affair, the product of the Hellenic idea of freedom, the rights of individuals against arbitrariness.

Rome occupied the successive states of the Asiatic Middle East, but this Asiatic world gradually stifled the spirit of Roman freedom, and Rome's political spiders did the rest. The process was similar in its extension from Sulla to Diocletian: a transition to rule by appointment, to absolutism, to tyranny, and to the downfall of Roman freedom.

But at the moment when freedom seemed to die and Roman citizens were converted into subjects of the Caesars, a profound agitation broke upon the distracted world from Palestine. To redeem and liberate an enslaved and despairing humanity with a new gospel of God, Jesus walked among men.

As a shining light, the gospel revealed the principle that each human soul comes into existence once, is unique, immortal, and that the will is free and through its action man shapes his destiny on earth and in the hereafter. The idea of man, the concept of freedom and personality, was reawakened by Christianity just when state omnipotence had reached its highest development. *And the struggle of Christianity is still against all who see the future of man in terms of government omnipotence.*

In this fight against the concentration of power, there are principles that cannot be compromised. Either we have a society established on orderly liberty and the initiative of the individual, or we have the State. They cannot be mixed.

Some twenty-five years ago we accepted these principles as simply as we accept any truth. We fought a great war for their protection. Yet in this thundering era of world crisis a spiritual ponderation has set in even among thoughtful people, causing them to test lifelong convictions and to question the effectiveness of natural truths in the light of all they see taking place.

The onslaught of tyrants, with their barbaric ideas and pagan plans, on one hand and the muddle of collectivists on the other has caused even free men the world over to doubt themselves and their value as free individuals.

Yet, again, unlike the Pyramids, the great structures of human progress can be built only by the free, although it is not easy for us who whirl in the mechanistic mass to be free and to conduct our lives and control our government so that we remain free.

The long-term answer comes in how strong is the desire for freedom and restraint (which are the same thing) in our own hearts and minds.

It is strong, and it will be stronger.

Nothing is plainer than that sympathy with domestic tyranny or with war may be long in years but that its years are numbered. Is it delayed? It is not delayed; this era has had only an instant to mature, only a breathless instant in the lopsided, headlong rush of the Hudson Tube Age.

The shame that men feel in the occurrence of this latest and largest war certainly shows we have got on a little already. Everything which makes for intercourse in the mechanistic network combines to shorten our time lag behind our tools and to bring us abreast of our new advantages. Even this latest war itself is doing so. New migration and new trade will be the important factors accruing in the same direction. These, with learning, art, and revitalized religion, can make war look like fratricide, which it is.

This thought is no invention. Rising first in the most simple and pure souls, such as we see on all sides of us, the meek of the earth, and first made visible by them, it is announced to us beforehand. It has now become so distinct as to be the feature of this war.

The interest of the world is not in the glory of this war. It is in peace, on a scale and with an anxiety for attainment beyond anything in the annals of man. The work of the world is devoted to guns and death. The thought of the world is on food and peace.

In the midst of war, there was never an hour in the history of man when so many millions were praying for peace.

The spiritual quality of man is already struggling to catch up with the mechanical and chemical genius of the few.

That idea itself is epochal. The fact that it is so distinct is the commanding fact. There is no good now enjoyed by society, including Christianity itself, that was not at one time as problematical and visionary as this. It will happen. It is happening. But it will be slow in terms of our generation, and the next and the next. No one can remake society and the world overnight.

Meanwhile, the Americans in the world cannot support the world or police the world.

America is incomparably better off than the rest of the world, and it is the solemn duty, the prime duty, of our Government to see that we remain so. We obtained this position by coming here in the first place, then working hard and honorably after we got here.

We have been fortunate in our location. But, remember, we

made our location. It was not delivered to us. Our blessings did not come easily.

From the days of the first immigrants, through the days of Concord and Lexington, of the wilderness of Ohio, from the days of the Great Lakes, the days of the new California and the great Pacific Northwest, through the tragedy of the last war and of this one, we have built our nation with more idealism and less greed than any people on earth. It has been a long and difficult struggle, the combined struggle of a great and successive body of free men. It has been a continuing process.

The result: America is the greatest nation on earth. How true you find that as soon as you leave our shores! As a people, we are more productive, we ask less and give more, we are more generous and more open-minded, more tolerant and more forgiving, than any group on earth. Our men are the most versatile, our women the most beautiful and free, our children the best-educated. As a nation we are plagued by neither infancy nor old age. From the timber forests of Oregon and Washington to the blue waters of the Caribbean, we want only to work and play, live honestly, love deeply, and die in our time.

We have the resources, and the temperament, for our greatness. *But they are ours.* They were not free to us, and they are not free to squander. They are not common property. An honorable state cannot give them away, because they do not belong to the state. They belong to us.

There is the work of my own generation, started twenty years ago in colleges, shops, stores, laboratories, factories, or on farms. Our work and our hopes may not be important to world planners. But our work and our hopes are important to us. We cannot live in debt, and many of us never have. We cannot take on obligations for others until we have fulfilled our own. Neither can our country.

It is difficult at best for most of us to make our way and provide for our families. We have no surplus. We have no certainty of our future. We have great problems, great sadnesses. It will take us generations to overcome the mistakes already made at home, and to overcome the effects of this war.

We shall be faced by every sort of readjustment, deep priva-
tions. We must provide for the returning American soldiers, for
the desperate and the wounded of our own land. We must work
tirelessly to regain our solvency and to recompense the huge drain
on every resource we have. In this alone we face the greatest task
in our history. We are in no position to lift the standard of living
in China, in Russia, among 400,000,000 impoverished people on the
overpopulated peninsula of Europe, no matter how desirable that
may be. One hundred and thirty million Americans are in no position to do this, and there is no possibility whatever of our suc-
ceeding in the attempt. There are a hundred places to start and no
place to stop. *We simply descend into the morass of repudiation or
continual war*. Our citizens deserve a better destiny than that.

In the process of our national life we have already been incredibly charitable to the rest of the world. We have asked no thanks
for this, and sometimes it seems as though we have received none.
But the record stands. We need not be ashamed of our generosity
to the rest of the world.

The obligation to assist towards a better world and the value
in doing so are obvious. Who does not know that? Our duty is to
be useful, however, not according to our desires but according to
our powers.

There is a limit to the failures Americans can absorb. At some
point our statesmen failed, or we should not have suffered as we
did in the depression. At another point our statesmen failed, or we
should have been so strong on land, on sea, and in the air that there
could have been no war. Now they fail their country again if they
saddle its citizens with the astronomical and impossible burdens of
the world.

Our citizens cannot give (1) freedom of speech and expression,
(2) freedom of every person to worship God in his own way, (3)
freedom from want, and (4) freedom from fear, to the world.
The whole conception of giving or infusing the Four Freedoms is
preposterous. It is not idealism. It is sheer political buncombe, and
is so recognized abroad.

The idea is that our Government promises to arrange freedom

and prosperity for the people of the world. This is a thoughtless undertaking—how thoughtless no one knows. Yet this airy and fatuous approach to the reality of the world is promulgated at the very time when the solemn and high purpose of the United States should be to have the people of all the world believe in us—what we say, what we do, and what we intend to do.

Anyone must know that the problem of freedom is deep in human nature, for the real limits of making the world free exists in the present limits of human nature and the small distance we have gained in our short time along the road to universal education. Those who promise it now do vast harm to the cause of freedom and to the strength of the democratic idea. Their intentions are better than the tyrants', but their results are chaotic, and this gives new tyrants a chance.

On the narrower question alone, the question of "freedom from want"—to say nothing of freedom itself—anyone must know that the politicians, good and bad, of each and every country of the world will be pulling on us in a tug-of-war to get the most out of America's International WPA, exactly as our local mayors camped in Washington to get the most out of our disastrous, boondoggling WPA at home. We are referring to at least a billion people, most of them in primitive surroundings and 400,000,000 of them in the Europe I have attempted to describe. Will we succeed? The promise of the United States is utterly fantastic.

Not in this way, or in any other way, should we attempt to have the last word in the conduct of the world. Certainly the Europeans —Prime Minister Salazar and others like him, in England and elsewhere, including Winston Churchill himself—do not speak as though we should.

Sitting in his quiet study in Lisbon, this is what Portugal's great scholar and statesman told me:

"I have always been in favor of a policy of plain good sense, as opposed to a policy of magnificent plans, so vast and magnificent that such energy is spent in admiring them that no strength is left to carry them out." Then Salazar pointed to a section in the collection of his speeches, *Doctrine and Action*. "This," he said, "is what

I mean: The idea of exaggerated internationalism, which hopes to simplify a problem but only confuses it a thousandfold, is just as surprising as the action of those who allow themselves to be dominated by a narrow and aggressive nationalism."

Yet the Viscount Cranborne, Lord Privy Seal of England, representative of the Inter-Allied Committee on Postwar Requirements, announced in the House of Lords that the United States Government had already requested from all Allied governments and governments in exile estimates of their food, clothing, and housing needs for the *first eighteen months* after the war was over, along with supplementary lists of raw materials, machinery, and industrial goods which all these various countries of the world will need.

The Viscount Cranborne, says the Associated Press, reminded the House of Lords that, while Prime Minister Churchill had already promised that "Britain would do all she could to help," the principal supplier can be only the United States. England herself, he pointed out, will need much.

The Archbishop of York protested over the omission of certain countries of the world in the report. Lord Cranborne corrected this promptly. "Russia, China, Burma, Malaya, and the Netherlands East Indies," he said, "will state their needs."

Now, it is no discredit whatever to the Viscount Cranborne and the Archbishop of York that they talk this way, or to the Inter-Allied Committee on Postwar Requirements to meet and make their arrangements. They have been educated to do so by the promises of the official spokesmen of the United States, who, after a parade of broken promises and colossal stupidities at home, now make new promises to the world.

Our national socialists will fail the world. We shall be unable to do what our leaders say we should do, and probably unwilling to do it. And in these circumstances we shall make enemies of our friends. Voices will rise against us in panic and denunciation, precisely as voices rose against us after the last war, when our leaders promised much less.

Our national socialists commit a national sin in their folly, for the promises we make should be honest and within our reach. Then we should live up to them, set our example, and in that way establish our place in the world of free men.

No one will thank us for starting down the road, going as far as we can, and then chucking the whole business through the revulsion of our own people to a program which Americans know in their hearts is unsound and untrue.

Millions of worried Americans, therefore, point to the last war, when our country turned to "realism," exactly as it has turned at the end of every war in history. Is this a portent of what will happen after World War II?

Some insist that we shall react again as we did the last time. For our leaders hurt grievously the case for America's place in the postwar world and immensely increase the already too good possibility that America will wash her hands of everything outside the twelve-mile limit, good or bad, at the earliest possible moment.

Such a tragic outcome would be assured already were it not for a few bright and encouraging facts which emerge.

This country, like the world, has changed much since the last war and is changing faster than ever as the Age of Air accelerates. There remains at least half a chance that Americans will remember the lessons of the last struggle and devote themselves wholeheartedly to building a strong and dynamic peace.

The problem, then, would be not the will but the means.

The principles are the things to grasp now.

The first step we should take in dealing with Europe is to recognize our own limitations and abandon the impertinent idea that a world is to be built in the American concept. Next we should put a limit on our total postwar aid, both in time and in dollars, and at the same time require that any postwar aid should be restricted to whatever nations took certain elementary steps in their own behalf. The Europeans' opening of Africa to themselves typifies such steps, hard but vital. The sale of vast European investments in the United States, still retained against our Treasury's loans instead of sold, is another. Replacing in the pot such untold millions of dollars as the Norwegian Government in London has acquired from ship charters, and from insurance on each vessel sunk, is another. Application of nearly a billion dollars of French gold, safe in our hemisphere, is another. The list is long. Are the Germans going to rehabilitate the devastated countries, or are we called on to do it? A few of these points are basic. But the *sine qua non* of this cascading age is not in Europe at all.

It is within the minds and hearts of the American people.

The success of the hope for a better world depends on re-establishing the self-faith of the American people and the integrity of the United States.

At these turning points in history there are always those who forget that there is little that has not been tried before, and who refuse to give credit to those who preceded them. Their idea is to build a new day: a mixture of generous intentions, naïve inexperience, but at the same time of low human passions.

On the other hand, others feel strengthened by opinions acquired in the past, to the point where they are chained to "their times" and can see only outrages and misfortune in the present and future. They stubbornly oppose many changes because they feel that the beliefs and customs in which they were reared have the quality of eternal truth.

The solution to America's problem lies in determining where these opposing views converge, in holding firm to the highest human truths of the past, the rewards of mankind's experiences, and at the same time boldly anticipating the conditions of the changing world and courageously meeting them.

The fundamental error of our national socialists is that they have never understood the place which integrity has in all the ramifications of life. They have always believed that to say a thing is the same as to do it, as though speech were final, as though rhetoric were capable of modifying the tendencies, habits, and character of real beings, and as though verbiage were a substitute for will, conscience, and education.

They will not see that their inability to organize liberty comes from their own nature; from wrong notions which they have of the individual, of society, of races, of law, of duty. Their way is to plant trees downwards and then be astonished at the result.

This means perpetual wavering between confusion and tyranny, between the red and the black, between Danton and Loyola.

The evidence of our history is mercilessly exact. Through long years we have been wasting and abusing the liberties our ancestors won. Conceived in liberty, we have been distracted from the stern fact of liberty, the first element of which is that we supply ourselves with good government.

When President Roosevelt said, "We do not need to abandon our democracy to match the strength of aggressors," he spoke the truth. *We do not need to abandon it, but we do need to go back to it.*

The immediate war measure and the primary postwar task of the United States in behalf of itself and the world is to return to its moral and intellectual foundations and believe in them again.

The heavy foreboding which many note in the hearts and minds of thoughtful men and women, the strange failure to rejoice and be electrified by the mere thought that one day the war may be over —what does it mean? It means we see a Fate coming closer, and that we know we have been made weak in our own house.

We are weak because we have not been trusted. "If you don't trust us how can you expect us to trust you? Well, you can't—and we don't. But that's not our fault, it's yours."

We are weak because every bulwark of integrity we have has been tampered with. The oath-bound leaders of our government cannot circumvent the purpose of law, destroy the authority of contracts, belittle the fundamental postulates by which all honorable men live, the sanctity of the spoken word, the clarity of the written word, whether it be between government and citizen or citizen and citizen, and in this way make us strong.

We are weak because of haphazard and bureaucratic "planned economy," which was, in essence, the substitution of an unplanned economy for the virility of self-faith and manly enterprise. Instead of freeing the creative power of America under a triumphant affirmation of its ability and power, Americans were shackled.

Under the disguise of modifying our economy, which was really a witch hunt, the creative impulses of countless millions were destroyed. After toying with the most explosive features of racial questions at home, fomenting class prejudices, inciting pressure groups, agitating the young and the old, and foundering in a "purchasing power" policy which collapsed for all except the office-holders themselves, we contemplate healing the world.

We contemplate healing the world when we are not decently governing ourselves.

The reality of this demands the elimination of collectivism in the United States, or the future ability of the United States to help the world is nil and the ability of the world to be helped is negligible.

It will take a new honoring of first principles to get back to self-faith and to re-establish the integrity of our nation. To do this, to turn our backs on political opportunists and to resist the "inevitableness" of national socialism, requires a courage which is the equivalent of the courage of America's pioneers.

It requires sacrificial devotion, spiritual and intellectual conviction, and a genuine respect for the dignity of one's self as a man, one's own work, one's place as the head of a family, as a member of a community, and as a citizen of a prosperous and stable nation. Men are the essential element of the nation, which will be precisely what they are. And above this, each man is a spirit and a conscience. How should we not respect and do our utmost to protect, elevate, and improve that spirit and that conscience?

For in this principle of self-faith and integrity is the only hope of our country this side of intermittent war and permanent national distress. And in our country's accomplishment of this goal rests the only hope of a world caught in spiritual liquidation and writhing in the distortions of the Hudson Tube Age.

The lopsided development of American government in the face of astounding technological improvements will grow either more lopsided or less lopsided. It will not stay, suspended, in the midpoint where it is today.

If our ability to rule ourselves grows worse, we and our children's children shall descend the path of Dante's bewildered traveler, who, "worn by dreadful trials of the past, turns from the dangers which beset his life's course." We shall face the rule of a chosen group of militarists after a sufficient number of wars.

Conversely, with the support of the principle of self-faith, and in the American spirit, our future and our ability to help the world are boundless, praise God, in uncoerced dedication to the common and lofty cause of the individual strength of man.

Index

Abdul Hamid, 232
Abetz, Otto, 184f.
Abidjan, French Ivory Coast, Africa, 100f.
Abyssinia, 55, 139; Abyssinian plateau, 90
Accra, British Gold Coast, West Africa, 23, 93ff., 97, 101ff., 111f., 129
Adams, Franklin P., quoted, 42
Adana, Turkey, 22, 242
Adnan Bey, 234
Adnan Edib, 234
Aegean Islands, 51
Africa:
 animals, 115f.; centuries in development, 93f.; colonial benefits from America, 101ff., 111ff., 131; construction of airports in, 101ff.; co-operative agricultural developments, 114f.; drum signals, 82; effect of American economic policy, 226ff.; geography and climate, 89ff.; gold production, 91; hydroelectric development, 91; monopolies and concessions, 94ff.; native characteristics, 89ff., 115, 117ff., 138, 148, 152; natural resources, 90f., 93ff., 100, 114; political divisions, 91ff.; population, 92; public works projects, 102ff.; quality of colonial administrators, 94f.; refueling of German submarines, 100f.
Ain Taya, fortifications, 189
Airplanes:
 Baltimore, 202; Boeing, 89; Boston, 199, 207f.; Consolidated, 123; De Havilland, 45; Dornier, 239; Douglas, 99f.; Focke-Wulf, 111; Heinkel, 239; Hurricane, 132, 202; Junkers, 166; Liberator 24s, 153; Messerschmitts, 153, 166, 199, 208f., 239; P-38s, 113; Potez, 130; Seafire, 189; Spitfire, 189; Stuka, 2f., 105, 145, 199f.; Zero, 164
Albania, 220
Albany, New York, 12
Albertine Rift, Africa, 90
Alexander the Great, 230
Alexandretta, Gulf of, 229
Alexandria, 132, 173f., 190ff., 201; closing of naval base, 178
Algiers, 100, 174, 183ff., 204
Ali-el-Gailani, Rashid, 268
Ali Fand, 234
Ali Riza, 231f., 235
Allenby, Field Marshal Edmund Henry, Viscount, 216
American Committee for a Jewish Army, 217
Amsterdam, Holland, invasion bridgehead, 171
Andaman Island, Bay of Bengal, 164
Anglo-Egyptian Sudan, 113ff., 132, 195; Sudanese Desert, 132ff., 173
Angola, Portuguese colony of, southwestern Africa, 90
Ankara (Angora), Turkey, 80, 231ff.
Ankara Numune Hastanesi, 234
Annam, French Indo-China, 55
Antwerp, Belgium, invasion bridgehead, 171
Arabian Desert, 173, 212
Arabian Nights, 1
Arctic Ocean, 89

Argentina, 84
Aristotle, 66
Arnold, Gen. Henry H., U.S.A., 159
Asbury Park, N.J., 140
Ashland, Wis., 22
Asia, 8, 52f., 57, 116
Asmara, Eritrea, 114
Atatürk, Mustafa Kemal Pasha, 59, 231ff.
Auchinleck, Gen. Claude, 174, 176ff.
Australia, 106; Army in Middle East, 155, 175
Austria, 58

Baden-Baden, Germany, 66
Baldwin, Stanley, 223
Balfour, Arthur James, Earl of, 216
Balkans, the, 55, 180ff.
Baltic Sea, 69; attitude of Russia towards, 219
Bamako, French Sudan, French West Africa, 100
Barclay, Lieut. Comm. McClelland, U.S. N.R., 114
Bardia, Libya, 176f.
Bataan, Philippines, 155
Battle of Britain, quality of airplanes in, 132, 161f., 163
Bauchi, Nigeria, 117
Bayazid, Sultan, 230
Beirut, Lebanon, 213
Belém, Brazil, 84
Belgium, 44ff., 54, 221; chronic unemployment, 103; colonial benefits from America, 106ff.; colonial office administrators, 94f.; colonies in Africa, 92ff., 112; forts of Liége and Namur, 45; relations with England, 46; relations with Germany, 46
Belgrade, Yugoslavia, 181f.
Benue River, Nigeria, 114
Berchtesgaden, 260f.
Berlin, 2, 4, 65f., 69ff., 85, 112, 159f., 169ff., 172, 177, 215
Berlin-to-Bagdad railway, 232
Bermuda, 106, 140
Bethouart, Gen. Émile, 186ff.
"Better World Order," 221ff., 277ff.
Bimini, Bahamas, 82
Blagovyeshchensk, U.S.S.R., 220
Blitzkrieg, 45, 74, 232
Boisson, General M., 113

Bonaparte, Napoleon, 11, 34, 53, 81, 83, 170
Bordeaux, France, 204
Bornu, Nigeria, 117
Bosporus, 180, 181, 230
Boulogne, France, invasion bridgehead, 172
Bourbons, of France, 53
Braidwood, Illinois, 26
Brauchitsch, Field Marshal Walther von, 70, 172
Bray, Squadron Leader Gerald, 192ff., 202
Brazil, 83, 88, 151
Brazzaville, French Equatorial Africa, 112, 129
Brereton, Maj. Gen. Lewis Hyde, U.S.A., 163f.
Breslau, Germany, 220
Brickley, Charles, 39
Bristol, England, 93
Britain, *see* England
British Broadcasting System, 211
British Guiana, 84
Brock, Ray, 251
Brüning, Heinrich, 70
Brussels, Belgium, 44
Bulgaria, 181, 220, 241
Burke, Edmund, 63
Buryat basin, U.S.S.R., 220

Cairo, Egypt, 1ff., 44, 88, 114, 124, 132, 137f., 144ff., 177f., 201, 211; horse racing, 150
Cairo, Ill., 13
Calais, France, 181
California, 214
Cameroons, Central Africa, 55, 129
Canada, 82, 106ff., 225; Army in Middle East, 175; availability for expansion, 82, 108; relations with United States, 225f.
Çanakkale, Battle of, 235f.
Carlyle, Thomas, quoted, 104
Carroll, Madeleine, 150
Cartwright, Rev. Peter, 14
Casablanca, French Morocco, 80, 100, 163, 174, 185ff.
Casey, Hon. Richard G., 154f.
Catroux, Gen. Georges, 214
Chad, Lake, 80, 112, 115, 124
Chad, colony, French Equatorial Africa, 112, 114

Chakmak, Marshal Fevzi, 80, 239ff.
Chamberlain, Prime Minister Arthur Neville, 75ff., 223, 263
Chaney, Maj. Gen. James Eugene, U.S.A., 164
Charlemagne, 263
Charles V, Emperor of Germany and King of Spain, 53
Chatham, William Pitt, Earl of, 63
Chiang Kai-shek, Generalissimo, 220
Chicago, Ill., 19ff., 93
Chicago River, 18
Chillicothe, Ohio, 13
China, 6, 101, 143, 165f., 219; development of civilization, 143; development of writing, 6; relations with Britain, 220; relations with Russia, 220
Churchill, Prime Minister Winston, 8, 79, 135, 150, 159, 163, 170, 204, 223, 229, 242; decision to hold El Alamein, 178; quoted, 69
Cincinnati, Ohio, 13
Clark, Lieut. Gen. Mark W., 187
Clarke, G. H., British Consul, 229
Clay, Henry, 63
Clemenceau, Georges, 65
Clipper (Pan American Airways), 68, 82ff.
Clodius, Dr. Karl, 246
Coal City, Ill., 23f., 29ff., 51, 123f.
Cobden, Richard, 63
Colbert, Jean Baptiste, French Minister of Finance, 53
Columbia Broadcasting Company, 211
Columbus, Ohio, 12ff.
Combined Chiefs of Staff, 170ff., 186ff.
Comiso, German air base, 176
Compton, Col. Louis J., U.S.A., 80, 84, 89ff., 98ff.
Congo, river and basin, 90, 92, 113, 129
Coningham, Air Vice-Marshal Arthur, 192ff.
Constantinople, see Istanbul
Continental Hotel, Cairo, 140
Coolidge, Calvin, 62, 233
Cooper Union, New York, 14
Copenhagen, 65
Corfu, Greece, 67
Cranborne, Robert, Viscount, 292
Crete, island of, 153, 212
Cromwell, Oliver, 53
Croydon, London airport, 45

Cunningham, Col. F. H., Sr., U.S.A., 112f.
Cunningham, F. H., Jr., American Embassy, Berlin, 112
Cuno, Wilhelm, 70
Cyprus, Island of, 220, 229
Czechoslovakia, 77

Dahomey, French West Africa, 114
Dakar, French West Africa, 80, 100, 186ff.
Damascus, Syria, 213
Dankelmann, Gen. Hermann von, 182
Dante Alighieri, quoted, 103, 296
Danton, Georges Jacques, 10, 294
Danzig, Free City of, 65, 220
Dardanelles, the, 232
Darlan, Admiral François, 100, 188ff.
Day, Richard, 113, 123; death of, 125ff.
Dayton, Ohio, 111
De Gaulle, Gen. Charles, 112f., 187
Denmark, 65, 77, 93, 106; attitude towards war, 65f.; colonial benefits from America, 106; relations with England, 93; relations with Germany, 77; settlement of Africa, 93
Denver, Col., 174
Detroit, Mich., 111
Deutsche, Felix, German industrialist, 70
Deutsche Akademische Auslandsstelle, 151
Deutsche Bank, Berlin, 68
Devlet Hava Yollari, 230
Dieckhoff, Dr. Hans Heinrich, 72ff., 253
Dill, Field Marshal Sir John, 160, 241
Diocletian, 286
Dnieper Dam, U.S.S.R., 262
Dodecanese Islands, 221
Doolittle, Maj. Gen. James, U.S.A., 161
Douglas Aircraft Company, 61
Dover, England, 140
Drum, Lieut. Gen. Hugh Aloysius, U.S.A., 153, 175
Dubreuil, see Lemaigre Dubreuil
Duluth, Minn., 18, 21ff., 91
Dunkirk, France, 178
Durusoy, Dr. Salahi, 250f.
Düsseldorf, Germany, 172
Dutch Guiana, 83

Eden, Foreign Secretary Robert Anthony, 219
Edison, Thomas Alva, quoted, 38
Edward, Prince of Wales (Duke of Windsor), 44, 93f.

Egypt, 1ff., 51, 113, 118, 129, 134, 142ff., 147ff., 168, 176ff., 183f.; Army, 157; debt to Nile, 142f.; migration to central Africa, 118; Ministry of Foreign Affairs, *Kars el Nil*, 151; Palace of the King, 156ff.; sandstorms, 133ff.; State Broadcasting, Ltd., 211

Eisenhower, General Dwight David, U.S.A., 183ff., 227

El Alamein, Egypt, 178ff., 183f.

Elizabeth, Queen of England, 53

Ellsberg, Captain Edward, U.S.N., 138ff.

Elmhirst, Air Commodore Thomas, 200

Emerson, Ralph Waldo, quoted, 7, 55

England, 2, 4, 6, 11, 67f., 75ff., 80, 165, 211ff., 275ff.; attitude of General Staff towards Russia, 75; August 1923 note to France-Belgium (quoted), 46; Cabinet, 95; chronic unemployment, 51ff., 94, 103ff.; colonial benefits from America, 106ff.; colonial office administrators, 94; colonial policy, 92ff.; Committee of the African Research Survey, 92; Corps Military Police, 192f.; effect of invention of steam engine, 53f.; Embassy in Cairo, 156; Imperial General Staff, 160, 205; Military Alliance with Turkey, 211; Military Intelligence, 151; Ministry of Information, 147; percentage of troops in action, 193f.; plans to withstand invasion, 165ff.; plunge into world markets, 52f.; regiments captured at Tobruk, 175; trade with continent of Europe, 54; troops in B.E.F., 205; urbanization, compared with Germany, 54

Eritrea, 134ff., 227

Falkenhayn, Gen. Otto von, 233

Faraday, Michael, 96

Farouk, King of Egypt, 156ff.

Faya, 132

Fedala, fortifications, 190

Ferguson, Ronald, 211

Fields, Gracie, 45

Fighting French; *see* France

Finland, 2, 4, 68, 75, 80, 137, 165, 172, 246; Karelian isthmus, 125; War of 1939–40, 75

Fischer, Louis, correspondent and author, 42

Fitzgerald, Brig. Gen. Shepler W., U.S.A., 101f., 112

Florence, Minn., 22

Fox, Charles James, English statesman, 63

France, 54ff., 68, 78, 80, 92, 156, 171, 181, 275ff.; and Belgian action in Ruhr, 46; colonial benefits from America, 106ff.; colonial office administrators, 94f.; colonies in Africa, 92ff.; Fighting French: Air Forces, 129; Alsace Squadron, 132, 199, 201ff.; in Syria, 214; mobilization at Ft. Lamy to attack Rommel, 131f.; seizure of African colonies, 112f.; treatment by Vichy, 131; Fort of Beaufort, 45; invasion bridgeheads, 171ff.; plunge into world markets, 52f.; refugees, 109; relations with England, 46; relations with Germany, 46, 74, 78; relations with Turkey, 231ff.; Revolution, 220

Franklin, Benjamin, 63

Frederick William I, King of Prussia, 271

French Guiana, 83

French Guinea, 100

Freyberg, Lieut. Gen. Sir Bernard, 178f.

Fulton, Robert, 11, 13

Gabon, French Equatorial Africa, 112

Garbo, Greta, 150

Gates, Jack, 39

Gela, Sicily, 176

Genel Kurmay Başkani (Turkish General Staff headquarters), 240ff.

George, Maj. Gen. H. L., U.S.A., 124

George, Air Vice-Marshal Robert, 211ff., 229ff.

Gerard, Lieut. Sumner, Jr., U.S.N.R., 147f., 153

German-Russian Non-Aggression Pact, 67, 74ff.

German-Russian Trade Treaty, August 1939, 67

Germany, 4, 8, 11, 50, 54ff., 65ff., 77, 80, 159, 166, 231, 275ff.; Air Force, 74, 105, 161ff.; armies in Yugoslavia, 181ff.; armistice commission in north Africa, 187f.; artillery, 105; attitude of people towards Hitler, 46, 58; attitude towards Africa, 169; *Blitzkrieg* army, 45; chronic unemployment, 67, 103; colonies in Africa, 54, 93; declaration of war on the United States, 73; degree of urbanization compared to England, 54; disorders in 1923, 4; Embassy in Washington, 68f.; foreign borrowings (table),

49; Foreign Office, 68f., 72ff.; fortification of France, 172; General Staff, 69, 169, 171; invasion of, 169ff.; mythology and folklore, 70; neurasthenia, 197f.; organization of *Luftwaffe*, 167f.; Pan-Germanism, 54; propaganda, 157; refueling of submarines in Africa, 100f.; refugees in America, 69f, 105f.; relations: with Czechoslovakia, 77; Denmark, 77; England, 46, 70; Norway, 77; Poland, 65, 77; Turkey, 231ff.; United States, 70 traditionalists, 69ff.; war guilt, World War I, 70; West Wall fortifications, 66, 144, 172

Gestapo, 112, 150f., 182, 249ff.
Gibbons, Floyd, 43f.
Gibraltar, 2, 68, 100, 111, 129, 133, 166, 180, 190, 230
Giraud, Gen. Henri Honoré, 186ff.
Gladstone, Herbert John, Viscount, 232
Gloucester, Duke of, 132
Glubb, Maj. John Bagot, 265
Gold Coast, Africa, 23, 93ff., 101ff., 111ff.
Golden Horn, 80
Goltz, Gen. Hermann von der, 233
Gordon, Gen. Charles George, 135
Göring, Field Marshal Hermann, 165
Gort, John Standish Vereker, Viscount, 205
Governments in exile, effectiveness of, 220f.
Great Britain, *see* England
Greece, 126, 153, 221, 230, 234ff.
Greenland, 106
Grobba, Dr. Fritz, 268
Gunther, Foreign Minister Christian, 220

Haifa, Palestine, 213
Haile Selassie, Emperor, 139
Hailey, Lord, 92
Halfaya Pass, Egypt, 177
Hannibal, 170
Hansson, Prime Minister Per Albin, 220
Harding, Warren Gamaliel, 46
Harkess, Harry, 123
Harkess, William, 29ff., 123
Harrington, Gen. Charles, 236
Harrisburg, Pennsylvania, 6
Havenstein, Dr. Rudolf, president of the Reichsbank, 70
Haydon, Maj. Gen. J. C., 189
Hayward, Wis., 22

Heliopolis, Cairo airport, 1ff., 138, 199
Henderson, Sir Nevile, 154
Hentig, Georg Werner von, 268
Hess, Rudolf, 170
Hibbing, Minn., 22
Hinchliffe, Capt. Walter, R.F.C., 44ff.
Hindenburg, Field Marshal Paul von, 258ff.
Hiser, Capt. Charles H., U.S.A., 80, 88ff.
Hitler, Adolf, 58, 66, 165, 170f., 174, 182, 185f.; attitude towards Munich pact, 73, 75f.
Holland, *see* Netherlands
Homer, quoted, 144
"Horst Wessel Lied," quoted, 44
House of Representatives, 16f.
Houston, Dame Fanny Lucy, 162
Hudson River, 6, 18
Hudson-Wohlthat conversations, 70
Hull, Hon. Cordell, 66f., 127
Hungary, 58; armies in Yugoslavia, 181
Huntzinger, Gen. Charles L. C., 184
Huri Turao, 131
Hurley, Wis., 22
Husein ibn-Ali, 215

Ibn-Saud, 215
Iceland, 155
Illinois, 21ff.
India, 103, 114, 166, 194, 219; air route, 114; competition with Europe, 103; Sikhs, 1, 155
Inönü, Ismet, 236, 239
Inter-Allied Committee on Postwar Requirements, 292
Iran (Persia), 137
Iraq, 143, 214
Irish question, 40
Ismet Pasha, *see* Inönü
Istanbul (Constantinople), 137, 181, 231f., 236f.
Italy, 8, 38, 58, 125, 153, 156, 165, 181; armies in Yugoslavia, 181f.; "capture" of Tobruk, 175ff.; relations with England, 46; relations with Turkey, 231; Roman explorers in Africa, 91; Secret Police, 150f.
Ivory Coast, French West Africa, 100

Japan, 75ff., 103f., 261ff.
Jefferson, Thomas, 63f.
Jenke, Frau, 269

Jerusalem, Grand Mufti of, 214f.
Jerusalem, Palestine, 212f.
Jewell, Lieut. N.L.A., R.N., 187
Jewish Legion, Jabotinsky's, 216
Jews in Palestine and Syria, 214ff.
Joliet, Louis, French-Canadian explorer, 93
Joliet, Ill., 23
Juneau, Alaska, 88
Jung, Carl, quoted, 37

Kano, Nigeria, 114ff., 124, 202
Kansas City, Mo., 151, 155, 196
Karachi, India, 114, 137
Karelian isthmus, Finland, 125
Kars el Nil, Egyptian Foreign Office, 151
Keefer, Matthew, 29
Keitel, Field Marshal Wilhelm, 261ff.
Kellogg, Frank Billings, 50
Kemal Atatürk, see Atatürk, Mustafa Kemal Pasha
Kent, England, 116
Kenya, East Africa, 95
Kenya and Uganda Railway, 95
Keokuk, Iowa, 143f.
Kerns, Vernon, 124, 132ff.
Khartoum, Anglo-Egyptian Sudan, 91, 114, 132ff., 143, 202
Kilimanjaro Natives' Co-operative Union, 115
King, Admiral Ernest J., 140
Kirk, Hon. Alexander Comstock, 66, 148, 154, 177
Kitchener, Horatio Herbert, Earl, 135
Knatchbull-Hugessen, Sir Hughe, 239
Knightsbridge, Battle of, 175ff.
Knox, William Franklin, Secretary of the Navy, 140
Knox, Fort, 91
Koran, 157f., 203
Korea, 220
Kreisler, Fritz, 98

La Guardia Field, 82, 101, 145
Lake, Veronica, 151
Lamson, Sir Miles, 156f.
Lamy, Fort, French Equatorial Africa, 114, 124ff., 129
Larminat, General M. de, 113
Laski, Harold, British pamphleteer, 107
Lausanne Conference, 236f.
Lawrence, T. E., 242

League of Nations, 40; Statistical Year-Book, quoted, 92, 216ff.
Leclerc, General J., 132
Lee, Gypsy Rose, 151
Lemaigre Dubreuil, Jacques, 186ff.
Léopoldville, Belgian Congo, 113
Lewis, John L., 24, 241
Liberia, 89ff., 97f.
Libya, 100, 113, 165ff.
Limoges, France, 130
Limpopo river system, southern Africa, 90
Lincoln, Abraham, 14, 63
Lisbon, Portugal, 150
Liverpool, England, 43
Livingston, Robert R., 13
Livingstone, Commando Capt. R. T., 187
Lloyd George, David, 65, 234
London, 44f., 94, 112, 116, 126, 129, 131f., 145, 171, 187, 211, 236
Londonderry, Siege of, 15
Longmore, Sir Arthur M., 160
Louis, Joe, 241
Loyola, Ignatius, 10, 294
Luftwaffe, see Germany
Luxor, Egypt, 138
Lwów, Poland, 220
Lydda, Palestine, 212
Lyon, France, 185, 204

Macedonia, Greece, 220
Mackie, Wing Commander J. B., 239
Madagascar, 55, 155
Madison, James, 63
Madrid, 150
Maginot Line, 45, 144, 162f., 172
Magnitogorsk, U.S.S.R., 103, 262
Málaga, Spain, 104f., 188
Malta, 160, 190, 212
Manchester Guardian, quoted, 107
Manchuria (Manchukuo), 220
Marcosson, Isaac F., 237
Marquette, Jacques, 93
Marquette, Mich., 22
Marx, Karl, 63
Massaua, Eritrea, 138ff., 178
Mast, Gen. Charles, 186ff.
Matifou, Cape, 189
Maxwell, Maj. Gen. Russell L., U.S.A., 141, 147, 153f.
Mayhew, Col. Reginald Rawson Mark, R.A.O.C., 80, 88ff., 98, 116ff.

McNarney, Lieut. Gen. Joseph T., U.S.A., 124, 159
McPherson, Aimee Semple, 152
Mechanistic network, development of, 33ff.; rotation of production-consumption, 35ff.; mass effect, 36ff.
Mediterranean, 2, 51, 55, 80, 89, 100, 153, 169, 176f., 204
Mehmet Reshad, Sultan, 245
Mein Kampf, 257
Mercantile system, 52ff., 93ff., 102ff.
Mersa Matruh, Egypt, 177f.
Mesopotamia, 51
Mexico, 52
Miami, Fla., 182
Middle Congo, French Equatorial Africa, 112
Migration, 11ff., 82ff., 88, 103ff., 108ff., 118, 143
Mihailovitch, Gen. Draza, 181ff., 249ff.
Mikusch-Buchberg, Dagobert von, 268
Mills, Ogden, 263
Milwaukee, Wis., 21
Minnesota, 18, 22f.
Mississippi River, 14, 143
Mitchell, John, 24ff.
Mohammed the Victorious, 235
Molotoff, Foreign Commissar Vyacheslav, 67, 219
Mombasa, Africa, 95
Monastir, military academy, 231
Montesquieu, Charles de Secondat, 294
Montgomery, Gen. Bernard Law, 183ff.
Montgomery, Lieut. Com. Robert, U.S. N.R., 150
Montreux, Conference of, 237
Moscow, 67, 74, 144, 163, 172
Moses, 83
Mountbatten, Lord Louis, 189
Mozambique, Portuguese East Africa, 92
Mukhtar Pasha, 235
Munich (pact), 66, 75ff., 151
Murphy, George, 150
Murphy, Robert Daniel, 184ff.
Mussolini, Benito, 165, 215
Mustafa Kemal Pasha, *see* Atatürk

Naci Sevket, 268
Nairobi, Africa, 95
Napoleon, *see* Bonaparte, Napoleon
Natal, Brazil, 84

Neditch, Gen. Milan, 182
Neenah, Wisconsin, 85
Netherlands, 51f., 93, 171; Relations with: England, 52; France, 52; Spain, 52; settlements of Africa, 93f.
Newfoundland, 106, 225
New Orleans, La., 13
Newspapers: New York *Times*, 46, 243; Trinidad *Guardian*, 82; Egyptian Mail (Cairo), 151
New York City, 68f., 88, 101, 129, 153
New Zealand, 106, 155, 192, 195; Army in the Middle East, 175 178f.
Nigeria, 113ff.
Nile River, 4, 80, 90, 114, 134f., 142, 173, 176, 178
Noguès, Gen. Auguste, 189f.
Norman, Sir Montagu Collet, 107, 263
Norman Conquest of England, 6
North Africa, *see* Africa
North American Newspaper Alliance, 65, 82, 243, 249
North Sea, 69, 125, 134, 137
Norway, 166, 219
Nubian Desert, 142, 203

Ödemiş, Turkey, 244
Ohio, 9, 11ff., 98, 107, 115
Okkak, Labrador, 226
Omdurman, Anglo-Egyptian Sudan, 135
Oppenheim, E. Phillips, 1, 150
Oran, Algeria, 100, 185
Ottoman Empire, 230f.

Pacific Ocean, 6, 55, 155
Paine, Corp. Leonard, 120ff.
Palace Hotel, Brussels, 45
Palestine, 148, 178, 211ff., 216, 236, 238
Palmerston, Henry John Temple, Viscount, 63
Panama, 89, 140
Pan American Airways-Africa, Ltd., 101ff.
Papen, Franz von, 182, 233, 246ff.
Paris, 50f., 236
Pearl Harbor, 68f., 112, 175, 184, 227
Persia, *see* Iran
Persian Gulf, 230
Peru, 52
Pétain, Marshal Henri Philippe, 73, 259; dismissal of Gen. Weygand, 184f.

Philadelphia, Pa., 6
Piave River, 230
Pietri, Pvt. Ricardo, Italian Army, 121
Pitt, William, the younger, 63
Pittsburgh, Pa., 6
Plymouth, Mass., 93
Poland, 4, 58, 65, 77, 125; relations with Germany, 65, 125
"Policing," failure of, 46f., 233ff.
Pompey the Great, 230
Population, trends and problems in Europe, 53ff., 81ff.
Popva, Euginye, 251ff.
Popva, Pvt. Serge, Russian Army, 121
Port Said, 212
Portugal, 52, 68, 80, 92, 150; relations with Spain, 52; settlement of Africa, 92ff.; West Africa, 88
Portuguese Guinea, 92
Portuguese West Africa, 88, 92
Preston, Hart, 251
Priam, King of Troy, 230
Prince of Wales (now Duke of Windsor), 44, 93f.
Princeton, N.J., 6
Principes de Coalition, 92
Provincetown, R.I., 139
Puerto Rico, 96, 109
Pyramids, 2, 44, 126f., 192

Qattara Depression, 178
Quebec, Battle of, 12

Rabat, Morocco, 189f.
Radoyichitch, Col. Zhivoyin, 252f.
Raeder, Grossadmiral Erich H. A., 69, 169f.
Rauf Bey, 234
Red Sea, 139, 178
Reynaud, Paul, 204
Rhodesia, Southern, 90
Ribbentrop, Foreign Minister Joachim von, 67f., 262, 268
Ritz Hotel, Madrid, 150
Rome, 38, 51; bombing of, 150
Rommel, Marshal Erwin, 80, 82, 131, 137, 144, 148, 163, 169ff.; career in German Army, 170; author's meeting with, 177, 183ff.
Roosevelt, President Franklin Delano, 42, 163, 170; Casablanca meeting, 242; quoted, 295

Ruhr, 46ff.
Rumania, 150, 238
Runciman, Lord Walter, 265
Russell, Rosalind, 150
Russia, 53, 58, 67, 74ff., 103, 125, 165f., 205, 219ff., 229, 231, 236ff., 242ff., 275ff.
Ryan, Lucian, 123

Sahara Desert, 90, 131, 173
Saint-Cyr, academy at, 130, 184
St. John's, Newfoundland, 226
St. Louis, Mo., 174, 196, 227
Saint-Nazaire, France, invasion bridgehead, 171
Sakarya, Battle of, 234
Salazar, Prime Minister António d'Oliveira, quoted, 8f., 291f.
Salonika, Greece, 180f., 231
San Bernardino, mountains, 214
Sanders, Gen. Liman von, 232
Sandusky River, 12
Saracoglu, Prime Minister Shukru, 239ff.
Saul of Tarsus, 230
Saydam, Dr. Refik, 80, 137
Schacht, Dr. Hjalmar Horace Greeley, 50, 70, 263
Schmitz, Paul, 268
Schnering, Otto Y., quoted, 62
Schröder, Admiral Hans von, quoted, 259
Schuschnigg, Chancellor Kurt von, 260
Scioto River, 12
Scotland, 125, 137
Scranton, Pa., 24
Seattle, Wash., 85, 111
Sedbon, Gilbert, Reuters correspondent, 211
Senegal, French West Africa, 100
Sfax, Tunisia, 100, 175
Shensi, China, 220
Shepheard's Hotel, Cairo, 1, 145
Sicily, 101, 165, 176f., 190
Sidi Barrani, Egypt, 177
Sidney, Australia, 226
Sidon, Lebanon, 212
Sinkiang, China, 220
Smith, Adam, quoted, 81
Smith, Brig. Gen. Cyrus R., U.S.A., 124
Smyrna, Turkey, 234
Sokoto, Nigeria, 117
Solum, Egypt, 177
Sothern, Ann, 150

South Africa, Union of, 90, 92, 129, 175, 238
South America, 4, 84ff., 129, 249
Spain, 4, 51f., 68, 80, 100, 104, 150f.; living conditions and political implications, 104ff.; proving ground for post-World War II, 105; refugees, 109; relations with Portugal, 52
Spanish Morocco, 92, 174
Stalin, Joseph, 74f., 103, 144, 163, 267f.
Stalingrad, battle for, 243
Statesman's Year-Book, quoted, 92
Steinhardt, Ambassador Laurence A., 225, 238ff.
Steinhardt, Mrs. Laurence A., 238
Stettinius, Edward R., 224
Stimson, Hon. Henry, 261
Stinnes, Hugo, 70
Stockholm, 65f.
Strang, William, 265
Stumme, General von, 176
Sublime Porte, Turkish Foreign Office, 232
Suez Canal, 178, 180, 212; effect on world trade, 56; methods of clearing German mines, 212
Sulla, 286
Superior, Lake, 18
Swanson, Gloria, 150
Sweden, 66, 68f., 80, 219
Switzerland, 50, 66, 68, 181, 211
Syria, 129, 132, 148, 178, 211, 213ff., 236, 240; attitude towards Jews and Zionism, 214; friction between Christians and Moslems, 214; relations with Iraq, 214; resources, 213; secret societies, 155

Taha-el-Hashimi, 268
Tajeddine el Hassani, Sheik, 214
Tamerlane the Terrible, 230
Tangier, Morocco, 100
Taurus Mountains, 229f.
Taylor, Edward Livingston (grandfather of author), 14ff.
Taylor, Edward Livingston, Jr. (Uncle Ned), 16f
Taylor, Henry Noble (father of author), 17ff.
Taylor, Mehitabel Wilson (wife of Robert), 12ff., 107f.
Taylor, Robert Livingston, 12ff., 107f.

Tedder, Air Chief Marshal Sir Arthur William, 4f., 132, 137f., 144, 146, 159ff., 164, 177, 183ff., 211, 242
Terentieff, Ambassador Alexei, 263ff.
Texas, 83
Thebes, Egypt, 144, 175
Thoma, General von, 176
Thomas, Lowell, 242
Thrace, Eastern, 236
Thyssen, Fritz, 70, 76f.
Timberlake, Brig. Gen. Patrick W., U.S.A., 80, 89ff., 98, 152f., 164, 183
Tobruk, fall of, 175ff., 181ff.
Todt, Dr. Fritz, 144
Tokyo, raid on, 161
Tongking, French Indo-China, 55
Topal Osman Pasha, 235
Trapani, Sicily, 176
Trinidad, 82f., 106
Tripoli, Libya, 100, 173f., 176ff., 183ff., 230
Trojan Wars, 230
Truro, Nova Scotia, 12
Truro Township (Columbus), Ohio, 12
Tucker, Sophie, 152
Tunis, Tunisia, 100
Tunisia, 175
Turkey, 51, 58, 80, 83, 137, 181, 211, 225, 229ff.; antiquity of ruins, 230; armed forces, 241f.; army intelligence, 241; benefits from Lausanne Conference, 236; experiences with Germans in World War I, 232f.; German Trade Pact, 246ff.; Military Alliance with Great Britain, 211; Milli Mücadele, "The National Struggle," 59; population, 229; Red Cross, 234; social and political nature, 234f.; topography and climate, 229
Tyre, Lebanon, 213

Ubangi-Shari, French Equatorial Africa, 112
United Kingdom, see England
United Mine Workers of America, 24f.
United States of America, airplane construction in Africa, 111; "Better World Order," contrasted with German, 221ff.; blending of fascism, communism, and collectivism, 60; breeding ground and raw material pool, 52; British mandate convention, Palestine, 1924, 216;

collectivism in, 6off.; effect of mechanistic network on, 6off.; Hospital,
Istanbul, 250; integrity of, liberals,
63; loans to Germany, 49; migration
within, 9, 11ff., 63; Office of War Information, 147; postwar policy overseas, 47f.; public sentiment after World
War I, 4off., 46; relations with: England, 11; Germany, 49, 76; Lebanon,
214; Palestine, 216
University of Geneva, 244
University of Virginia, 41

Valin, General Martial, 129ff., 201ff.
Vansittart, Sir Robert, 263
Versailles, Treaty of, 93
Vessels: *Charles Hutchinson*, 2off., 91;
Clermont, 13; *Falcon*, 140; *George
Washington*, 40; *Intent*, 140; *May-
flower*, 93; *Niebenfels*, 141; *Nieuw Am-
sterdam*, 68; *Normandie*, 141; *Onaka*,
21; *S-51*; 139; Squalus, 139
Vichy, France, 73
Vichy Government, 112f., 184ff., 204,
240; *see also* France
Vienna, 168, 230
Vilna, Poland, 220
Virginia, 85
Vogler, Albert, German industrialist, 70
Volta River, Gold Coast, Africa, 93

Wadi Seidna, Khartoum airport, 136, 142
Wakefield, Mich., 22
Wales, 30, 103
War of 1812, 13

Washington, George, 12, 15, 63, 170
Washington, D.C., 114, 122, 131, 171,
196
Watt, James, 53
Watt, Sir Watson, 16of.
Waukegan, Ill., 21ff.
Wavell, Gen. Archibald P., 149
Wealth of Nations, reference to "fire
engine," 81
Webster, Daniel, 63
Welles, Hon. Benjamin Sumner, 66
West, Paul, 147
Weygand, Gen. Maxime, 144, 184
Whalen, Christopher, 21ff.
Whiteman, Paul, 44
Wilhelm II, Kaiser, 39, 129, 258
Wilhelmstrasse, *see* Germany
Wilson, Gen. Henry, 148, 179
Wilson, Thomas Woodrow, 39ff., 46, 65,
216, 237; quoted, 43
Winant, Ambassador John Gilbert, 154,
219
Wisconsin, 18, 22f.
Wohlthat, Helmuth, 70
Wyandot Indians, 11ff., 98
Wyatt, Capt. Ben H., U.S.N., 203
Wyndham, Capt. Thomas, 93

York, Archbishop of, 292
Yugoslavia, 176ff., 18off., 220

Zambezi river system, 90
Zaria, Nigeria, 117
Zhukov, Gen. Gregory, 172, 241
Zionist movement, 216ff.
Zubida, mother of Atatürk, 231